AI and Human Thought and Emotion

AI and Human Thought and Emotion

Sam Freed

CRC Press
Taylor & Francis Group
Boca Raton London New York

CRC Press is an imprint of the
Taylor & Francis Group, an **informa** business
AN AUERBACH BOOK

CRC Press
Taylor & Francis Group
6000 Broken Sound Parkway NW, Suite 300
Boca Raton, FL 33487-2742

First issued in paperback 2022

© 2020 by Taylor & Francis Group, LLC
CRC Press is an imprint of Taylor & Francis Group, an Informa business

No claim to original U.S. Government works

ISBN 13: 978-1-03-247539-4 (pbk)
ISBN 13: 978-0-367-02929-6 (hbk)

DOI: 10.1201/9780429001123

Library of Congress Cataloging-in-Publication Data

Names: Freed, Sam (Philosophy professor), author.
Title: AI and human thought and emotion / Sam Freed.
Other titles: Artificial intelligence and human thought and emotion
Description: Boca Raton : Taylor & Francis, CRC Press, [2019] | Includes
bibliographical references. | Summary: "This reference work examines how human
thought processes and emotion can be captured by artificial
intelligence (AI) algorithms and code. It provides a theoretical
framework and demonstrates how code can be generate on the basis of the
framework"—Provided by publisher.
Identifiers: LCCN 2019021293 | ISBN 9780367029296 (hardback ; acid-free paper) |
ISBN 9780429001123 (ebook)
Subjects: LCSH: Artificial intelligence—Psychological aspects. | Affect (Psychology)—
Computer simulation. | Thought and thinking.
Classification: LCC Q334.7 .F74 2019 | DDC 153.4/2028563—dc23
LC record available at https://lccn.loc.gov/2019021293

**Visit the Taylor & Francis Web site at
http://www.taylorandfrancis.com**

**and the CRC Press Web site at
http://www.crcpress.com**

Contents

PART III GETTING PRACTICAL

Author

Sam Freed is a researcher in the COGS (Centre for Cognitive Science) at the University of Sussex. This centre spans departments as diverse as neuroscience and philosophy, psychology, and computer science. Freed's background includes a career as a technologist starting as a research assistant in computer science at the age of 15 (at the Hebrew University, Jerusalem), work on Lotus 1-2-3 during Ireland's 1990s boom, and managing international projects in internet security during the .com bubble. His education includes a BA in philosophy and comparative religion, an MA in cognitive science (both from the Hebrew University), and a PhD in informatics (from the University of Sussex). His work centres on the relevance of the humanities to technology and on the historical analysis of the mindset behind current technology.

Chapter 0

Introduction

Artificial intelligence (AI) is in a sorry state, as will be detailed below. This book is no attempt to spoil the party that is currently being enjoyed by technologists, consumers, and financiers from California to Shanghai. By all means keep the party going, but there is an opportunity in this pessimistic assessment that AI is stuck: If the fundamental issues underlying AI are in such a grim state, then fixing *even a few* of the problems could offer a breakthrough in AI development. The party can get even louder. This book will travel far from technology into the humanities but will come back and offer concrete examples of new algorithms. Some of the text below is philosophical, some historical, some technical.

The vast majority of books about AI are technical and care not about the humanities at all. Most books in the humanities consider technology to be low class and uninteresting. This book is about AI, how we came to think about it the way we do, and how we can think about it afresh. It will walk a middle line, moving insights between the humanities and technology. I am not aware of any such book in the field of AI, bringing ideas from philosophy and the history of ideas all the way through to usable algorithms.

0.1 Frustrations and Opportunities in AI Research

Much is being made in popular media about the recent successes of AI: Computers are now the world champions in chess, go, and "jeopardy". Handwriting is being read by computers, computer translation has improved significantly, and many more aspects of AI that were confined to research laboratories are now in many pockets. However, most if not all of these recent achievements were done more by adding hardware and "brute force" to existing AI concepts than by entirely new ideas.

1

The motivation for this project can be illustrated by two frustrations and two opportunities.

The **first frustration** is that AI suffers a dearth of groundbreaking new ideas. The opinion that AI has been at some deep level "brain dead" since at least the 1970s is supported by pillars of the AI community such as Marvin Minsky (McHugh & Minsky, 2003) and Geoffrey Hinton (LeVine & Hinton, 2017).

> ... modern-day [*AI*] research is not doing well at all on either being general or supporting an independent entity with an ongoing existence. It mostly seems stuck on the same issues in reasoning and common sense that AI has had problems with for at least 50 years...
>
> **(Brooks, 2017)**

An illustrative parallel to this concern with AI could be a "30,000 feet view" of the development of *fundamentally new ideas* in wheeled transport in the 20th century. Though no one would doubt that wheeled transport has made great strides during this period, trains were invented in the early 19th century and became widely deployed towards the end of that century. Similarly, the bicycle was developed during most of the 19th century from an early concept to models that we would recognise as quite modern by the end of that era. Both the car and the motorbike are creatures of the late 19th century. Arguably, the next fundamental *conceptual* innovation in wheeled transport was the "Segway", introduced in 2001. So surprisingly, we had no *conceptual* innovations in wheeled transport during the entire 20th century – only incremental progress. This is not to belittle the efforts of automotive engineers between 1900 and 2000 – just to point out that there were few if any new *fundamental ideas* that caught on. The first frustration here (coming back to AI) is that from this same 30,000 ft view we have had very little progress in AI in recent decades. This is in stark contrast to most other fields in and around computers: Consider how much computer displays have changed, or computer communications, not to mention brute CPU power.

The fundamental ideas of symbolic AI were already in place in the 1950s. The basics of neural nets are found in a 1943 paper (McCulloch & Pitts, 1943; Piccinini, 2004) and were developed as a mainstay of AI by the PDP group in the 1970s (Nilsson, 2010, p. 339). The ideas of statistical AI can be seen as an extension of symbolic and logical AI, already part of the mainstream in 1956 (G. Solomonoff, 2016). Conceptual innovations are few, far between, and not that successful, with the possible exception of the work of Brooks on minimally intelligent systems, but these make no claim on intelligence beyond that of an insect.

The **second frustration** (or perhaps a symptom of the first) is that we have been led by popular culture to expect some sort of sentience or at least human-like conduct from computers. As of today (2019), this has *completely* failed to materialize. A case in point is "Star Trek (The Next Generation)", a TV series released in 1987 which included the character "Data", a robot that though not completely human-like, moved in human society, and took on human roles. We have been waiting for 30 years to no avail.

The above complaint about the absence of human-like AI is not only motivated by some romantic notions. Having human-like AI available to us would enable several applications of robotics that have a strong requirement for mutual understanding between untrained humans and robots. These applications require robots to think like humans in order to understand humans and be understood by humans. Consider robotic care for the elderly – we cannot expect octogenarians to understand novel technologies – the technologies must understand the humans. This also gives rise to several ethical questions – though this book will not delve into these.

If the situation of AI is so disappointing, perhaps we ought to re-examine the boundaries of the discussion, so as to try to "think outside the box". One of these boundaries is the way subjectivity has been treated as taboo.

Understanding human thinking as such is part of the science of psychology and is a long way in the future. But AI is a technological (and business) pursuit in the present, so we cannot wait for a full understanding of the human psyche to emerge.

There are two **sources** of commentary on AI that make poignant points, yet have not led to tangible results. Perhaps exploring these will provide an opportunity to get out of the impasse in the foundations of AI. That is what we are here to do.

The first and better known of these opportunities is the tradition of critiquing AI from the standpoint of phenomenology and other backgrounds alien to mainstream cognitive science. Much of the field ignores or trivialises these critiques. We will explore why the dialogue between this tradition and the mainstream of AI was so fruitless.

A second opportunity is examining more closely the utterances of some central AI researchers when speaking more freely than seems possible in the peer-reviewed literature. When interviewed informally, some researchers reveal severe tensions in their positions on subjective thinking in general and introspection in particular. A revealing example of the paradoxes endemic to our thinking is given by Seymour Papert (a leading AI researcher at MIT). The following quote is fundamental to this book:

> We are to thinking as Victorians were to sex. We all know we have these horrible moments of confusion when we begin a new project, that nothing looks clear and everything looks awful, that we work our way out using all sorts of odd little rules of thumb, by going down blind alleys and coming back again, and so on, but since everyone else seems to be thinking logically, or at least they claim they do, then we figure we must be the only ones in the world with such murky thought processes. We disclaim them, and make believe that we think in logical, orderly ways, all the time knowing very well that we don't. And the worst offenders here are teachers, who present crisp, clean batches of knowledge to their students, and look as if they themselves had learned

that knowledge in a crisp, clean way. It didn't happen that way, but the teachers don't admit it, and the students groan inwardly, feeling so hopelessly dumb.

(McCorduck, 2004, p. 339)

Papert describes a widespread tension in our culture that we all pretend to be logical and sensible, while being acutely aware that this is not the case "inside". Moreover, he admits that this is also the case for *him* and therefore possibly also for much of the AI research community. This is not only a theoretical tension between two well-understood positions but affects the very epistemic structure[1] of our academic and engineering disciplines. The "logical" side of this tension is not only ascendant in present society at large but is more ascendant the more one moves into academic and specifically science/engineering and business discourse. Having such a tension in the heart of any discipline is problematic, and arguably in the cognitive sciences (and AI), this can be positively harmful, at least in that it stops us from looking in the less supposedly sensible directions. There can be nothing scientific, scholarly, or even sincere about "making believe" on such a grand scale. I have found no AI technologies based these insights by Papert.

Note also that Terry Winograd, whose work on "micro-worlds" is one of the pinnacles of logical-symbolic AI argues that:

> The techniques of artificial intelligence are to the mind what bureaucracy is to human social interaction.

(Winograd, 1991)

Perhaps it is time to loosen up the stricter aspects of said "bureaucracy". Let us not regiment the mind but simulate it more like it is experienced, like it is experienced by *us* as individual humans.

0.2 Central Questions

Our question, in the field of AI, is how thinking occurs or how intelligence arises. Our thinking, whether as individuals or as a society, is seldom of the same high quality that we claim it to be: We often claim to understand more than we do – both as individuals and as societies. Possibly this is inevitable, and thinking with certitude outside of a mathematical system may simply be impossible. In order to discuss AI, we need to take a look at two other forms of intelligence – that of individual humans and that of our society as a collective.

---

[1] Epistemology is the field of philosophy that explores questions of knowledge: What is knowledge? What is Truth? How can we know the truth, if at all?

We will need to explore how less-than-perfect thinking masquerades as good thinking; how sloppy thinking has led AI to a dearth of new ideas; but maybe being sloppy is enough for many tasks, and "sloppy AI" may be enough for many applications, though not all. In one sense, this is a linear book that talks about the presuppositions underlying AI research and then shows how relaxing these presuppositions leads to better research. On the other hand, this book is forever looping back to the same questions: What is intelligence? Who decides what is correct? What is learning and what is play? Who (again) decides? How are decisions achieved in machines, in humans, in societies? When reading the humanities and philosophy parts of this book you will see ideas that were never discussed in the context of AI. Reading the technical parts you may have some new ideas on how we, humans, might work. AI, insofar as it tries to imitate human thinking processes, *cannot* be a simple linear discipline. This book is about us humans as much as it is about computers, and it is about confusion, anxiety, and pretence as much as it is about intelligence.

0.3 Structure of This Volume

This chapter (Introduction) included some context and preliminary clarifications.

Part 1 of the book gives an overview where we are today:

Chapter 1 gives an overview of the state of AI. It surveys the current state of AI and briefly discusses the main intellectuals influencing AI.

Chapter 2 gives a survey of critical thinking about AI, discussing the definition of intelligence (artificial and natural) and the various philosophical critiques of the field.

Chapter 3 discusses intelligence as it is found in humans – both as individuals and as societies. It explores emotional components such as anxiety and its consequences, such as pretence. The interrelations of these different views of intelligence are explored, touching on several seemingly unrelated topics, such as the rise of demagogue-dictators.

Chapter 4 enumerates various preconceptions that we currently have in our society and how they impact AI. These assumptions' historical origins are also touched upon.

Part 2 explores alternatives to the current mindset – specifically using introspection:

Chapter 5 outlines the argument for introspection. It starts with questions such as what is philosophy of AI and what types of truths are required in different situations. It continues by giving a detailed overview of the argument for subjectivity and introspection, leaving out two main terms and two main points. These are explored in the next four chapters.

Chapter 6 defines a new term – "Anthropic AI". This aims at the most basic human-like intelligence, as opposed to western, modern, well-educated, and adult intelligence.

Chapter 7 introduces in detail subjectivity and introspection as they may apply to AI.

Chapter 8 explores the acceptability of the proposed methodology – it surveys six possible attitudes towards using introspection in AI and shows that they each have some support. It also disposes of the main objections to introspection using the distinction between the context of discovery and the context of justification.

Chapter 9 discusses the desirability of using introspection for AI development. By looking at how introspection is already in widespread use in our society, it shows that (unlike what many might think) introspection is not noise but a cornerstone of any civilisation.

Part 3 takes the discussion to the technical level:

Chapter 10 goes into detail on how to implement the recommended methodology.

Chapter 11 gives examples of the use of introspection in AI, both in existing AI and in developing new algorithms.

Chapter 12 gives a more advanced example in detail. This example introduces a novel data type that implements an approximation of "trains of thought", amongst other features.

Chapter 13 provides a summary, discusses some consequences, and concludes.

0.4 How to Read This Book

This book assumes no background in the humanities. Terms (mainly in philosophy) are introduced as they are used, in footnotes. This volume does assume a basic knowledge of how computers and programming work, though no knowledge of AI is required.

This book is based to a large degree on my PhD work at the University of Sussex (Freed, 2017). Chapters 1–4, the introduction and conclusion have been rewritten and expanded significantly. The rest of the material has mainly been edited for readability. If you are looking for more detailed references they may be found in the original thesis.

The question of this book is how intelligence emerges (or seems to emerge) from more primitive processes. There are three three-fold points to keep in mind while reading this book.

1. When one tries to figure out what to wear on a particular day, considering the weather forecast, you could intuitively say that one is thinking "directly", about clothes. Call that ***thinking1*** – thinking about concrete concerns in the world. When you are now thinking about these thoughts, you are arguably engaging in a form of "thinking about thinking", in a sense you are engaging in psychology or cognitive science. This is the same level of thinking that you perform when you are watching a TV drama: "this person thinks this, and

will therefore do that, while the other sees things differently", etc. Let's call this level *thinking2* – thinking about thoughts. Most of AI research is done at this level: the questions are *about* thinking1 and the AI researcher thinks2 these thoughts2. There is a third level in which we will engage in much of this book. This is *thinking3* or thinking about thinking about thinking. We will examine the way AI researchers think2 and offer suggestions as to how they should think2. In this sense, this book is one level more complicated than reading a novel.[2]

2. Intelligence is (hopefully) found in individuals (1), societies (2), and computers (3).

3. Intelligence (1) is very often accompanied by pretence (2) and anxiety (3). It is an open question if, and in what senses, it can appear without these less glorious elements.

This is necessarily a tangled book, with more than one plot, and some subplots jumping backwards and forwards in time. This makes the author's work difficult, but I endeavour to make the reader's work easier by assuming as little background knowledge as is practicable. Cross-references are provided as necessary, and the index is provided for exploring any particular issue. Color versions of the figures in this book are available on the CRC Press website: https://www.crcpress.com/9780367029296. References are provided in parentheses as is customary, referring the reader to further material in the bibliography.

Let the tour begin.

---

[2] Occasionally in writing I will also worry about making myself clear to my reader. Perhaps I am engaging in *thinking4*, but the mind boggles, so let's just leave it at three levels.

INTELLIGENCE IN COMPUTERS, HUMANS AND SOCIETIES

I

Chapter 1

Artificial Intelligence as It Stands

This chapter will present the current state of the artificial intelligence (AI) world: What types of AI exist, and who are the central figures who had the most influence on how the AI world understands itself.

1.1 About AI

1.1.1 AI's Relation to Psychology, Cognitive Science, etc.

AI did not appear out of nowhere nor is it unrelated to other fields. Some would say that AI is "the intellectual heart of the cognitive sciences" (Wheeler, 2005), but strangely, AI predates cognitive science (at least under those names). The history is complex and need not concern us here in all its detail (Boden, 2008). This section will give the context needed for the rest of the book.

Psychology is a science, in the sense that it aims to understand a phenomena that is objectively out there is the world: Human thinking and behaviour. Psychology is usually dated either to Plato or to the mid-19th century. Human behaviour includes the pesky trait of insisting, using language, that there is such a thing as subjectivity and a personal point of view (Seth, 2010). Some, however would resist this idea that psychology is a science, in that it has precious few theories that produce useful predictions – in any case nothing like physics or biology. Thomas Kuhn, in his analysis of scientific paradigms, gave a possible solution to this question: Psychology may be today where chemistry was before Dmitri Mendeleev invented the "periodic table of the elements" and gave chemistry its first theoretical framework (Kuhn, 2012). Psychology does not have an overall theory (yet). That does not devalue the work of psychologists (who are grappling in the dark about the main questions of their discipline) – rather, it makes their work more heroic – they are collecting the myriad facts and observations that may allow for a theory of human subjectivity and behaviour to emerge some time in the future.

The **interests** of psychology are divided very roughly between scientific psychologists who want to explain the mind like physicists explain matter, and therapists who are interested in helping individuals, and tend to be more interested in individual cases than in scientific theories. These two are joined by many other sub-fields such as social psychology, who want to help people achieve goals, whether personal, social, economical, or political. These form elements of the social sciences.

The **history** of psychology is divided very roughly into three periods, with perhaps a fourth one starting about now (the 2010s).[1]

"Classical" psychology (started in the mid-19th century) was done mainly in Germany and included people exploring their own subjectivity, along with electrical currents in nerves. It was an open and uncritical time, when every researcher who could afford to set up a laboratory and develop their own methodologies published books, and was either accepted or not by their peers. Some would argue that several of the schools of thought that flourished at that time were indistinguishable from one another other than by academic politics.

This era came to a close (especially in the United States) with the **behaviouristic revolution**, led by John B. Watson, from 1913 onwards. The idea of behaviourism is that any discussion of the subjective is suspect, since we can never agree on what is happening in the subjective realm, and also as scientists we want to explore the behaviour of all animals, not just humans, and we have no access to the subjectivity underlying the behaviour of birds, a research field of Watson's. We will discuss Watson in a more detail below.

The **cognitive revolution** in psychology was a rebellion against the austerity of behaviourism. In getting rid of anything subjective or introspective behaviourism had pretty much banned any discussion of the mind. The cognitivists (as they were later named) rebelled against the idea that there can be no discussion of "mental processes" since the acquisition of language by infants cannot be explained by the simple dog-like processes of stimulus and response. This

---

[1] Some would argue that the story I am about to tell is fully mythical (Costall, 2006), but we need to get started somewhere, and regardless of historical accuracy, the following is how psychologists usually understand their own discipline.

movement was spearheaded by Noam Chomsky (1959) and included people from a variety of disciplines. Interestingly, many of the same people were heavily involved in the development of computers. This is no coincidence: In a sense, cognitive psychology is based on the metaphor of "mind as machine" or more specifically of "mind as computer".

A key player both in the world of computers and in the nascent cognitive psychology was Herbert A. Simon, who will be discussed in more detail in Section 1.6, since he probably was the most influential single person in the formative decades of AI (G. Solomonoff, 2016).

The fourth era in psychology which is arguably gaining steam is a full-fledged return to interest in the subjective. This movement goes under the banner of "consciousness science" (Seth, 2010).

Cognitive science is an unusual field, in that in many contexts it is not even seen as a separate discipline. Rather, it is a meeting place of several disciplines, where researchers exchange ideas and explore shared interests. The fields include psychology and neurology (of course), but also linguistics, cybernetics, electrical engineering, computer science, and our field, AI.

Strangely, in a sense cognitive science existed as an intellectual movement at least since the late 1950s, but it only got its name from the book titled "Cognitive Psychology", published in 1967. AI was given its name in 1956, at a conference in Dartmouth. History is rarely tidy. We will return to both of these events.

1.1.2 What Are Intelligence, Consciousness, and Introspection

The question of the definition of intelligence is complex, and even the Stanford Encyclopedia of Philosophy, where one would expect to find definitions and discussions of difficult words, has no article on the topic. Even the idea of measuring intelligence without defining it is mind-boggling in its complexity (Hernández-Orallo, 2017). Instead of delving into defining intelligence, I will preliminarily use the following cobbled-together definition:

> Intelligence is proficiency in the acquisition and application of knowledge.

Any discussion of intelligence is also a discussion of knowledge, and there are complexities here, but we can leave those to Section 6.7.

I will not attempt to define consciousness. I will simply follow widespread custom in using "consciousness" as the sum total of all our subjective experience, and hence, consciousness is accessible to us, by looking at our own experience. And looking at (and reporting on) our own subjective experience is a pretty good initial definition of introspection. So for now, introspection is how we look at consciousness, and consciousness is the totality of what is available to introspection. If the circularity of these preliminary definitions worries you, recall that even in mathematics, some terms (What is 1?) are left undefined. And our entire language, as defined in the dictionary, is utterly circular, since all words are forever defined using other words. This book is ultimately about technology, so we cannot afford to get bogged down in definitions. For better definitions of introspection, see Chapter 7. Human consciousness as such is not a topic in this book.

1.1.3 Defining and Viewing AI

AI is a strange field. It is young – the name was only made up in 1956. It is part of the computer revolution from the start, actually from before the official start of electronic computing during the Second World War (McCorduck, 2004).

In the summer of 1956, several young researchers, mostly still in graduate school, gathered in Dartmouth. It was no normal conference with a clear beginning and end; it was more of a walk-on walk-off informal gathering of like-minded people, all interested in computers. Many were interested also in the ongoing cognitive revolution in psychology and neighbouring fields. The most influential character in the gathering was Herbert A. Simon, already a professor at the time (see Section 1.6).

At that conference, a definition of AI was agreed. It may not be the most satisfying definition, but it stuck.

> … the artificial intelligence problem is taken to be that of making a machine behave in ways that would be called intelligent if a human were so behaving.
>
> **(G. Solomonoff, 2016, p. 6)**

An interesting result of this definition is that once you program something that qualifies as AI, like a chess program to beat the world champion, from the moment it works, and you have some time to catch your breath, it is no longer AI. Since it just worked, it has just been done by a computer, and therefore, it is no longer interestingly human, it's just a "relatively sophisticated piece of programming" – and all the glory is gone. This is one of the reasons that university departments of AI are rare and getting rarer – AI is usually taught in departments of computer science, as a sort of "advanced programming".

AI used to be taught (like many other fields) historically. But now it is most often taught using the book titled "Artificial Intelligence: A Modern Approach" (Russell & Norvig, 2013). The "modern" bit of the approach seems to be that AI is presented in that book purely as engineering, as a series of useful techniques, with no history at all.

Some psychologists and cognitive scientists see AI not as a technology, but as the theoretical wing of cognitive science (a bit like theoretical physics). By their lights, a theory in cognitive science should be a program, a piece of code, that produces a similar result to a human's cognitive system. AI is (by these researchers) the "intellectual heart of cognitive science" (Wheeler, 2005).

As a matter of historical fact, AI approaches can broadly be separated into two-and-a-half groups, depending on the original inspiration driving them.

1.2 First Approach: Logic and Mathematics

The first approach to AI, based on logic (and mathematics), is that of explicitly specified knowledge. At its most primitive, the AI system knows certain facts, and some rules of inference. An early example of this approach was the "Logical Theorist" (Newell & Simon, 1956) which was aimed at proving theorems in logic. Later examples were the "expert systems" used widely in science and medicine (Shortliffe et al., 1984). In these systems, the rules of the domain on knowledge (say chemistry or medicine) are precoded in the system, and by adding some facts about a particular case, the system can (automatically, flawlessly, and quickly) infer everything that can be inferred using the rules based on the data.

This first approach of representing knowledge explicitly using rules and facts later evolved to handle uncertainty, whereby every fact is represented as a probability, and the rules therefore produce diagnoses (for example) with a specific certainty factor. Another extension of this approach allowed even rules to have a probability, like "if A and B then the chances of C are 90%". The expert systems that used to deal with knowledge that was either clearly present or not were thereby generalised to handle uncertainties, without losing any of its mathematical rigour and explicit clarity. Another development allowed a more sophisticated use of statistics, known a Bayesian systems and later Bayesian networks (Boden, 2016).

Another (early and important) example of logical/mathematical AI is the algorithm used to play chess and other turn-taking board games. This was initially proposed by Alan Turing, in 1953 (Turing, 1953). The basic idea is that for every situation on the board, there are so many moves that are possible. That number may be (say for example) 5. So one could draw a tree of possible board situations, with the current situation on the top, and all the possible immediately subsequent board situations below. We can apply this idea of making a tree junction out of every board situation time and again, until we have a tree of all possible developments in the game up to a certain dept, see Illustration 1.1.

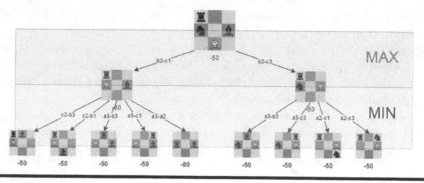

Illustration 1.1   A two-layer game tree.

Next, we use some procedure to evaluate all the "leaf" positions that will not be further expanded. This may be done crudely, as in adding some small integer for every piece "our" side has on the board, while deducting something similar for opponent pieces. A large number can represent winning. Once we have an evaluation of all the "leaf" nodes (the ones that we did not further explore), we calculate the values of the preceding positions as follows: For each node that represents "our" turn, we choose the highest of all subsequent values, since we can trust ourselves in the future to make the best move for us (within the limits of our calculation). For each move by the opponent, we choose the minimum value, since the worst that can happen (from our point of view) would be for the opponent to play well, and do what is best for him, and his best is our worst, so we select the minimum. Evaluating all the way to the top, we can see for the current situation what would be the best move (as far as we can see into the future). We perform that move. This is the min–max algorithm.

All software systems that play turn-taking board games of this type use some variant of this algorithm. The power of the software is limited only by the amount of computing resources and time that we can invest. In absolute theory, we could calculate the entire game from beginning to end, but all the computers in the world working together may not suffice, since every new layer is larger than all the previous tree. That is why the systems that play better than humans are expensive and are backed by major corporations (IBM for chess, Google for "Go").

1.3 Second Approach: Biological Inspiration

The second approach to AI is based on science (in this case, biology). This approach begins with the idea that natural intelligence, whether human or animal, whether conscious or not, is always based on some neural structures. The anatomy of neural nets, as understood (in 1943), was further simplified (as technologists and model designers often do) to produce what we now know as "neural nets" (Piccinini, 2004). These nets are most often designed as a collection of "layers" of "neurons" (see Illustration 1.2). Each such neuron does nothing but sum up the incoming

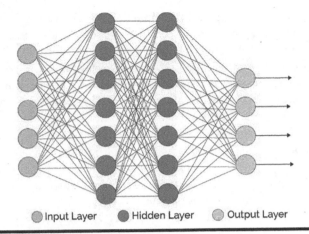

Input Layer   Hidden Layer   Output Layer

Illustration 1.2   An example of a small neural network.

signals from its input side (using some weights), apply a function to this sum, and cut the result range into two possibilities: Either the neuron "fires" or not, and if it does, it sends out a signal into all neurons that are connected to its output side.

These networks are most often trained to produce the correct result by assigning random weights to all connections initially, and then every time an input is presented and the result out is erroneous, the magnitude of the error in the output is used to re-randomise the weights in the connection leading into the output neuron, and so on upwards in the net. So the net works from the top down, but is adjusted or trained from the bottom up. This technique, called "back propagation of the error", was developed in the early 1980s.

Because of the dearth of computing resources before the 1990s, large and deep neural nets were not practical. Moreover, some researchers have convinced themselves that (within certain limits) anything that can be done with a neural net can also be done by some other net with only one "hidden layer", and a three-hidden-layer net would be plenty. In recent years, there has been an explosion in interest in neural networks with the relaxation of this constraint (Mhaskar et al., 2016). Networks with hundreds of layers are now being explored as a matter of course (Boden, 2016). These networks produce some truly astounding results and lead to technology companies being valued astronomically. This is "deep learning", often conflated with "big data".

1.4 A Half-Approach, and a Point or Two

What I called above a half-approach to AI is a series of either ad hoc or otherwise limited approaches that have no real ambition to produce human or higher-level intelligence. An outstanding example of this family is the work of Brooks on insect-level intelligence (Brooks, 1991), leading to impressive-looking walking robots such as "big-dog" (Raibert et al., 2008).

We have seen two main approaches to ambitious AI. Both are well founded in formal thinking and science, respectively. The first uses clear-and-distinct, fully explicit knowledge to achieve what would be provably the best possible result. The other scatters the knowledge across a net, the knowledge, insofar as we can point to it all, is implicit. The system is opaque, in that its complexity mostly precludes any explanation of why things were done the way they were. Logic and mathematics are too abstract to model human complexity, and neural nets are "too neat, too simple, too few, and too dry" (Boden, 2016, pp. 90–91). There are some combined methods, such as Bayesian networks, combining some of the characteristics of both approaches – but these are combinations, not a novel idea. The results are interesting, but not groundbreaking.

Can there be another way? What will we have to give up to get a new type of technology? This book answers this question.

1.5 Watson[2]

The history of introspection for AI is rooted deeply in the debates about introspection inside psychology, but "the early debates about introspection as a method in psychology were a good deal more subtle and insightful, and also much less decisive, that the textbooks might have us believe" (Costall, 2006). This section will survey the initial banning of introspection by Watson. The next section will show how Simon brought this assumption into AI. These sections also serve to introduce two of the scholars that this book will be attacking the most. A point worth bearing in mind when discussing past thinkers is that the way that (for example) Watson is remembered is a gross simplification of his actual persona, thoughts, and positions. But our mind is feeble (see Section 3.1), and there are so many historical figures to remember…. Perhaps Watson-as-remembered is more important than Watson-as-he-was, for the purpose of understanding his impact on AI.

John B. Watson (1878–1958) delivered a paper in 1913 at a talk in Columbia University. This speech is seen as the manifesto that started the behaviourist revolution and abolished introspection. His aversion to introspection was continued by the cognitive revolution. Watson's teacher (Harvey Carr) insisted that "objectivism" would be a better term than "behaviourism" for Watson's legacy, since behaviour had been studied before, but Watson's determination to exclude the subjective was new to psychology.

He asserts his message clearly: "Psychology, as the behaviorist views it, is a purely objective, experimental branch of natural science which needs introspection as little as do the sciences of chemistry and physics" (J. B. Watson, 1913, p. 176).

---

[2] Don't confuse Peter Watson, a living Cambridge historian, with John B. Watson, the behaviourist. A third Watson will have some comments to make about case-based reasoning, in Section 11.2. Moreover, IBM has an AI system named "Watson" after the founder of that company.

1.5.1 Explicit Motivations

To understand Watson's motivation (and vehemence), we must recall that during Watson's time, the Darwinian revolution was still fresh and in progress: It was moving the place of mankind in the world from being the pinnacle of creation and its master (Genesis 1:29) to being another random artefact of mutations and natural selection (P. Watson, 2006, pp. 707–708). Watson views the resistance he encounters to the abolition of introspection and to the interpretation of humans as animals as being essentially the same as the resistance to Darwin, stemming from the same religious sentiment that requires humans to be distinct in kind from animals (J. B. Watson, 1931, pp. ix–x).

Science, as opposed to the religious debates, is supposed to be objective. And the best example of science is (a somewhat idealised view of) physics and chemistry, where if you are lucky, the phenomenon you are working on can be explained using neat causality both forwards and backwards. Watson, optimistic for his new scientific psychology, envisaged behaviour being predicted precisely as in other sciences: "In a system of psychology completely worked out, given the response the stimuli can be predicted; given the stimuli the response can be predicted" (J. B. Watson, 1913). He details how psychological theories should not refer to "colours" but to "light frequencies" – converting the language of experience to a language of physics. The rationalistic aspiration for clear and distinct, numeric and deterministic science cannot be clearer (and will be discussed in Section 2.4). Watson also assumes that the mind can be decomposed into modules, another hallmark of rationalistic thought (see Section 4.3.3).

1.5.2 Arguments against Introspection

Watson presents two main arguments for rejecting introspection:

1. To maintain the unity of psychology and the coherence of the scientific programme one must apply the same standards of research in human behaviour as in **animal behaviour** (J. B. Watson, 1913, 1914, p. 1, 1920, 1931, p. ix). Since animals have no consciousness *that we can access* (even by the introspectionists' lights), we should not even attempt the same with humans.
2. His most direct attacks on introspection say that the content of introspection is "obscure" (J. B. Watson, 1931, p. x), the technique of introspection is unclear and imposes self-contradictory demands, its terminology is incoherent even in simple distinctions of sensations (J. B. Watson, 1913), and (switching to ad-hominem attacks) its practitioners are effete (Costall, 2006, p. 646) and "insufferably prolix" (J. B. Watson, 1920).

Recall that we are assuming (together with many others) that introspection and consciousness cover the same subjective field. Interestingly, in presenting his anti-introspectionist revolution, Watson did not deny *any* role at all to introspection or consciousness, in fact he saw two legitimate roles for introspection, one explicitly and one implicitly:

1. Explicitly, he recognised that every science needs a modicum of introspection: "If you will grant the behaviourist the right to use **consciousness** in the same way that other **natural scientists** employ it – that is, without making consciousness a special object of observation – you have granted all the my thesis requires" (J. B. Watson, 1913, p. 175, emphasis added). Watson accepted and was unfazed by the idea that a chemist needs to be conscious to say things such as "I see the liquid turning red". This statement is strictly about the *experience of perception*: "I see" – hence it is (at least grammatically) a report on a mental state and hence introspective. Watson stated that his type of psychology "is a purely objective, experimental branch of natural science, which needs introspection *as little as do the sciences of chemistry and physics*.... Consciousness may be said to be the instrument or tool with which *all scientists work*" (J. B. Watson, 1913, p. 176, emphasis added).
2. Watson introduces the idea of soliciting reports from subjects using "thinking aloud" (see Section 7.3).

1.5.3 Interesting Points

Watson moved between two positions: methodological behaviourism (ignoring the subjective) and ontological[3] behaviourism (the subjective does not exist). Ontological behaviourism denies that something mental is going on inside the brain (or elsewhere) and claims that only external behaviour *exists*. Methodological behaviourism remains neutral on the point of the existence of the mind, but just refrains from investigating it since there is no scientific way of doing so.

Usually he simply argues against introspection and consciousness and asks for the whole issue of consciousness to be "put away for a time" (J. B. Watson, 1913), perhaps even "many lifetimes". He views the denial of introspection as good *methodology*. In other times, he denies the very existence of the mind and the subjective and slips into ontological behaviourism: "The behaviorist believes in no such transcendental human power [*as mystic self knowledge*].... It is a serious misunderstanding of the behaviouristic position to say, as Mr. Thomson does- 'And of course a behaviorist does not deny that mental states exist. He merely prefers to ignore them.' He 'ignores' them only in the same sense that chemistry ignores alchemy, astronomy horoscopy, and psychology telepathy and psychic manifestations" (J. B. Watson, 1920, p. 94).

---

[3] Ontology is the field of philosophy that asks "what exists, fundamentally". What are all other things made of?

Regardless of the ontological status of subjectivity, Watson *preferred* to study behaviour rather than consciousness, since it is clearer, and mainly because it is practical: He wished to integrate with other sciences (like Comte, see Section 4.1), and he wanted to make psychology useful for "the educator, the physician, the jurist, and the businessman". He wished to simplify psychology (and make it a science like any other) by eliminating consciousness as a special object of research for psychology (J. B. Watson, 1913, pp. 168, 171, 175).

Watson's 1913 paper attacked philosophy: "These time-honoured relics of philosophical speculation need trouble the student of behaviour as little as they trouble the student of physics... I should like to bring my students up in the same ignorance of such hypotheses as one finds among the students of other branches of science" (J. B. Watson, 1913, p. 166). There will be a detailed discussion of how philosophy is considered useless in Section 4.4.2.

A concession he makes to treating humans differently to how he treats animals is in using **language**. He accepts that the experimenter may use language to communicate with a human subject (e.g. in colour tests), as simply an "abbreviated method" of getting what we would now call inputs and outputs from a human (J. B. Watson, 1913, p. 172n). This concession is limited to very concrete communication in "real time", no memory, understanding, or other faculty is supposedly involved.

In further discussing the use of language, a somewhat surprising quote refers approvingly to **psychoanalysis**, which we today see as diametrically opposed to behaviourism: "The subject can observe that he is using words in thinking. But how much word material is used, how much his final formulation is influenced by implicit factors which are not put in words and which he cannot himself observe, cannot be stated by the subject himself. The behaviourist, as well as the psychoanalyst, holds that there are hundreds of such factors involved, some of which require a minute search into the subject's biography as far back as infancy..." (J. B. Watson, 1920, p. 97).

This reference to Freud's work is not some sort of slip that Watson would later regret. He quotes Freudian sources several times, a pertinent example is when he warns anyone attempting the "thinking aloud" method (discussed in Section 7.3) that "... one has to be careful to impose problems upon his subject which are as far as possible removed from *repressed emotional factors*. It is never possible of course completely to do this as the analysts have more than once pointed out" (stress added). He also agrees with the "analysts" that "a human animal never gets away from his biography" (J. B. Watson, 1920).

An interesting aside is Watson's answer to the question in his title: "Is thinking merely the action of Language mechanism?" Watson's answer is surprisingly "embodied": "A whole man thinks with his whole body in each and every part. If he is mutilated... he thinks with the remaining parts". However, he continues to say that if we sever muscles in a tennis player, his play will suffer badly. In a normal person, thinking is subvocal speaking (maybe today we would call it "narration"). Similarly, in the deaf and dumb, thinking is done by "fingers, hands, arms, facial muscles, muscles of the head, etc."

1.5.4 Watson – Summary

Watson prohibited any speculation about "internal structures" (Crosson, 1985, p. 438) and turned the word "introspection" into a taboo in psychology. Watson did not think all introspection is entirely nonsense, but many of his followers do take him to say that and follow that creed blindly (Costall, 2006). Here we also see echoes of Descartes' polarization of doubt and knowledge – "what we are not sure of we must treat with the utmost doubt" – and since we are not sure of introspection, we must treat it as noise (see Section 4.2.4).

As a result of the widespread acceptance of the denial of introspection and the phenomenal mind, some heavy lifting is required in this volume: I will need to show in some detail that introspection is legitimate (see Chapter 8) and likely useful (see Chapter 9).

1.6 Simon

The cognitive revolution in psychology was led (to a large degree) by the same people who pioneered computers and AI (Crosson, 1985, p. 438; Pear, 2007, p. 113). One of the most influential people in this movement was Herbert A. Simon. Cognitivism was a revolution in that it legitimated the use of the term "mind" and allowed discussion of what went on "inside the black box". It did carry forward many of the assumptions of behaviourism, such as the aversion to the subjective in general, and to introspection in particular (Costall, 2006).

Herbert Simon (1916–2001) was one of the most prolific thinkers of the 20th century. His contributions span public administration, business studies, psychology, economics, operations research, mathematics, statistics, computing, and AI. Indeed, his "more than 900 publications" span in addition to computers and AI "every social science discipline other than anthropology" (Augier & March, 2001). "As much as any one person, Herbert A. Simon has shaped the intellectual agenda of the human and social sciences in the second half of the twentieth century" (Turkle, 1991). Specifically in AI, "Newell [*Simon's student and AI collaborator*] and Simon were by far the most influential Dartmouth Summer attendees" (G. Solomonoff, 2016). The "Dartmouth Summer" mentioned is the 1956 conference that to a large degree founded the field of AI and gave it its name. Arguably over half of the achievements of GOFAI ("Good Old-Fashioned AI") were Simon's own or his students'. He is the only person (so far) to win both the Turing prize (in 1975) and the Nobel Prize (in economics, 1978). He continued Watson's objections to introspection and took part in bringing much of behaviourism's heritage into the cognitive fold. For all his breadth, he saw himself as "…a monomaniac. All my life I have been studying one thing: human decision making" (Feigenbaum, 1989). His impact was not accidental – his energy and conviction showed him in the light of "a proper missionary" (Augier & March, 2001). He was heavily influenced by Rudolf Carnap, the logical positivist (see Section 4.1).

1.6.1 Economics

Simon viewed as his main contribution (in the field economics) the notion of **bounded rationality** (Simon, 1996a, p. 165). The idea of bounded rationality was a rebellion against classical economics, and that theory's faith in "'*economic* man', who in the course of being 'economic' is also 'rational'" (Simon, 1955). Simon's contention was that the circumstances in which a human agent finds itself places restrictions on their rationality, and therefore, the idea of an optimising, totally rational "economic man" is unrealistically optimistic; humans are not as rational or as well informed as classical economics would have it. Human rationality is bounded by the information available and the amount of time and resources one can practically devote to any decision. He propounds "satisficing", which is his technical term for a solution that is not optimal, but "good enough" or "fit for purpose". This will later be related to the notion of a heuristic in AI.

Note that Simon's view of human nature is less unrealistically perfect than his (economist) predecessors, but he still views humans as being entirely rational within his newly discovered "bounds". See Section 4.5.4 for a discussion of the idea that humans are rational.

1.6.2 Hostile to Subjectivity – Rationalistic

Simon was a scientist of the rationalistic tradition through and through (see Section 2.4). His basic world view was that humans are rational; his main metaphors for life were a maze or a chess game (Simon, 1996a, p. 113). "For me mathematics has always been a language of thought. I don't know precisely what I mean by that... Mathematics – this sort of non-verbal thinking – is my language of discovery" (Ibid., p. 106).

He was uncomfortable with subjectivity and often distanced himself from it – in himself and others. In his autobiography (Simon, 1996a), he only refers to himself in the first person once he is grown up (as a child he is always "the boy") – the vicissitudes of a child's emotions were a bit too much for him to identify with or discuss in later life. Moreover, in his uncomfortable relationship with all things subjective, he was not versed even in the everyday terminologies of subjectivity, confounding "introspection" with "introversion": "the boy himself was incorrigibly introspective" (Ibid., p. 19).

Simon accepted Watson's ambition that psychology should be a science on a par with chemistry and physics (Costall, 2006). However, he fell into hubris and took his ambition to be already substantially fulfilled, making his own projects into the building blocks of his world view, with faultless circular logic: "If chess plays the role in cognitive research that Drosophila does in genetics, the Towers of Hanoi is the analogue of E Coli..." (Simon, 1996a, p. 327). His assumption that chess is a good model of human cognition and that chess is at least in-principle solved (see Section 1.2) means that cognition has been "cracked" at least as much as Mendeleev "cracked" chemistry with the invention of the periodic table of the elements, in 1869 (see Section 1.1.1).

1.6.3 *Artificial Intelligence*

The issue of subjectivity and introspection does not explicitly show up in Simon's writings about AI. Rationalistic symbol-manipulating AI was (for him) the future: "... enlarging symbol manipulation to embrace much more than deductive logic. Symbols can be used for everyday thinking, for metaphorical thinking, even for 'illogical' thinking. This crucial generalisation began to emerge at about the time of world war II, though it took the appearance of the modern computer to perfect it" (Simon, 1996a, p. 193). Throughout his AI career, he was "... interested in simulating human problem solving, and not simply demonstrating how computers can solve hard problems" (Ibid., p. 209). So much so that he explicitly claims in a 1956 letter to Russell that his software proves theorems like a human does. And yet, there are no signs of subjectivity or fallibility, beyond his own theory of "bounded rationality" (Ibid., p. 207, see also pp. 234, 274, 331).

Simon "saw problems as generally decomposable into hierarchical structures" (Augier & March, 2001; Simon, 1989). This view is visible in his AI efforts, such as the General Problem Solver and the Logic Theorist. His faith in decomposability and in the validity of general solutions for wide areas shows also in his contention (above) of being only interested in one question, human decision-making, while publishing research in many different fields.

Simon towered over the field of AI also in terms of methodology and in terms of how the field viewed itself: Simon viewed AI as a science (Simon, 1996b), and as inseparable from his other fields of study – in this sense he predated Wheeler's (2005) definition of AI as the "intellectual heart of cognitive science". Simon (with his usual AI collaborator, Newell) established his ideas as the rules of the field:

> The work of Newell and Simon impressed upon AI the methodological paradigm of empirical science. The methodology dictates this 'scientific loop':
>
> a. design ... based on the information processing model
> b. test ... based on computer programs you write to represent your design
> c. measure ... based on actual computer runs of these programs (not 'pencil-and-paper', not 'armchair thinking', not 'theorems')
> d. redesign... based upon the discoveries made about the behaviour...
>
> This is the 'coin of the realm', as Newell labelled it....
>
> **(Feigenbaum, 1989, p. 10)**

I will follow other critics in taking Simon as the main spokesperson for the mainstream of (at least old) AI.

1.6.4 Against His Critics

Critics of Simon's work in AI came in two main types: Phenomenologists such as Dreyfus (See Section 2.3) and Ethicists who took exception to AI, such as Weizenbaum (see Chapter 2). Insofar as he was aware of or cared about other opinions about human nature, he derided them by comparing them to Marxism and religion (Simon, 1996a, pp. 274, 358–359). He mentions four main critics of his work: Mortimer Taube, Richard Bellman, Hubert Dreyfus ("a humanistic philosopher" – whatever he may mean by that), and Weizenbaum. He said: "you don't get very far arguing with a man about his religion, and these are essentially religious issues for the Dreyfuses and Wiezenbaums of this world". He proceeds (Ibid., p. 275) to make a virtue of misunderstanding his critics: "I think that those who object to my characterising man as simple want somehow to retain some mystery at his core...", implicitly accusing all who stand in his way of the ultimate sin in rationalistic/positivistic doctrine (see Sections 2.4 and 4.1) – having "religion up their sleeve" (Boden, 2008, pp. 251, 324).

Even though he understands that in exploring new frontiers he may come across fields that he does not understand at all, he refuses to engage with research areas that are inimical to his way of thinking, dismissing huge bodies of knowledge out of hand, such as "... hermeneutics (if I can ever find out just what that word means)" (Simon, 1996a, p. 331). We *will* find out what that word means, and what it means to AI, in Section 2.5.

1.6.5 Flirting with Subjectivity

In this vein, of rejecting any subjectivity, it is surprising (and somewhat entertaining) to find him not only admitting to introspecting about how he learnt Greek (Simon, 1996a, p. 219), but also *promoting* introspection under another guise as a research technique: "Thinking Aloud". This will be discussed in detail in Section 7.3.

1.7 AI as It Stands – Summary

AI as currently practised is built on sound scientific grounds. It tackles building a mind either from the most basic building blocks, networks of neuron-like calculations, or from the top, starting from explicit knowledge, logic, and mathematics.

Subjective approaches are seen as unscientific, and the word "Introspection" is positively seen an antithetical to the programme of science and progress. This book will argue the exact opposite position. However, the author is not the first to see fault in the exclusion of the subjective. Several critics have traversed this terrain before and have written well-respected records of their findings. The next chapter will give an overview of the current critiques of AI. You will find that the thinkers critiquing AI attack mainly Simon (being the pillar of the AI community), but the positions they attack are largely those he inherited from Watson.

Chapter 2

Current Critiques of Artificial Intelligence

This book seeks to explore the space of possibilities for AI beyond the status quo. This chapter reviews the existing critiques of AI from philosophers. This review will start with understanding the two camps – cognitivism and classic AI on one side, and phenomenology and related critiques of AI on the other.

Section 2.1 gives some background about the intellectual traditions that influence the critiques of AI.

Section 2.2 introduces in detail the heart of the disagreements between cognitivism and phenomenology.

Section 2.3 presents Dreyfus (1929–2017) and his critique of AI. Dreyfus is like "the voice of one crying in the wilderness: 'Make clear the way for Heidegger!'…",[1] arguing against a tradition in AI that Winograd and Flores will later (1986) call the rationalistic tradition. Sadly, Dreyfus made no concrete, coded contribution.

Section 2.4 presents Winograd and Flores, who aim to bridge this divide and make some more concrete progress. They come up with ideas for a working system, but that system starts a new field of technology called "group-ware", rather than contributing to AI as such. One of the contributions of their analysis is adding the hermeneutics of Gadamer to the discussion.

Section 2.5 surveys hermeneutics and Gadamer in more depth.

Section 2.6 discusses the AI community's response to these critiques, a response the present author (for one) finds lacking.

Section 2.7 locates this book's project and its relation to the other criticisms of AI.

---

[1] To paraphrase Isaiah 40:3, John 1:23, etc.

2.1 Background: Phenomenology and Heidegger

Before we start with critiques of AI, we need a bit of background.

After Kant (in the 1800s), there was a crisis in philosophy: Should we take as our secure foundation (1) the world of experience or (2) the world of physics? The school of thought choosing to prefer physics and science became known as the analytical philosophy (or Anglo-American school), while those choosing human experience as the foundation are known as continental philosophy (more in Section 4.4.3). The most prominent continental philosopher in the 20th century was Heidegger, who is key to our discussion. Let's first give an introduction to his speciality (phenomenology) and then to Heidegger's own philosophy.

2.1.1 Phenomenology

"Phenomenology is the study of structures of consciousness as experienced from the first-person point of view" and is arguably as old as Buddhism, but (at least in the west) it "came to full flower in *Husserl*" (1859–1939) (D. W. Smith, 2013). It is a systematic research project into human experience, from the subjective point of view. In being subjective, it is opposite science. This discipline was developed in German and to this day is to a large degree conducted in that language.

Note some points of terminology: In everyday speech, the terms world and universe are used near-interchangeably. In the parlance of phenomenology, the term "universe" means the objective perspective, planets, and other things "out there", while the word "world" means something more akin to "the world of the child" or "the world of the 17th-century London carpenter" – it is (approximately) the subjective world of an individual. This is related to the Kantian distinction between phenomena and noumena (see Section 4.4.3). Likewise, a "situation" is conceived as pertaining to a particular subject, while a "state" is physical, external, and objective. So a state is in the universe, and a situation is in a world. Similarly, "coping" in a situation is the phenomenological term for "responding" to a state, being "situated" is the subjective side of being in a specific place and time. There is plenty more, but for our purposes, these terms should suffice.

2.1.2 Heidegger

Heidegger, Husserl's student, revolutionised the ontology[2] implied by phenomenology – for Husserl (Heidegger's teacher) questions of being or ontol-

---

[2] **Ontology** is the question of what exists, or what are the elementary things by which we should explain all other things. **Atomists** believe that all things are ultimately composed of small indivisible things, called atoms. **Physicallists** believe everything is ultimately physical, and any mental phenomena should be reduced to physical processes. **Idealists** believe that the basic building block of our world is impressions, ideas, or "sense-data". Physical objects are just our way of making sense of what we see and feel in the world. **Dualists** believe that the physical and the mental worlds are both basic, and speculate (a lot) about how they can interact – this is known as the mind/body problem.

ogy were "bracketed" or set aside, leaving the phenomenologist with essentially an idealist ontology.

One of Heidegger's key points is denial of the dualism of subject and object. We never encounter subjectivity without it being directed towards an object nor of an object unobserved by a subject. What *is* going on is a unity he calls "being-in-the-world", the ongoing encounter between the human ("dasein" in his parlance) and his world. That is not to deny that there may be an objective universe out there – Heidegger is just saying that is not what is going on *phenomenologically* – phenomenologically we *are* being in the world – an ongoing encounter between dasein and dasein's world. This encounter is not neutral, disinterested, Platonic or scientific but caring – the world in encountered inside a context of dasein's concerns. In simpler terms, we are not disinterested – we look at things with our own interests in mind.

Heidegger makes this very interaction into his new ontological foundation. In recasting this human condition of interaction as basic (instead of the more traditional idealism or materialism), Heidegger points out that fundamental to a human's interaction with the world is the act of interpretation, of making sense of the situation one is "thrown" into (see below) (Heidegger, 1962, pp. H135, H298). The "objective" and the "subjective" are relegated to the status of theoretical poles that do not exist. It is the individual's involvement and interpretation of the word that is the main actor.

This involvement is with the immediate environment, the "ready to hand". A hammer (the classic example) is not given to us in terms of its objective properties, nor is it really present for us when it is in its correct context and in use. A hammer shows up to us with all its technical detail when it breaks or when it is completely in a wrong context, like in our salad or displayed in a museum. When a workman is driving a nail, the hammer is hardly more present to him than his arm or the tendon *inside* his arm. So equipment, in its correct context, is transparent. The same equipment becomes present (and an annoyance) when the hammer breaks, or isn't where it should be, or in an unusual context.

Practical understanding is more fundamental than detached theoretical understanding. Our mind is not built to deal with abstract theories. Understanding the nature of our mind, which is the same as understanding the nature of interpretation, should start and end with our encounter with everyday life, not with advanced academic matters, which are highly contrived (e.g. formal grammar, mathematics).

We do not relate to things primarily through having representations of them. What we have, in our practical and day-to-day mind, is familiarity and skills of dealing with situations and the world – not some engineer's schema of the objects around us.

Meaning is fundamentally social and cannot be reduced to a meaning-giving activity of individual subjects. This point is similar to Wittgenstein's point about meaning being given within the context of a language game, where there are socially agreed rules (e.g. "anthropology" is not a colour).

Our implicit beliefs and assumptions cannot all be made explicit. There is no neutral position we can occupy where we may examine our own thought processes without these processes being active. The inevitability of this circularity, and hence, the fact that the project of human self-exploration is endless – these should not discourage us, as in every iteration we can find out more about how we operate, only this information will never be clear and explicit, complete, and objective. Being human is not an engineering project.

"Thrownness" describes the human predicament, that life itself, and everything and every moment in life always comes imbued with meaning, for the individual. It is an exceedingly unusual situation when one looks at a field of (say) computer output with no understanding or care for what is presented.

2.2 The Cognition vs Phenomenology Debate

Let's now get into understanding the debates around AI. First it would be useful to contrast the mainstream cognitivist position with the most widespread critique starkly and in detail, using two founding texts. We will find that these two camps talk past each other: Using philosophical terminology cognitivism is essentially reductionist materialist,[3] while phenomenology has either an idealist or Heideggerian ontology. In plainer terms, cognitivism understands the mind "from the outside", as an engineer would, while phenomenology is interested in "what it is like" to be/have a mind. Sociologically, phenomenology is heavily based on a philosophical tradition written mainly in German, while cognitivism is heavily based on the metaphor of the mind as a machine and is written nearly entirely in English (see Section 4.4.2).

The book "Cognitive Psychology" coined the term "cognitive psychology" which gave the name "cognitive" to the later "cognitive science", and "cognitivism" (Boden, 2008, p. 16). The first paragraphs of this book – arguably the defining part of the defining text of the entire field – go as follows:

> It has been said that beauty is in the eye of the beholder. As a hypothesis about localization of function, the statement is not quite right—the brain and not the eye is surely the most important organ involved. Nevertheless it points clearly enough toward the central problem of cognition. Whether beautiful or ugly or just conveniently at hand, the world of experience is produced by the man who experiences it.

---

[3] Materialist – believing that the basic building block from which we can construct an understanding of the world is matter (like physicalism). Reductionists are those who believe that anything can be explained (reduced) to their favourite theory. So, reductionist-materialists believe that all things, including subjectivity, must ultimately be explained using matter. Contrast that with idealism or dualism.

This is not the attitude of a skeptic, only of a psychologist. There certainly is a real world of trees and people and cars and even books, and it has a great deal to do with our experiences of these objects. However, we have no direct, immediate access to the world, nor to any of its properties. The ancient theory of eidola, which supposed that faint copies of objects can enter the mind directly, must be rejected. Whatever we know about reality has been mediated, not only by the organs of sense but by complex systems which interpret and reinterpret sensory information. The activity of the cognitive systems results in ... the activity of muscles and glands that we call "behavior." It is also partially—very partially—reflected in those private experiences of seeing, hearing, imagining, and thinking to which verbal descriptions never do full justice.

Physically, this page is an array of small mounds of ink, lying in certain positions on the more highly reflective surface of the paper. It is this physical page which Koffka and others would have called the "distal stimulus," and from which the reader is hopefully acquiring some information. But the sensory input is not the page itself; it is a pattern of light rays, originating in the sun or in some artificial source, that are reflected from the page and happen to reach the eye. Suitably focused by the lens ... the rays fall on the sensitive retina, where they can initiate the neural processes that eventually lead to seeing and reading and remembering. These patterns of light at the retina are the so-called "proximal stimuli." They are not the least bit like eidola. One-sided in their perspective, shifting radically several times each second, unique and novel at every moment, the proximal stimuli bear little resemblance to either the real object that gave rise to them or to the object of experience that the perceiver will construct as a result...

(Neisser, 1967)

So we see that Neisser accepts the following perspectives as legitimate:

- A person is an animal, with their brain, sense organs, etc.
- With a "complex" "cognitive system", inside it
- In a "real world", with
  - "trees and people and cars and even books", and
  - "small mounds of ink" that generate
- "patterns of light at the retina" – a process rather than a thing.

And Neisser rejects "eidola". "Private experiences" are only accepted as end results not as having any causal efficacy, beyond being described. It seems that Neisser wants to reduce the number of elements in his world view as much as possible – he is trying to make his world view simpler. This could have two motivations: Either to make a technology based on this model more feasible or because he had inherited an aversion to complex explanations from his predecessors, be they Occam, Watson, or the other early cognitivists (Pear, 2007, pp. 111–115).

Dreyfus, the fiercest critic of cognitivism, and AI, on the other hand, will have none of this. He quotes from Neisser's opening paragraphs above:

> There is certainly a real world of trees and people and cars and even books... However, we have no direct, immediate access to the world, nor to any of its properties.

Dreyfus retorts:

> Here [...] the damage is already done. There is indeed a world to which we have no immediate access. We do not directly perceive the world of atoms and electromagnetic waves (if it even makes sense to speak of perceiving them) but the world of cars and books is just the world we do directly experience. ... we saw that at this point, Neisser has recourse to an unjustified theory that we perceive "snapshots" or sense data. His further account only compounds the confusion:
>
>> Physically, this page is an array of small mounds of ink, lying in certain positions on the more highly reflective surface of the paper.
>
> But physically, what is there are atoms in motion, not paper and small mounds of ink. Paper and small mounds of ink are elements in the human world. Neisser, however, is trying to look at them in a special way, as if he were a savage, a Martian, *or a computer*, who didn't know what they were for. There is no reason to suppose that these strangely isolated objects are what men directly perceive (although one may perhaps approximate this experience in the very special detached attitude which comes over a cognitive psychologist sitting down to write a book). What we normally perceive is a printed page.
>
> Again Neisser's middle-world, which is neither the world of physics nor the human [*experience*] world, turns out to be an artefact. No man has ever seen such an eerie world; and no physicist has any place for it in his system. Once we postulate it, however, it follows inevitably that the human world will somehow have to be reconstructed out of these fragments.
>
>> One sided in their perspective, shifting radically several times each second, unique and novel at every moment, the proximal stimuli bear little resemblance to either the real object that gave rise to them or the object of experience that the perceiver will construct as a result.
>
> But this whole construction process is superfluous. It is described in terms which make sense only if we *think of man as a computer* receiving isolated facts from a world in which it has no purposes; programmed

to use them, plus a lot of other meaningless data it has accumulated or been given, to make some sort of sense (whatever that might mean) out of what is going on around it.

There is no reason to suppose that a normal human being has this problem, although some aphasics do. A normal person experiences the objects of the world as already interrelated and full of meaning. There is no justification for the assumption that we first experience isolated facts, or snapshots of facts, or momentary views of snapshots of isolated facts, and then give them significance. The analytical superfluousness of such a process is what contemporary philosophers such as Heidegger and Wittgenstein are trying to point out. To put this in terms of Neisser's discussion as nearly as sense will allow, we would have to say: "The human world is the mind's model of the physical world." But then there is no point in saying it is "in the mind," and no point in inventing a third world between the physical and the human world which is an arbitrarily impoverished version of the world in which we live, out of which this world has to be built up again.

(Dreyfus, 1979, p. 269, stress added)

So Dreyfus rejects the "ink mounds" and extols phenomenology. One could be fully sympathetic with Dreyfus, but it is important to also understand Neisser: He goes to the "ink mounds" level probably because he has an eye out for the scientific reductionist or *engineering* perspective. The ink mounds are not only some "Martian" invention of cognitive scientists but also an approximation of what a camera would see as pixels. The ink mounds are also what an engineer would need in order to *replicate* a page. And replication, in the 20th century, is considered a hallmark of understanding: On the death of the eminent physicist Richard Feynman, this text was found on his office blackboard: "What I cannot create, I do not understand" (Feynman, 1988).

Arguably, Dreyfus is the more thoroughly philosophical (or more dogmatic) of the two, trying to distinguish "real" categories, while Neisser is more pragmatic and technological.

In the field of philosophy of mind, many have resolved this argument by saying that the cognitivists are discussing "sub personal" mechanisms, while phenomenology exposes the "personal level". This distinction may be satisfying for philosophers, and perhaps even for scientists, but does not help us as technologists. A more useful distinction is between cognitivism as a scientific theory aiming at objective truth and subjectivity exposing how things are for us. In AI, we can aim to simulate one, the other, or both. That is direction of this book.

Let's now move to a more systematic presentation of Dreyfus's position. More on how Dreyfus and the AI community talk past each other is found in Section 10.3.2.

2.3 Dreyfus

Dreyfus's book, "What computers can't do" (1979), may have been better titled "What cannot be formalised". Beyond being quite polemic against the AI community, he exposes their over-optimism that he blames on wild extrapolations, and shows their underlying assumptions that he finds questionable. He presents very sketchily an alternative based on the works of Heidegger and Merleau-Ponty, but this alternative does not lead to anything that can be formalised and programmed. The present volume will show a method of formally *approximating* the informal (Sections 10.3.5.3–10.3.5.4).

For an introduction to the relevant parts of Heidegger's philosophy, see Section 2.1.

The rest of this section is a summary of Dreyfus's main work, "What Computers Can't Do" (Dreyfus 1979) and his updated position (Dreyfus, 2007).

2.3.1 Part I – Ten Years of Research in Artificial Intelligence (1957–1967)

To Dreyfus, the assumptions of AI start with Plato, who looks in Euthyphro for the "necessary and sufficient" conditions for piety. To him, this is the first quest for "effective computation" – a blind procedure that would allow a conclusion to be reached with no human discretion. He skims over Aristotle and quotes Hobbes' assertion that "reason is nothing but reckoning". Leibniz saw his algebra as a means to calculating the "characteristics" of things, perhaps the first allusion to symbols as a basis for AI. Dreyfus moves along swiftly to Boole, Babbage, and Turing.

Dreyfus then gives a history of AI and turns to the wild optimism of early years, including Simon's 1956 predictions:

1. That within 10 years a digital computer will be the world chess champion, unless the rules bar it from competition.
2. That within 10 years a digital computer will discover and prove an important new mathematical theorem.
3. That within 10 years most theories in psychology will take the form of computer programs or of qualitative statements about the characteristics of computer programs.

Dreyfus then launches into a detailed debunking of these predictions; at the time Dreyfus wrote, none of these seemed at all likely.

Next Dreyfus surveys AI work from 1957 to 1962 in what he terms "cognitive simulation", including language translation, problem solving, and pattern recognition. He shows that the efforts in these fields were characterised by early success, enthusiasm, failure, and sometimes pessimism and sometimes outright denial of the difficulties.

His diagnosis of cognitive simulation is that this project has been on the wrong side of four distinctions:

- Fringe consciousness vs heuristically guided search
- Ambiguity tolerance vs context-free precision
- Essential/inessential discrimination vs trial-and-error search
- Perspicuous grouping vs character lists.

The next phase of AI was what Dreyfus calls "semantic information processing": Bobrow's "student", Evans's "analogy", and Quinlan's "semantic memory program". His analysis of the problem with this form of AI is that all these attempts were very specific, and no attempt was made to solve the underlying issues of semantics, which humans obviously have a natural solution for.

2.3.2 Part II – Assumptions Underlying Persistent Optimism

Dreyfus details four assumptions that are in the heart of AI as a research programme, at least one of which a researcher must embrace in order to pursue AI:

1. The **biological** assumption, that at some level humans operate in a digital manner. Every generation thinks in terms of its latest technology, and so we should excuse Aristotle of thinking of the human as a "clay vessel animated by divine breath" (Bolter, 1984, p. 14), and we should therefore forgive those alive in the later part of the 20th century for thinking in terms of computers. But even if the brain *were* some sort of computer, there is no evidence that it would be in any way similar to our computers. All evidence we have points to the brain *not* being digital (B. C. Smith, 2005).

2. The **psychological** assumption, that there is some *mental* level which is digital (this is at the heart of cognitive science (Boden, 2008)). Dreyfus doubts that there is any non-metaphorical way in which we can discuss information-processing notions like "list processing" as anything but one of the things that the mind is *capable* of doing – but the psychological assumption and the cognitive research paradigm require that the mind be *constituted* in these discrete, digital information-processing terms.

3. The **epistemological** assumption is that perhaps neither the brain nor the mind are digital, but just as the planets are not actually calculating their trajectories around the solar system, nonetheless their trajectory *can be* calculated. In a sense, this is the assumption of AI-as-technology as opposed to cognitive or brain simulators. In AI-as-technology, all we need is to simulate the *behaviour*, not the precise actual mechanism that produced it. The optimism of this programme is to a large part based on the success of physics and the subsequent technology. Dreyfus doubts that any non-arbitrary human behaviour can be formalised.

4. The **ontological** assumption is that all facts are enumerable and can be presented to a computer. The idea that all facts can be made explicit has a history going as far back as Plato but received its most recent prominent statement in the Tractatus: "The world is the totality of facts, not of things" (Wittgenstein, 2001b, para. 1.1). Minsky attacks this notion with his estimate that "sensible behaviour" would require between 10^5 and 10^7 facts. This gives rise to the "large database problem", and the related frame problem (the problem of programming our notion of relevance (Shanahan, 2016)). These problems arise, for Dreyfus, not from human intelligence but from the ontological assumption, which is only one possible interpretation of human intelligence. His alternative is a flexible intelligence that is always already in a situation and therefore has no frame problem nor has any need to look up relevant facts in a large database (see Section 4.3.3 on Logical Atomism).

Dreyfus turns to giving his alternative by pointing out that the Platonic-logical tradition and the computer industry are forces so strong that they overwhelm all before them, but one must at least try to be aware that the direction they are taking human culture is not the only possible one and the assumptions involved (above) are not axioms we should never question. Presenting an alternative as a *scientific* theory would be falling back into this Platonic tradition because a scientific explanation, these days, *requires* separating any object into atomic parts and so subsumes it under the very framework Dreyfus is trying to reject. Dreyfus presents as an alternative phenomenology. Phenomenology (to Dreyfus) is diametrically opposed to a mechanical explanation. Its explanations aim to find the necessary and sufficient elements that go into human experience and behaviour. Dreyfus draws mainly on the phenomenological work of Martin Heidegger and Maurice Merleau-Ponty.

2.3.3 Part III – Alternatives to the Traditional Assumptions

Admitting that his account is less precise, Dreyfus examines three areas:

1. The **role of the body** in intelligent behaviour
   Descartes made an argument that machines can only be in a small number of states and therefore cannot respond to all the complexities of the world (without an immaterial soul). Convenient as this would be for Dreyfus, he must admit that the number of possible states of a modern computer is so vast that this argument no longer holds. Dreyfus argues that what is missing from a machine is not a soul but being "an involved, situated, material body". AI has done well in all the "higher" parts of the mind, like logic, etc., but has failed miserably in the parts of behaviour that we share with animals. Our perception is global (Gestalt), with the overall meaning determining the parts, for example in language determining the parts of speech and the phonemes. Perception involves a distinction between the foreground

and background, with most of the retina input ignored as background. Our perception involves an "outer horizon" – the limits of what we notice. A computer, by contrast, has to either process data explicitly or not at all. Perception also involves an "inner horizon" of perceiving objects as being whole, even when we only see the upper side of a table and three of its legs, we perceive it as *having* an underside and four legs.

Skills need to be acquired, and perception is also a skill, no less in vision or feeling than in language understanding. Unlike computers, in humans, there is a clumsy rule-following phase later replaced by a smoother skill (see the video examples in Section 12.4) or a gestalt of skills. This requires practise, and practise requires being involved with a body. The body is already skilled in acquiring skills. Skills are acquired by what Merleau-Ponty calls "maximum grasp", which is a continuous monitoring of the situation while measuring how well one is coping with the situation. This process is situation and goal dependent. Science may require a detailed description of every motion, but our skills do not – birds are not aeronautic engineers – they just fly. Skill also allows us to adopt tools in a sense as part of our own body, as a skilled carpenter adopts his hammer or as we all do with our main language.

2. Orderly behaviour **without recourse to rules**

Our (rationalist) philosophical tradition believes that every orderly behaviour can be formalised in terms of rules. In open-structure problems, there are (at least) three phases: One needs to find out which elements can possibly be relevant, which actually *are* relevant, and which of these are essential. All these distinctions vary with the situation (and constitute "the frame problem" in AI).

Dreyfus's alternative view is that the situation is *not* a collection of data that needs to be sorted into relevant/irrelevant categories, etc., but is always already imbued with meaning. A punter deciding on the horses does not use a database of all facts about horses and people, but always already knows what it would be like to be upset by a parent's death or to be disappointed in love. He knows that such events would affect a jockey's performance not because of some arms-length analysis of an alien situation but because the punter is involved in the same field of concerns which constitutes being human. He always already knows "what it would be like" for a jockey to lose his mother as opposed to losing his watch.

The human world has a unity to it that arises out of it being *my* world, with *my* concerns, and with implements being there for purposes, *my* purposes. The AI universe of disjoint pixel inputs being modelled into a "universe model" of objective objects is devoid of all meanings, significance, or unity. "Nowhere [*in AI*] do we find the familiar world of implements organised in terms of purposes".

Dreyfus continues with his attack on cognitivism quoted above (Section 2.2) and summarises that "to avoid inventing problems and mysteries we must leave the physical world to the physicists and neurophysiologists, and return to the description of the human world which we immediately perceive".

3. The **situation as a function of human needs**

People's needs cannot be pre-specified. One cannot say there is a need for "food", "shelter", etc. and thereby predict human behaviour except in the most cruel and extreme situations. People discover what they want, what they need, as an act of creative self-discovery. One can say that a man needs love, but that need is never fully specified as just "love". After that man falls in love with a specific woman, his need is for *her*, not for "love" or "a woman" in general. We explore the world and stumble upon things that we later say that we always needed – and these are always specific and arrive in the day-to-day involvement in the world. So no pre-specified means-ends-analysis, with a predefined set of "ends" will come close to implementing the way human intelligence operates.

Moreover, not only the motivations and needs of a human are not pre-determined, even the correct description of a situation, even for a committed scientist, is not pre-fixed but is determined by the observer, subject to her preconceptions, or "paradigm" to use Kuhn's terminology (see also Section 7.3.4). Man's nature is indeed so malleable that Dreyfus worries that if the current infatuation with computers and the AI way of thinking continues then humans will think of themselves more and more in terms of the pre-specified means-ends paradigm, and the danger to humanity will not be from superintelligent machines but from subintelligent humans.[4]

2.3.4 Dreyfus's Updated Position

Dreyfus (2007)[5] uses the frame problem (the problem for a computer of finding what is relevant or not (Shanahan, 2016)) as key to understanding how different researchers have tried to achieve AI. He takes it for granted that the only AI worth having would be "Heideggerian AI". He quotes approvingly from Brooks, Agre, Wheeler, and Freeman. We will come back to the first three later in this volume.

Brooks is quoted approvingly for objecting to representations and looking for a non-Good Old-Fashioned AI (GOFAI) way of making robots, but his "robots respond only to fixed features of the environment, not to context or changing significance. They are like ants", Dreyfus also points out that Brooks's systems do not learn.

Dreyfus calls Agre a "pragmatist". Agre (with Chapman) is explicitly Heideggerian but objectifies the Heideggerian readiness-at-hand and programs none of the *experience* of skilful coping. Agre was "putting his virtual agent in a virtual world where

---

[4] Some would say that the wholesale adoption of American business-school methods of management in areas other than business is already doing this (thanks to Blay Whitby for pointing this out).

[5] The self-same talk has been repeated on other occasions, and appears with later dates.

all possible relevance is determined beforehand" and therefore cannot account for learning or new relevancies.

Moreover,

> Agre's Heideggerian AI did not try to program this experiential aspect of *being drawn in by a solicitation*. Rather, with his deictic representations, Agre objectified both the functions and their situational relevance for the agent. In Pengi [*Agre's AI experiment*], when a virtual ice cube defined by its function is close to the virtual player, a rule dictates a response, e.g. kick it. No skill is involved and no learning takes place (emphasis added).

Dreyfus is perhaps most positive about Wheeler's work – He "agree[s] it is time for a positive account of Heideggerian AI and of an underlying Heideggerian neuroscience". However, he objects to Wheeler's reintroduction of representations and to Wheeler's adoption of Classic AI's concept that humans are involved with problem solving.

Dreyfus suggests that recent research into neurodynamics in rabbits (by Walter Freeman) provides a promising start to understanding cognition correctly. However, this effort is still quite far from producing any usable technology.

Dreyfus maintains that "most basically we are absorbed copers", not problem solvers, or cognitive agents, or planners, etc. He continues that "at its best, coping does not involve representations or problem solving at all".

In short, Dreyfus's later work continues his wholesale rejection of all AI efforts.

2.4 Winograd and Flores

Terry Winograd (1946–), the author of SHRDLU (a hugely influential AI system in the 1970s), and Fernando Flores (1943–), a Chilean philosopher and politician, wrote an important book called "understanding computers and cognition" in 1986.

They describe an intellectual current central to western civilisation that they call "the rationalistic tradition" (Winograd & Flores, 1986, pp. 14–26). It is characterised by approaching any and all problems in a series of steps:

1. Characterise the situation in terms of identifiable objects with well-defined properties.
2. Find general rules that apply to situations in terms of those objects and properties.
3. Apply the rules logically to the situation of concern, drawing conclusions about what should be done.

In most of the analytic or English-speaking tradition of philosophy, questions about points 1 and 2 are often neglected as being antithetical to the scientific project, which is precisely about explaining and making predictions about situations in clear and distinct terms, using general rules. Most attention in English-speaking philosophy (especially as "the hand maiden of science", see Section 4.4.2) goes to finding better ways of applying the third part of this definition. This rationalistic approach is at the heart of science and enjoys all the prestige that comes from science's success. For many, this is the correct (or possibly the only) way to think. Anyone objecting to this way of thought is accused of "having religion up their sleeve", or of mysticism, or of being incomprehensible (Boden, 2008, pp. 251, 324; McCorduck, 2004, p. 230).

The rationalistic orientation pervades, therefore, not only computer science and AI but also scientific psychology, management theory, linguistics, and cognitive science (not least due to Herbert Simon being central in several of these fields simultaneously). Careful thinkers within this tradition do admit to its limitations, but in daily work from computer science through cognitive science to psychology and the social sciences, far too often, this methodology is taken for granted, not only in what answers are accepted but also in what questions are even allowed.

Winograd and Flores discuss three alternatives to the rationalistic view.[6]

2.4.1 Cognition as a Biological Phenomenon

In nature, any system that has a boundary and tries to control the environment (outside) for its benefit using its body (inside) can be considered a form of life. Forms of life include bacteria, horses, people, and cities. Any attempt to look at people as a form of life would be biological and would be based on physics and chemistry. Zoology, anatomy, and evolution are a "macro" view of this level of description.

In philosophy of mind, this approach is called "autopoesis" and is promoted by Maturana and Varela, and their students (Winograd & Flores, 1986, pp. 38–53).

In AI, "artificial-life" approaches (with minor if any technological significance) are based on this definition of life. Other approaches (much more successful) are based on *aspects* of biology, like neural nets, and genetic algorithms.

2.4.2 Understanding and Being

Winograd and Flores follow Dreyfus in introducing Heidegger as a major possible source of ideas for cognitive science and AI. However, they expand on Dreyfus by going into hermeneutics, which is the study of the process of interpretation. **Hermeneutics** began as a theory of the interpretation of texts, especially religious texts, such as the Bible. One of the important insights of phenomenology is that people when interpreting art, music, and texts use similar approaches to when interpreting anything else, for example making sense of situations they are in. In a sense, studying the practices people apply to understanding art or texts can be used as a test case for developing ideas about understanding how people make sense of the world in general.

---

[6] In a slightly different order.

One of the key observations of hermeneutics is the **hermeneutic circle**. The idea is that a whole is always understood in terms of its parts, and the parts can only be understood as part of a whole. So how can we understand *anything*? This is somewhat analogous to "the frame problem" in AI – the problem of finding the context in which to understand some input.

Winograd and Flores stress (following Heidegger) that the subjective and the objective cannot exist independent of each other. They are theoretical (non-existent) polar opposites of what is really going on – a process of encounter, which is identical to the process of interpretation (of the world and "objects" by the human). "The interpreted and the interpreter do not exist independently: existence is interpretation, and interpretation is existence".

Hans-Georg Gadamer (1900–2002) continued Heidegger's work in the field of hermeneutics, with Heidegger's approval (Malpas, 2013). Two of Gadamer's key concepts are tradition and prejudice. He shows that all thinking is done within a context of a tradition (if only minimally in that no one person invented language). Plato was operating in an intellectual tradition that already included Homer, Pythagoras, and Socrates, just as present physicists operate in a tradition that includes Occam, Newton, Einstein, and Feynman.

Gadamer re-examined **prejudice**, showing that prejudice does not only have the negative meaning it has in our daily parlance but is also a necessary condition of any understanding. Total "openness" (let's take that as the theoretical opposite of prejudice) cannot understand anything because it does not have any categories or language with which to interpret and understand anything. Physicists *need* their commitment to mathematics to gather and *measure* their observations. A businessman *needs* the notions of value and money in order to examine opportunities. An interesting example of prejudice in action in this positive sense is that our current society (following centuries of struggle against dogma, racism, and slavery) has a very strong prejudice against the notion of prejudice itself.

Winograd and Flores add to Heidegger's notion of throwness (see Section 2.1), combining it with urgency, and a sense that everything starts before one is quite ready (see Section 3.1.2). We are never fully prepared for anything, nor do we fully understand anything. Winograd and Flores demonstrate this with an example of having to chair an important meeting:

- You cannot avoid acting
- You cannot step back and reflect on your actions
- The effects of your actions cannot be predicted
- You do not have a stable representation of the situation
- Every representation is an interpretation
- Language *is* action.

This may be more clear and acute in chairing a meeting, but it is true of every waking moment.

2.4.3 Language as Listening and Commitment

Being humans with urgent concerns, an important aspect of our culture is the way that promises, commitments, etc. are used in society and specifically in organisations. These are of paramount importance to Winograd and Flores, and they propose software arrangements to facilitate such social structures.

Oddly, after all the detailed assessment of "computers and cognition", the book takes a sharp turn away from AI and goes on to exalt the virtues as software for managing group-work situations, projects, promises, and to-do lists. This was later implemented and called "group-ware", the most widespread example was "Lotus Notes", now renamed "IBM Notes" (IBM, 2014).

2.5 Hermeneutics and Gadamer

Winograd and Flores introduce Hermeneutics and Gadamer only briefly, but a bit more is necessary for our purposes. This is a (necessarily) schematic introduction to hermeneutics and how it relates to phenomenology. Initially, I will treat these as entirely separate things. Seemingly just to confuse things, in the 20th century, these merged to a degree and were also (at times) barely separable from existentialism and literary criticism – especially in the personae of Heidegger and Jean-Paul Sartre (1905–1980) (P. Watson, 2001). Luckily, for our purposes here, we needn't delve too deeply into this tangle of intellectual traditions, nor do we even need to have a full grasp of phenomenology or hermeneutics – a sufficient summary is provided here (and in Section 2.1).

2.5.1 Hermeneutics

Hermeneutics (the theory of interpretation) was for most of its history not a philosophical tradition, but rather the theory of how to correctly understand religious texts. Arguably, hermeneutics is at least as old as the Pauline epistles in the New Testament; however, it is with **Martin Luther**'s (1783–1546) "… 'Sola Scriptura' that we see the dawn of a genuinely modern hermeneutics" (Ramberg & Gjesdal, 2014). This protestant injunction that the Bible should be interpreted only on its own terms (without any reference to Catholic tradition) is probably the first explicit statement of a *policy* or *principle* by which interpretation of a text should be carried out.

Speaking against Cartesian notions of understanding ("clear and distinct"), **Giambattista Vico** (1668–1744) "argues that thinking is always rooted in a given cultural context. This context is historically developed and, moreover, intrinsically related to ordinary language" (Ibid.).

The romantic tradition, captivated as it was with holy texts from varying traditions, gave rise to the first theory of understanding in general, by **Friedrich**

Schleiermacher (1768–1834). He discussed the alien nature of foreign texts and called for particular attention to our prejudices, so we can understand texts under their own alien context. He does not guarantee that such strict awareness of prejudice and openness will lead to a correct understanding of a text (that may be impossible). However, such openness is *necessary* for understanding and is required not only for foreign texts but for any type of communications. Because neither is such an openness ever complete nor is our information about the context of the writing of the text full, no interpretation is ever final. Schleiermacher's work was seen as the beginning of a "critique, in the Kantian meaning of the term, of historical reason" (Ibid.).

Wilhelm Dilthey (1833–1911) distinguished "living experience" which is how each of us experience ourselves from "understanding" which is how we more systematically understand the world outside us and others. He claimed that true self-awareness can only be achieved when one understands oneself on the same terms one understands others. In understanding history and historical texts, one should combine (what we would now call) empathy, that is, a "living experience" identification with the historical characters, with "understanding", which is a more rigorous "from the outside" observation. The "living experience" component allows the historian to form hypotheses about history, while the "understanding" part allows one to critique such thoughts and see how well they stand to reason. This contrast between a creative and critical phase in intellectual work can be seen as a precursor of the context of discovery/context of justification distinction (Ibid.) (see Section 8.2.4).

2.5.2 *The Hermeneutics of Heidegger and Gadamer*

For Heidegger, interpretation is not only a matter of understanding texts but of our entire mode of being, which is continuously involved with comprehending the world and acting in it – hence, hermeneutics becomes one and the same project as phenomenology, and this joint project becomes the new ontology (Ramberg & Gjesdal, 2014; Winograd & Flores, 1986, p. 31). Heidegger was concerned with many issues in phenomenology and viewed the specifics of hermeneutics *as such* as a sub-field, the detailed exploration of which he later entrusted to a large degree to Gadamer (Malpas, 2013, Chapter 4).

Gadamer viewed hermeneutics not only as the theory of understanding ancient texts and art in general but also, and perhaps mainly, as the act of continuously understanding/interpreting all situations. In this sense, interpretation is an unceasing activity, during at least most waking hours (Gadamer, 2004, pt. 1).

Here is an example (my own) of what is meant by interpretation in this context. Consider the following:

- ■ הכלב מכוער ■
- ■ Ha-kelev meh'oar

- Il cane é brutto
- The canine is brutish
- The dog is ugly

At this point, you may be perplexed by this strange list, as one would be with any other strange sequence that is presented with little warning. In a sense, I just caused you to be "thrown" onto this unusual list and to the urgency of making sense of the situation, but help is at hand… The lines all convey the same meaning (in different alphabets, languages, and dialects). Note how much easier it is to interpret (for an English monoglot) these examples the further down one goes. Note also that as an English speaker you may be further interpreting the situation and objecting that "brutish" does not mean the same as "ugly", but you also may be aware that in the Italian "brutto" does actually mean ugly and may further be aware of how such words change meanings over the centuries and the geographic distances involved. All these thoughts are interpretative – they are attempts to make sense of a situation, at this instance, the situation at hand is the bizarre list above. *This* interpretative effort is what is meant when Heidegger, Gadamer, and others say that interpretation is our "mode of being" or suchlike expressions.

Interpretation (in the sense that interests us here) is the ability to "follow along", to "make sense" of the "inputs". In following along with (say) a song, this is easier with a familiar tune than it is with foreign music. The crux (here) of the knowledge or skill accumulated as we become more familiar with a situation does *not* consist of beliefs – we have no position on the ugliness or beauty of a dog we have never seen. What *is* being formed is an *interpretation*, an understanding, and a grasp – before (and not requiring) any judgement.

Gadamer's view of interpretation is contrasted with the objectivist school that viewed the purpose of interpretation as reaching the "true" or "objective" meaning of the text (Winograd & Flores, 1986, p. 28). Gadamer views the process of interpretation as a meeting, or a clash, or a merger, of two "horizons":

1. The brute facts of the text (which actual word is where *in the text*) and
2. The sum total of all knowledge, attitudes, and prejudices of the reader.

Hence, the name of Gadamer's magnum opus (2004), "Truth and Method" – Truth stands for the brute facts of the text, and method is all the wisdom the reader brings to bear.

The word "prejudice" has a chequered history – in earlier hermeneutics, and also in common modern usage, this term is seen as negative, and indeed, one of our culture's strongest prejudices is a prejudice against prejudice itself. However, this is (by Gadamer) a very narrow reading of the term: Prejudices are unavoidable. We only read texts that are available to us by some accident of history, and once some knowledge is acquired, it will colour our understanding of related topics for the remainder of our life. So in a sense everything that we bring to the process of understanding, all

our history, everything that falls under "method" – these could all be called prejudices, in that they colour how we will see all things (Gadamer, 2004, pp. 267–304).

Heidegger had already pointed out that in the process of interpretation we
encounter the "hermeneutic circle": We understand the whole in terms of the parts,
but we also understand the parts in terms of the whole. Gadamer adds another view
of the hermeneutic circle: The meaning of a text is determined (at least in part) by
the "method" or "prejudice" (or "mindset") of the interpreter – and also the entire
cultural being of the individual is constituted in the various influences on herself,
including the very text under study. So the text part-determines the reader, who in
turn part-determines the meaning of the text (Winograd & Flores, 1986, p. 30).

One should recall that Gadamer was exploring a specific aspect of Heidegger's
world view – namely the hermeneutic aspect. In exploring "Gadamerian AI", we
are exploring one aspect of what Heideggerian AI would be. This is in line with
Dreyfus's (2007) call for a more Heideggerian AI, but in saying that it is "a step in
the right direction" one is still threatened by the "first step fallacy" – AI researchers' tendency towards wild optimism based on a small first step being successful
(Dreyfus, 2012). How this book's proposals relate to a Gadamerian understanding
will be detailed in Section 13.4.2.

2.6 AI's Inadequate Response to Dreyfus and Other Critiques

Note that Dreyfus and Simon (and their successors) talk past each other: They
each "cannot believe" how the other side can be so misguided (McCorduck, 2004,
Chapter 9). This has several causes: Ontologically Simon (et al.) are reductionist physicalists, while Dreyfus is ontologically either an idealist (insofar as he
pushes phenomenology in general) or a Heideggerian. Pragmatically, Dreyfus is a
philosopher that views his role as writing insightful texts, Simon is an engineer –
even a social engineer. The present volume tries to maintain an understanding with
both sides of this debate, taking the subjective seriously with Dreyfus, but never
losing sight of technology, like Simon. The possibility of reconciling these positions
arises from recognising (and questioning) what they have in common – they both
think that there is only one truth that is relevant to AI. We will delve into such
assumptions as the "one truth" assumption in Section 4.2.2.

Cognitive science has tried, to an extent, to embrace Dreyfus's critique by trivi-
alising it (and sometimes merging it with the Varella critique, see Section 2.4.1).
Many AI researchers now recognise a need for robots to be real, physical, and
"embedded" in an environment in a real "embodied" manner. This does no justice
at all to Dreyfus's work. Some in cognitive science continued towards other "e"
words, like "enactive" and "extended" cognition and AI. This obsession with "e"
words has become a bit of a running joke in cognitive science.

2.7 Locating This Project amongst Existing Thinkers

As is often the case, one's nearest conceptual neighbours are also the antagonists that one critiques most harshly. Here is a list of some of this book's "nearest neighbours".

- I shall agree with **Herbert Simon**'s commitment to programming and empirical, pragmatic research. I shall critique him for his lack of imagination and for his unjustified rejection of subjectivity and introspection. I concentrate mainly on Simon since he seems to be the most influential amongst the old school of AI.
- I shall agree with **Hubert Dreyfus** in his commitment to the subjective point of view and in his general objection to the rationalist views of Simon and the other cognitivists. I shall object to his lack of commitment to programming concrete positive examples and his perfectionist rejection of all technologies so far. This book shall show that programming more phenomenological AI is possible.
- I shall agree with **Winograd and Flores** in their recommendation of Gadamer as a possible basis or inspiration for further AI development. I differ with them in their veering away from AI and (again) the lack of any concrete programmed AI examples.
- My thinking parallels **Wheeler**'s: I agree with his non-dogmatic pragmatism and with many of his ideas, mainly his notion of action-oriented representations. We differ in that his scope is broader – Wheeler (2005) deals with "the cognitive world" while I restrict my discussion to the specific field of human-like AI, as a technology.
- I agree with Brooks' distinction of two levels in human-level intelligence – the "lower" innate ability which enables the accumulation of culture and skills and the higher level of a cultured adult (Brooks et al., 1999). I will distinguish anthropic AI (the endeavour of simulating human intelligence *per se*) from any commitment to the specifics of our current, contingent "western, modern, well-trained, and adult" ideals about how thinking supposedly *should* be done. I disagree with Brooks et al's contention that the type of intelligence they preprogram can support human behaviour and culture.

2.8 Current Critiques of AI: Summary

Dreyfus blames the overwhelming success of physics for the biases of the AI research programme, though he does not give this way of thinking a consistent name: "Platonist", "intellectualist", "mechanist", and "they" (sic) figure often.

Winograd and Flores name this approach "the rationalistic tradition" and characterise it as aiming to solve problems by using three steps:

1. Characterise the situation in terms of identifiable objects with well-defined properties.
2. Find general rules that apply to situations in terms of those objects and properties.
3. Apply the rules logically to the situation of concern, drawing conclusions about what should be done (Winograd & Flores, 1986, pp. 14–15).

This critique of science-like thinking extending beyond the bounds of its competence is widespread in the humanities and social sciences, where it is called scientism (the term is derogatory) (Bannister, 1991). Usually the people using the word "scientism" in social science are fighting against what they see as an overextension of scientific practise to cover areas that should be given a more qualitative or a more nuanced treatment.

The project of this book belongs somewhere between Dreyfus's and Simon's schools of thought and uses elements of both together with Winograd and Flores's recommendation of Gadamer as the intellectual context. Having developed some example AI programs, we will recognise Wheeler's "action-oriented representations" in them.

This book is about AI. Let's first take a glance at how *humans* think, as opposed to how humans *would like to* believe that they think.

Chapter 3

Human Thinking: Anxiety and Pretence

This chapter is about thinking in individual **humans** and thinking in **societies**, and how these interact. This will serve as context for the discussion of thought in computers – artificial intelligence (AI). This discussion will include issues never handled before in the literature about AI: **Anxiety**, **pretence**, and **social pressures**. If we could program a computer to do something similar to what goes on in our own human minds, we will have very interesting human-like AI indeed. That's where we are headed.[1]

The process of human thinking is relevant to AI in three ways. When working on creating AI,

- What we are aiming for, intelligence, is what humans have.[2]
- The most readily available working example of intelligence is our own *individual* existence, a case of human intelligence.
- We work on AI collectively, as a group in our *society*. Our society's common presuppositions are most often taken to be automatically true, with no argument.

The complexity of examining our subjectivity, our emotions, and their interactions with intelligence on the individual, societal, and artificial levels would boggle the best of minds. This chapter is not for the faint-hearted. Let's begin.

---

[1] This chapter provides a broad context and may be seen by some as less rigorous than other parts of this book. It is not strictly necessary for the support the overall argument.

[2] We assume for present purposes that to "think" and to "use one's intelligence" is one and the same thing.

3.1 Individual Thinking

One might agree that most (other) people are not as clever as they would like to think, if only because they do not agree with oneself on matters of politics; religion; city planning; or taste in alcohol, music, dogs, or football. And yet we all know "in our hearts" that we are not that different to our peers, and that we ourselves were also (at least in childhood) quite less clever than we would like to claim to be today. We also know full-well that at no time (including our 18th and 21st birthdays) was there a dramatic improvement in our thought processes. As far as the quality of our thinking goes, any difference between us-as-adults and us-as-children was gradual and a matter of degree. We are also aware of our past mistakes but often we excuse them away and uphold a sense of personal near-infallibility, which is no more than a pretence.

3.1.1 Our Thinking Processes Are Embarrassing

Recall (from the introduction) the comments made by Seymour Papert's in an interview with a historian:

> We are to thinking as Victorians were to sex. We all know we have these horrible moments of confusion when we begin a new project, that nothing looks clear and everything looks awful, that we work our way out using all sorts of odd little rules of thumb, by going down blind alleys and coming back again, and so on, but since everyone else seems to be thinking logically, or at least they claim they do, then we figure we must be the only ones in the world with such murky thought processes. We disclaim them, and make believe that we think in logical, orderly ways, all the time knowing very well that we don't. And the worst offenders here are teachers, who present crisp, clean batches of knowledge to their students, and look as if they themselves had learned that knowledge in a crisp, clean way. It didn't happen that way, but the teachers don't admit it, and the students groan inwardly, feeling so hopelessly dumb.
>
> **(McCorduck, 2004, p. 339)**

Note how central "making believe" is, and societal pressure, and anxiety.

The vast majority of what we do and think is comprised of unconsidered, jumbled repetition of patterns that we have experienced, heard, or seen in the past (we may call some of these habits). We often "have voices in our heads", and we occasionally like to call some of them "the voice of reason", "a primordial call", or some suchlike. Listening closely to these "voices" as we experience them, they often sound like parents, teachers, of some other voice (often of admonishment) from the past, now seemingly living inside our head. Our thinking is hopelessly mixed with emotion (Goldie, 2012). The sentences in our thoughts are fragmented and not particularly rational. We have little control over these processes – trying to stop our own thinking is even more difficult than stopping our own breathing.[3] The contents of the thoughts are also not under our control: For example, I can make you think about an animal even without mentioning it: "Mary had a little…". Another example: "Please do not think about the sum of $2+2$". We muddle through life by repeating grammatical and causal patterns that sort of worked before, more or less acting according to these thoughts. Even when we actively make a point of acting *not* in accordance to some thought, the very process of suppressing a thought's effects is driven by just another thought. The thoughts, ideas, and behaviours that get repeated and transmitted amongst people are the "memes" that Dawkins described as the building blocks of cultures (Dawkins, 2016, p. 249).

3.1.2 Anxiety, Pretence, Stories, and Comfort

We know[4] nothing with any certainty but **pretend** we know a lot. This pretence is necessary for (1) survival and (2) social self-promotion.

The pretence of knowing what to do is necessary for **survival** since it is necessary for any action. Life is urgent:

> [Life] does not admit of any preparations or preliminary experiments.
> Life is fired at us point blank…. Where and when we are born, or happen to find ourselves after we were born, there and then, like it or not, we must sink or swim.
>
> **(Gasset, 1963, p. 42)**

We cannot wait to resolve our doubts or to prepare, we must act now. We think we know where the sugar is in the kitchen. We cannot be certain, but we are pretty sure, so we freely use or communicate such knowledge to each other, and societies muddle along that way – full of minor surprises when things are not as we thought they would be. We occasionally admit this, like when we say "you can never know". We expect our colleagues to be in the office tomorrow or at least tell us if they are sick, but they might die, or go psychotic, or quit town. Overnight.

A key angle to consider is how we emotionally relate to utterances we believe to be true or how we used to relate to them as children. Remember when you were (as a child) alarmed at something, and your parent would tell you that everything

---

[3] Except perhaps during advanced meditation, or deep sleep, and even in these cases it is doubtful whether there is any "us" there controlling our thoughts (Rahula & Demieville, 1997).

[4] Most of this chapter relates to "knowledge that" (rather than "knowledge how"), in the context of a society (see Section 6.7). Much of what is said here would also apply to "knowledge how", perhaps to a lesser degree. To what degree it would apply to a person living alone on a deserted island is an open question.

is OK (perhaps adding a brief explanation), and you accepted that, and it made everything fine. This is a central point about our human thinking. We have a need for **comforting stories** that we can believe in and so make us feel safe and make the anxiety go away.[5]

Several types of people tell us these (believable) stories – it starts with parents and continues with friends and teachers. Later in life, we often believe politicians, businesspeople, scientists, doctors, quacks, charlatans, etc. Some of these stories end up working for us, some do not.

Another angle on how fickle and **feeble** our minds are is advertising. We all would like to believe that advertising does not affect us, but empirical facts are not on our side here. The weakness of the human mind is systematically abused to persuade people not only to buy products and vote for politicians but also to join cults (Hassan, 1988).

3.1.3 Can We Even Tell the Truth?

We **don't know anything** for sure. Definitely not as children but also as adults. When we say "$2+2=4$" we cannot be sure that we are not confused, drugged, going demented, or suffering any other mental deficiency. We repeat $2+2=4$ mostly for the same reason we say things like "motherhood and apple pie" – it is always apple. These are slogans that were repeated often enough that they seem self-evident. But $2+2=4$ is the easy case, of a formal system, where there *is* (we like to think) a true answer, and we can hope to know it.[6] In natural (informal) situations, it is worse. We never know for (at least) the following reasons:

1. Most often there is no "fact of the matter" that can be stated in words.
   1.1. If I say that my niece is 13 years old, that is not accurate. Even if I say that she is 13 years, 2 months, 3 h, 54 min, and 15.7 s old – that is a non-sense since birth does not occur in any one instant. It is also nonsense in that even if it were true when uttered, it would not be true by the time it is comprehended. A couple of seconds would have elapsed.
   1.2. In describing anything, I can never give all the details. The image you will form in your mind based on my description will never match the image in my own mind, let alone the state of affairs in the world.

---

[5] Perhaps different mammals have very different tempers. In terms of overall levels of anxiety: cats (when undisturbed) display great confidence, happily sleeping anywhere. Mice, on the other hand, seem to always be worried, forever shifting their whiskers, forever checking and double checking. They try not to sleep in the open, or alone. I propose that the overall stress level in humans is somewhere in between, but nearer the mouse. We worry. We don't usually sleep in the open. We discuss worrying scenarios with each other. We seek reassurance.

[6] Disabusing us from hope that there would *always* be a true answer is what Gödel taught us (Raatikainen, 2015).

2. Words only possess meanings in the context of a language game (Wittgenstein, 2001a). No two people are playing precisely the same language game. Worse, even as individuals, our language game has no fixed rules – in that our language game is not even strictly a game (it is not consistently governed by its rules).
3. The state of affairs in the world may be quite different than we think. We are fallible.

So every utterance (even if I am saying something to myself) is in at least a partial sense a lie or an inaccuracy. We can't even know *how* inaccurate that utterance is. Life is too urgent to communicate precisely (see the quote in Section 3.1.2), so we get on with things, at the cost of knowing that we are not telling the truth. The only way to not lie is not to use language. This has been understood by major Asian civilisations for millennia: The Buddha sits mum. The Tao is silent (Rahula & Demieville, 1997; Smullyan, 1993).

So every sentence is a lie, or an inaccuracy, or a gamble, including this one. All we can do is approximate.[7]

3.1.4 Motivations

We would like to think that we think logically, about facts, goals, sub-goals, etc. But actually what we have inside is not a logic machine, but a mess. Worse, even our motivations are not some sensible motivations we decide upon autonomously and reasonably but the result of various biographical accidents that happened to us in our childhood or youth: Someone said "X" with great authority, and we accepted X as axiomatic. Or we made some momentous decision like deciding to always seek harmony and therefore *never* hold any strong opinions or *never* to end up like such and such a person.

Rather than pursue sensible motivations logically, we pursue nonsensical motivations using rather chaotic means. Such is our mind, if truth be told – but it works. Humans are a successful species.

---

[7] Considering how unreliable the human mind is, the question arises as to how can the author of this book, a mere mortal, guide the reader through this quagmire? The answer is equivocal – ultimately I make no claim to have a full understanding of anything. Consider Rome: it is a city so complex that even life-long scholars make no claim that they fully understand it. The same is true with many natural parks – the safari guides are often surprised themselves by what they find. All one can do in guiding tourists through such places is share what *is* known, try to keep the tourists safe, and attempt to draw a picture that is more complete than the tourist would get by wandering alone. Similarly, this book makes few hard-and-fast claims – it merely points out paths that for historical reasons have been neglected, but may well be fruitful (see Section 5.2.4). Unlike in a safari, I can guarantee that you will not get physically assaulted by any monsters jumping out of these pages, and that the algorithms towards the end of this book work.

3.2 Society's Thinking

Some may object that social thinking has little to do with AI, and they would be correct, in that what we are looking to recreate in AI is an individual thinking machine, similar to an individual thinking human. Social phenomena are too "macro" – they are outside our scope.

However, when we are discussing AI from the outside, as in philosophy of AI (including this volume), we need to discuss the prejudices and opinions of the AI community. The AI community is a social thing and is embedded in a wider society: the late 20th (and early 21st) century western, English-speaking, society, mainly in the United States. So both the AI community *per se* and the more general society in which it is embedded are of interest to us. Our discussion of how AI was part of wider currents in the post-Second World War society has already been mentioned (around Watson and Simon) and will be discussed further. Here, we need to examine how societies' thinking works in general terms, just as we discussed the individual above. As we saw that individuals are not as clever as they pretend, we will find a similar situation with societies, not that collective stupidity would be news to historians (Tuchman, 1990).

Societies think politically, scientifically, and culturally. Some of the (questionable) beliefs of the AI community will be discussed in Chapter 4.

3.2.1 Politics

In politics we should look at followers and leaders.

Our yearning for believable, soothing stories explains our tendency to follow people who seem to know what they are talking about. In the insecurity of not knowing which perspective to adopt, we clamour for a wise or strong person to lead us, to tell us a believable, hopeful story, and to absolve us from the need to worry about all the various problems ourselves. The clamour for strong leadership in times of crisis (real or perceived), regardless of the quality of such leadership, is just a more extreme case of the normal desire to flee from our anxiety towards the certainties offered by an apparently knowledgeable person with an appealing narrative. The more sinister cases of humanity's hankering after simplicity are the demagogue-dictators of the mid-20th century (Fromm, 2011). These leaders build such a cult of personality that allows them to claim knowledge that they manifestly do not have: A recent example is Donald Trump, with his instantly infamous quotes: "I am like a smart person" (Trump, 2017), and "I know words, I have the best words" (Trump, 2015).

Becoming a leader allows also the person himself to feel relief from the anxiety of not knowing: "If all these people are following me, then I must be right!" An alternate explanation as to how leaders lead is by wilful manipulation. At least on the surface, most such leaders also end up believing their own megalomania.

In the case of AI, one may wish to recall the personality cults found around leading thinkers in psychology (e.g. Freud) and perhaps the outsized influence of Herbert Simon on many fields, including AI.

3.2.2 Social Perceptions of Science

In most modern societies, religion has lost its former grip. However, explicit religious hierarchies have been to a large degree replaced by a belief in science, having faith that it and the "scientific way of doing things" will solve all the world's problems. The educated elites occasionally "speak for science" with a dogmatic tone not dissimilar to the tone of a priesthood speaking for a god. This belief that science will solve *all* problems has flimsy foundations (see Section 4.1).

Science claims to know some things through experimental observation and mathematics. A main methodology for building and integrating the edifice of scientific knowledge is peer review, the process whereby scientific and scholarly works are critiqued by other experts in the field before they are published. This mechanism is usually enough to weed out any bizarre claims that make no sense to the rest of the field but is no bulwark against groupthink or prejudices. Cognitive science has its share of such biases, to be detailed below.

What about verified scientific knowledge? Insofar as it is treated as hard and fast, that is a misunderstanding – since in principle all science (unlike dogmatic religion) is open to modification and the ascent of new, better theories. So science gives us better approximations of what is going on, but no hard and fast, permanent knowledge. Moreover, science is no solution to personal anxiety, since it tells us nothing about *our* lives or about subjectivity. And the things that can comfort our *personal* anxiety are *personal* and subjective.

A point worth keeping in mind is that wrong beliefs *are often very useful*. Even if one believes that the earth is stationary and the sun revolves around it, one can predict day and night and manage agriculture successfully. Likewise, understanding Newtonian physics is sufficient for all daily activities, even though Newton's physics has been superseded by modern physics. Pragmatically, we can muddle through with partial truths. Consider how the most successful polity ever (the Roman Empire) had no science at all. For an example of wrong information being useful closer to AI, see Section 8.2.6.

If you like vertigo-inducing stories, you may be interested in the fact that our very tradition of logical thinking is rooted in the works of Plato. Plato used the character of Socrates to present his thought. Socrates introduces a story, a myth, that logic is qualitatively different from any other myth or story. If we were to follow him seriously, we might find ourselves unsure of where we stand (Partenie, 2014). Note also that the reason we are led to believe that Socrates is the "wisest person" is none other than another story, a story attesting that the mythical oracle of Delphi said so (Ryan, 2014). It is stories all the way down: Comforting stories, which often work – but with no foundation other than further stories.

3.2.3 Interrelation of Politics and Science

Politics and science are not as separate as we may like to think. Politicians, whether elected or hereditary, like to keep the people with knowledge close at hand – this seems to be a universal phenomenon. In China, scholars who could predict an eclipse were highly prized and were given much influence in the emperor's court. In medieval Arabia, the situation was similar (Irwin, 2010, p. 25). The Bible mentions the central role of Egyptian magicians in the court of Pharaoh (Exodus 7). But this is not only a premodern phenomenon. In the modern United States scientists managed to prove their worth in the most dramatic way (exceeding the most spectacular myths) by developing the atomic bomb and (seemingly) winning the Second World War for the United States at a stroke.

This proximity of knowledge and power is not all innocent. Scientists often bent their theories to suit the political times. An extreme case was soviet genetics under Stalin (Brown, 2010, p. 221). Even Watson, a central figure in the history of cognitive science, was playing politics with his imposition of behaviourism on the world of American psychology. Herbert Simon, a central figure in AI research, was also an advisor to the US federal government.

3.2.4 Distinct Disciplines and Education

People (including AI researchers) have a tendency to stick to the relevant topics rather than the irrelevant. This saves time but may lead to a dearth of new ideas. Breaking disciplinary boundaries (as does this volume) may be necessary for a breakthrough in AI. In this vein, it is useful to see how the different disciplines are introduced to us in education and how the supposedly less-relevant disciplines are systematically undermined by policy makers and educators.

The idea of distinct disciplines originated at least as early as with Aristotle, who taught different subjects at different times, and used to announce at the beginning of his talks that "X will be explained" (McKeon, 1941). It is pretty obvious why we continue to separate human knowledge into distinct groupings: No one can know everything, and in administering even an elementary school, different teachers specialise in teaching different topics. This leads most students to believe that the topics are truly distinct, and that there is no historical accident in how (say) arithmetic evolved, and that psychology and technology have nothing to do with each other. These beliefs are false.

In modern democracies, an attempt is made (more or less sincerely, depending on the time and place) to manage society reasonably and rationally. Amongst the first concerns of nations and governments is taking care of the future of the economy, to ensure (insofar as possible) future prosperity. It has become a truism that society should invest in education, and not just any education, but the sort of education that leads to good jobs. Once a consensus has formed around this idea, it is very easy to run a survey amongst well-paying employers as to what education they would like their recruits to have – and the result is a supposedly sensible education policy (Gonzalez & Kuenzi, 2012).

Such a sensible education policy of course assumes the separability of subjects – otherwise there is no way to decide which are the useful subjects to teach. Like many policies, they seem to address the main concern (economic growth, employment) with little care for the side effects. A current favourite buzzword associated with such "sensible" subjects is "STEM" (Science, Technology, Engineering, and Mathematics). Apparently the irony is lost on many of the policy specialists that their own skill set (politics and government) is being condemned as useless (perhaps they would like, at some level, to reduce the competition for their own jobs).

Another administrative motivation for compartmentalising education is the constant pressure to measure education. Schools are often run like businesses, aiming for standardised tests (Chomsky, 2017). This book (in passing) demonstrates some of what is being lost when a society decides to not teach the humanities to engineers, and vice versa.

But things get even worse. Having this (cultural) notion of distinct topics and disciplines allows us to internally compartmentalize "work issues" away from personal emotional complexities. The pretences involved in taking on socially acceptable roles (Goffman, 1971) are *justified* by "X being an entirely different topic than Y".

3.2.5 Education as Indoctrination

I have a further suspicion about education: That it has evolved into an unconscious but powerful mechanism to mislead the young. The main untruth being sold to the young is that the adults know what they are doing, and the main benefit for society is that the young are indoctrinated to adopt the roles which would be beneficial to society (or to the powers that be) rather than invent a more original life for themselves.

Let's examine how this was achieved in one particular case. In the schools that I personally attended, geometry was taught in great detail, with proofs for every theorem being demonstrated using both axiomatic and graphic means. By the end of our course in geometry, we were thoroughly convinced that (Euclidean) geometry is complete and consistent (which it is). Even the most suspicious students were reassured by unimpeachable proofs for every claim.

However, when we were taught algebra, we were taught (more pragmatically) how to solve equations, initially linear equations with one variable. The teaching of algebra then extended in two directions: quadratic equations (with X^2) and two equations with two variables. We were also shown that the same system can be extended to N equations with N variables. All was well and presented with great clarity. The fact is that whoever designed the curriculum extended the idea of solving equations only to the second degree (X^2), and though a cubic equation (X^3) was solved on the blackboard to demonstrate that it is possible, equations of a higher degree were quietly ignored. This is not an innocent omission – higher order equations cannot be solved analytically, even the experts solve these "numerically", that is, by groping in the dark.

That form of presentation in school created the impression that in mathematics all is clear and simple, known and understood, since the open problems in mathematics were elegantly sidestepped. The pupils were encouraged by the very structure of the curriculum to assume that our society understands all the practical parts of mathematics and by extension knowledge in general. The fact is that Euclidean geometry is one of *very few* areas of knowledge in which we really know everything there is to know. But informing teenagers that our entire society is groping in the dark about so many subjects – that was considered a bad idea. Perhaps it is indeed a bad idea to tell the truth to teenagers, but certainly, if we as adults want to advance the cutting edge of knowledge and technology, we need to face reality as it is: We know very little – both as individuals and as a society. "The adults" or "the experts" may know more that than we do, but at the edges of their knowledge, they grope in the dark just as badly as the rest of us do.

The thought that we are all just groping in the dark creates a motivation to join the pretence of some "winning side", often the rationalists, and to deny our actual predicament, groping in the dark.

The separation of education into "STEM subjects" vs "woolly" or "useless" subjects is impeding our ability to revisit and review our most fundamental assumptions. Moreover, our training makes us afraid of the subjective. This in turn keeps us from developing radically new ideas, no less valid than the existing consensus. This situation is similar to C.P. Snow's "Two cultures" argument (Snow, 1964) and is at least a contributing factor to the paucity of revolutions in science and technology.

3.3 Adapting to Social Norms

3.3.1 Social Pressure – the Game of Life

Alan Watts (1915–1973) introduced the idea of a social game, which one is *required* to play. This game is widespread, and a variant thereof is probably necessary for the functioning of any society. The game is a double-bind game, in that its rules are self-contradictory. One has to muddle through these contradictions:

1. The first rule of the game is that it is not a game.
2. Everyone must play.
3. You must love us.
4. You must go on living.
5. Be yourself, but play a consistent and acceptable role.
6. Control yourself and be natural.
7. Try to be sincere.

(Watts, 2009, p. 73)

In a sense, the "game of knowledge" can be defined in this vein as "8. Tell the truth, and make progress". That is contradictory, as we saw in Section 3.1.3. The option of staying silent is also ruled out by the requirement to play an acceptable role (point 5 above).

3.3.2 Conforming

Learning anything means adapting to some norm, external to ourselves – learning is adapting to doing something *correctly*. And the definition of "correctly" comes from outside: "correctness" may be defined by the rules of some game (Wittgenstein, 2001a). The rules may be defined by some loose group of people, a certain "they" (Heidegger, 1962, pp. H113-) or society or culture at large.[8]

The problem raised by Papert's quote (Section 3.1.1) is that we try to conform to our society's norms (in thinking) at the individual level and deny how we actually think – making our thinking processes convoluted, pretentious, and anxiety-ridden. This effort at conformity makes our mental processes even more obscure for AI researchers, who are often trained specifically to ignore the subjective.

Social adaptation leads to the creation of local cultures, such as a certain family's particular sense of humour, or an attitude shared by a certain profession. In academia, the split between the humanities and the exact sciences is such an example (Snow, 1964).

3.3.3 Escape to a Role, Arrogance

There is a common strategy for escaping the predicament of knowing how fake we are. This strategy starts with accepting as axiomatic some highly specific societal system of values and of thinking, adopting it as a role and trying to make it within that system of values with its own peculiar definitions of what is true or valuable (see Section 9.3.1). Such socially defined roles can be, for example, a devout member of a well-organised religion, being a family person, a political activist, a scholar or scientist, going into business, law or the military – each according to their own set of beliefs and values. Even a relatively unstructured system like "having fun" or "doing one's own thing" is socially structured and provides criteria for success by which one can "make it" (at least to a degree) and console oneself. The more competitive try to excel at their choice of lifestyle, some try to just get by, some even revel in mediocrity, but even that is part of a socially accepted narrative. Even criminals are following a role, of "outsmarting society". Some people excel at their role, and many become self-righteous and arrogant, within the value judgements of their adopted role and beliefs.

---

[8] Perhaps the intelligent thing is the culture and not the individual. Perhaps the individual evolved specifically to carry culture (selfish gene assisted by selfish meme).

So pretence in our speech has two levels – one arises directly from the inability to say something that is true and accurate (see Section 3.1.3). The second level of pretence is the construction of a self-defensive persona that actively tries to hide our inadequacy. One common symptom of such a personality is a wholesale withdrawal from and disavowal of the subjective, and an attraction to areas where an always-correct persona can exercise its superiority. Such fields include mathematics and any other areas where truth and falsehood can be clearly separated. I personally associate this attempt to pretend to be always right mostly with highly educated men. These are just the sort of men we find in the cutting edge of exciting pursuits, like AI, actually. Few people in our field seemed as secure (and political) in their scientific assertions as J.B. Watson and Herbert Simon.

There is also the softer case, of becoming qualified as an expert: A common report from the aftermath of graduation ceremonies is that people, having acquired some qualification or another, do not *feel* much wiser than they were before. They have read some texts and have practised some skills, but their subjective sense of how secure they are in their knowledge has not improved much. This has to do with how much they have become aware during their studies of more areas of ignorance they were not even aware of before their studies begun.

3.3.4 Needs Must

We know we are lying, approximating, or "cutting corners". But we pretend to know what we are talking about, and our society would not function without this pretence. Moreover, even alone in one's room one cannot progress in thinking from A to B to C without committing (internally) to A, in order to move on to B. So all thinking requires a certain amount of pretence: "Ok, for now, say A is true, so B…". When we reach a conclusion, we know that the premises and the logic that led to the conclusion are all questionable. We choose to ignore that – we need to get on with life. Life is urgent (see the quote in Section 3.1.2).

3.4 Relevance to AI

3.4.1 Anxiety and Pretence Are Immediately Relevant to Thinking

Some may admit the idea that anxiety and pretence are innate to the human condition but so is occasionally having a gall stone. They may ask how are anxiety and pretence *directly* relevant to thinking or intelligence?

Anxiety is more proximate to thinking than gallstones. Anxiety is the motivation for most thoughts leading to most actions (see the quote in Section 3.1.2). We have to respond, we need to decide. Now. Anxiety (and pretence) is also the result of thinking. So thinking both comes from and contributes to anxiety. Pretence is only a result, anxiety is both a cause and an effect of thinking.

Many descriptions of happiness, bliss, etc. involve *not* thinking and *not need-ing* to think – which is compatible with no anxiety. Also, even if cases of thought without anxiety can be demonstrated, that does not detract from this argument about *much* of thinking. That's especially relevant in the case of thinking about work (where demands are high and persistent). In building AI, we are looking for robots that will function in work situations, rather than bliss robots (whatever that may mean). Human-like AI is for human-like work – work where we need to "rub along" inside a human society (see Section 6.2).

Anxiety is therefore more intimately tied up with thinking than gallstones or most other human functions.

3.4.2 Implications for AI, a Rudimentary Human-Like Mind

AI as it stands is good but far from human-like. If we want to make it more human-like, we may wish to implement various approximations of our subjective experi-ence. "Trains of thought" that "fade in and out", for example, will be demonstrated in an algorithm in Chapter 12. Dealing with anxiety in a deeper fashion is a future challenge. This may require bringing in mental self-observation, which would be a step towards an approximation of consciousness (see Gamez, 2008).

We still have a long way to go before mental self-awareness becomes robotic consciousness and introspection. Language would be necessary for introspection. This book is not reporting on a complete project – it aims at opening up our think-ing, resulting in a multitude of possible projects in AI.

3.4.3 Meaning-for-Me vs Big Data

Existing AI aims mathematically to get the best answer possible. This AI is correct, incorrigible, and inhuman. It also requires huge amounts of data in order to have an acceptable level of certainty. It has nothing to do with anxiety.

Humans generalize from very little data. As we saw above, such a generalization is *necessarily* a guess, a pretence, and would bring up some anxiety. A human-like system would also need to generalize from few data points or it would not be like humans.

Humans (and dogs) choose their course of action based on the expected results (this was a central insight of behaviourism). In a sense, the "expected outcome" is the "meaning" of an action. That's how we extrapolate from few data points – we establish what the cause means *to us* by what happened *to us*. Humans are not born scientists (one is under no obligation to aim for a general truth in one's pri-vate life) – we only take responsibility for ourselves based on our own experience. So a human-like system would require *meaning-for-me*, while most existing AI is based on *general correctness*. These are polar opposites. More about this is detailed in Chapter 8.

3.4.4 Relevance to AI – the Future

But what do these notions of pretence and anxiety tell us about AI? In a trivial sense, the algorithms presented in Chapters 11 and 12 already "experience" some anxiety in that they aim to get the least bad result (in a fallible, human-like way). Again, in a trivial sense, any AI algorithm, when it proposes a solution to a problem, "pretends" or presents that solution as "the best" or "the truth", etc. But these trivial senses in which anxiety and pretence are parts of AI's "psychology" are not very satisfactory.

If we wish to create human-like AI, we need to make machines with more human-like versions of our thought processes. Ultimately, such a project would require that we build the AI so that it "has experiences" like humans do. This would require, for starters, allowing the AI to experience itself at all. That can be achieved by adding some parameters that are internal to the state of the AI system as inputs to the self-same system. Currently few, if any, AI algorithms "experience themselves" at all.

3.5 Human Thinking: Anxiety and Pretence: Summary

This chapter provided a social-subjective explanation as to why people flee from subjectivity, self-policing their thought processes. Deep inside, we know that our thinking is as flimsy as a house of cards. This leads to internal anxiety (we know all our thinking is messy) and to social anxiety (we are afraid that people will find out). This motivates us further to pretend that we are thinking in a socially acceptable manner. The fashionable way to think in modern times is rationalism.

Rationalistic thinking is seductive on several levels:

■ It is what society to a large degree demands of us.
■ It allows us to ignore subjectivity, emotions, and hence, many difficulties that perhaps may be seen as weak or effete.
■ It allows us to partake in the scientific project, a most impressive thing.
■ It allows us to partake in fashionable business school-type thinking and its promises of financial success.

It seems that we will never be able to describe human thinking processes from a subjective point of view completely. That is not a "bug" of the human condition, but rather a "feature": For most of the history of humanity, there would have been no evolutionary value in that, and the "architecture" required for our mind to be fully self-transparent would be quite peculiar. But we *can* describe *some* thinking processes, and we *can* get closer. That is where this book is heading.

The more we dare to program approximations of processes that we find in actual humans (if we look for them), the more our AI can become genuinely human-like. Our AI, like us, should be able to construct intelligent behaviour out of its own internal mess of emotions and pressures. We humans may just be "faking it till we make it", but that did not stop mere humans like ourselves from landing on the moon. If human intelligence successfully emerges from the muck of human emotions, there is no reason to think that a human-like AI should emerge out of anything else.

This book is about how (the seeming miracle of) intelligent behaviour emerges from various not-too-intelligent mechanisms. This chapter dealt with intelligence in societies, and in individual humans – the reader may be excused being in a rush to move on to computers. We need just one more preparation: Since AI is an urgent project in our own society, current western society's thoughts and presuppositions about AI and thinking in general would be of great interest. Noticing one's prejudices is a first step to abandoning them.

Chapter 4

Prevailing Prejudices Pertaining to Artificial Intelligence

Things that you're liable to read in the Bible… ain't necessarily so.

Ira Gershwin

In every pursuit, we are forced to make assumptions. Some of these are made consciously and explicitly, some others are just part of our beliefs or opinion systems or attitudes. Some further assumptions are inherited from the surrounding culture's habits. Moreover, in thinking about difficult topics, we often adopt a metaphor, such as "Mind as Machine", as Boden's omnibus history of cognitive science is entitled (Boden, 2008). Every such metaphor brings in further assumptions. We should (logically) be alarmed at this multitude of assumptions, but we are powerless to avoid them. What we can do is try to be aware of the specific assumptions we make, and when the time comes and we find ourselves in an impasse, we can try to relax these assumptions one by one until we find a way out of that impasse. As we have seen, artificial intelligence (AI) is now at an impasse.

The purpose of this chapter is to show that some outmoded ideas, opinions, attitudes, and metaphors[1] (some going back thousands of years) have influenced cognitive science and AI with often insufficient argument. Many of these influences have more to do with theology, politics, or historical accidents than with anything

---

[1] I am not sure that there are any clear boundaries amongst those things: ideas, opinions, attitudes, habits of thought, and metaphors. They all influence our thinking insofar as they cause us to adopt or reject new notions more or less readily.

65

relevant to science or technology. This chapter builds on Winograd and Flores' (1986) description of the rationalistic tradition (reviewed in Section 2.4). It also builds on Wheeler's (2005) survey of how beliefs held by Descartes (1596–1650), though officially rejected, survive in cognitive science.

A pertinent example of how the history of ideas illuminates our philosophical discussions is the question of whether humans are rational (see Section 4.5.4). The rationality of humans has been abundantly refuted in every generation (Ariely, 2009; Tuchman, 1990), and yet (at least in cognitive science), this idea refuses to die (Bringsjord, 2008). Another example of an influential idea refusing to die is positivism. We shall use the story of positivism as a sample of the evolution of such ideas and how little their history had to do with careful argumentation. The other assumptions will only be enumerated and summarised briefly. Positivism is detailed here as an example of the accidents of history that underlie all these beliefs.

4.1 A History of an Idea: Positivism

France had a revolution in 1789–1799. It was followed by various periods of chaos, including the Napoleonic wars (some would say that even today's protests in France are an aftershock of that revolution). The revolution not only overthrew the king and the aristocracy but also much of the authority of any and all churches. By the early to mid-1800s, there were several attempts to produce a new ideology for the new society. What was required was a quasi-religion that would give meaning to life without the power structures that were overthrown and without the scaremongering doctrines that were used to keep the citizenry down for many centuries. Christianity was tainted as being part of the old regime. France needed a modern ethos, a modern story to live by. One should recall that Darwin was still in the future, so full-blooded atheism was a much less tenable position than it is today.

Auguste Comte (1798–1857) was a French intellectual trying to make sense of this post-revolutionary world. He created a philosophy-cum-religion called "positivism" that held that all sciences were going to eventually be unified in a single logical structure with mathematics at the base, followed by physics, chemistry, biology, etc. leading up to a full understanding of individual humans and eventually societies.[2] Science would provide all answers and solve all problems (Bourdeau, 2014; Mill, 2013).

Positivism had rituals and churches, and spread to many countries beyond France (Kremer-Marietti, 1993). Comte's movement grew popular far beyond what we would now imagine as possible for a made-up religion. His followers included diverse and influential people, such as John Stewart Mill and the designers of the

---

[2] Sociology being on top is one of the reasons that Comte in considered amongst the founders of that discipline.

Brazilian flag who put "order and progress" (a positivist slogan) on the flag, where it remains today.

Positivism, believing in human progress based on science, did not survive the horrors of the First World War. The war had made it painfully apparent that scientific progress will not inexorably lead to good outcomes – it can lead to machine guns, barbed wire, poison gas, and pointless deaths on a scale comparable to all previous wars in Europe added together (Eksteins, 2000; Hastings, 2014).

Shortly after the war (in the 1920s, mainly in Vienna and Berlin), philosophers felt a need to re-establish some sort of unified agenda for science. They wanted a clear method to distinguish what is scientific from what was not, since the prestige of science was attracting many hangers-on, which were not scientific and methodical enough by any strict definition.

The result of their work was a philosophical movement called "*logical positivism*".[3] Logical positivism specifically aimed *not* to be a religion. It did not endow life with meaning, nor was it overtly political. It did retain a belief that the sciences will coalesce and ultimately leave no empty space between them, especially not for ignorance or superstition. All real or true knowledge should be scientific. Logical positivism aimed for a clear distinction between science and the nonsense disciplines: religions, pseudo-science, superstitions, romanticism, etc. Part of "clearing away the nonsense" was a wholesale rejection of subjectivity (Creath, 2014).

The main doctrine of logical positivism was that all utterances can be divided into three categories, in terms of where they get their meaning. The three categories were as follows:

1. Utterances whose meaning is given by the difference they would make to the evidence of one's senses. Examples include "this is blue"; "At a microscopic level, all living creatures are made of cells"; "The planets are only approximately spherical". Evidence for such sentences is *publicly* verifiable. There is nothing subjective about them. These are known as **empirical** statements.
2. Utterances whose meaning is given by their very syntax: "X = X" or "if (if A than B) and A, then B". These are known as tautologies or proven theorems in **logic** or mathematics.
3. All other utterances were viewed as **meaningless**.

Logical positivism became hugely popular amongst scientists and people interested in technological progress. It gave a clean definition of what was of interest (sentences of the first two types) and what was not. The interwar period was a time when many

---

[3] Note that when a movement has a double-barrelled name it often means that it has a predecessor with a simpler name. An example is social-democracy being a much softer version of socialism, emerging after the rejection of anything related to the horrors of Stalin (Brown, 2010). By having a double-barrelled name a movement relates to its predecessor while (hopefully) shedding the predecessor's worst characteristics.

people wanted to think of politics and war as little as possible. Cheering oneself up after the horrors of the war was seen as necessary for retaining sanity (Eksteins, 2000). Scientists (and other, "more serious" people) wanted to separate themselves from all this frivolity and so flocked to logical positivism (P. Watson, 2001). An abyss opened between logical-positivist scientists and the rest of humankind, who were interested in feelings, politics, literature, and other topics viewed as meaningless by logical positivism.

The sociopolitical changes leading up to the Second World War led to migration of many intellectuals away from Germany and Austria, especially in the case of thinkers who had no time for the "non-empirical nonsense" that Nazism was imposing on society. This led to the dispersal of leading intellectuals from Berlin and Vienna, mostly to English-speaking countries. Carnap (a leading light of logical positivism) went to Chicago. There (beyond the general influence of logical positivism on Anglo-American thought) he had a strong personal influence on the founders of AI (G. Solomonoff, 2016).

Note that logical positivism is wrong, on its own terms: Let's try applying the three-way categorisation of utterances (above) to itself. What gives this three-way categorisation its own meaning?

1. Is there anything that we can feel with our senses that would differ if the whole categorisation were correct vs if it were not? There isn't – hence the doctrine of logical positivism is not an empirical utterance.
2. Is this categorisation a tautology, that is, is it a form of logical necessity or mathematical truth? It isn't.
3. Then it must be nonsense.

If we were to believe in logical positivism, we are forced by its main doctrine to declare that this self-same main doctrine is meaningless.

Recall Papert's observation of the weakness of our thinking (in Sections 0.1 and 3.1.1), he was protesting against a form of overemphasis on logic and against the pretence that we think logically. The demand to be logical, to be scientific, arose from logical positivism, which itself originated from the confusions of the religious needs of post-revolutionary France and the social mayhem following "the great war".

As we will see (in the following sections), logical positivism was not the only questionable influence on AI. Hopefully, this section has convinced some readers sceptical of the humanities that having a deeper historical context to the debates over AI is of value or at least of interest.

4.2 Knowledge

In Chapter 2, we saw that the cognitivists (and the AI community) are mostly opposed to Dreyfus and his phenomenological critique of AI. We also saw that these two camps, much as they view themselves as opposites, share some common beliefs about the nature of truth itself. Let's examine some of those.

4.2.1 Truth Exists, Is Knowable, and Can Be Expressed in Language

This assumption is necessary for most if not all discursive knowledge and is fundamental to science, to theology, and much of philosophy. Cognitive science is therefore implicitly committed to this. But this is not believed universally: The Tao-Te-Ching is the fundamental text of Taoism (one of the three traditional religions of China). The book starts as follows: "The truth that may be told is not the everlasting truth" (Lao-Tzu, n.d.) – specifically denying the verbal communicability of any permanent truth.

The idea that truth is knowable and can be expressed in language **originated** mainly from monotheism and arguably also from Platonic rationalism. Our modern thought grew out of medieval thought, and medieval thought can be grossly seen as an amalgamation of these two traditions – the Hebrew and the Greek. The work of the "Fathers of the Church" (in late antiquity) was mainly reconciling these two traditions, that both had rationalist streaks. We are heirs to that tradition.

4.2.2 There Is Only One Truth System

The belief that there is only one truth is most clearly manifested in the Cognition vs phenomenology debate (Section 2.2) but is also very clear in Watson's polemics against his predecessors. In ancient Greece, and in other polytheistic cultures, truth is not held to be singular: One can be an orthodox Hindu by holding any one (or more) of six different canonical world views (Zimmer, 1951). Even in science, the idea of a single truth is held only in principle (as an aspiration), while pragmatically, most calculations in (for example) physics are done either classically or using one but not the other or relativity and quantum mechanics.

This idea underpins the very notion of a "correct" answer to anything and any attempt to optimise a system or to prove theorems. It is also inherent to any bureaucratic management of education, in exams, marking, etc. The demand that we should "resolve" the mind/body problem (amongst others) reeks of "there must be only one truth".

The notion of one truth **originates** with the dogmatism of the monotheistic "jealous god" that first appeared around the 8th century BC (P. Watson, 2006, pp. 109–111). These ideas were strengthened and further embedded into European culture during the establishment of Christianity as the exclusive religion of the Roman Empire (4th–5th centuries AD).

I will argue for a version of the opposite position, "perspectivism" in Section 5.2.2.

4.2.3 Kinds of Illumination

There is a related point, about what kind of approach a culture adopts when searching for knowledge. This distinction can best be made by relating to two kinds of illumination that were available on earth throughout history – the sun and the moon (Harding, 2001; Jung, 1984, pp. 340–400).

The first approach, call it the **solar** approach, is to seek to illuminate any unclear issue with the strongest available light – the sun. The idea is that once we shine a strong light on any problem (literally or figuratively), we will get the best view of it. Therefore, once we find such a light, all our problems will be over. We will have a clear view, a solution, quite probably a single solution (see Section 4.2.2) that will explain what is going on and what needs to be done. An example of this type of thinking is Christianity: Accepting Jesus as one's saviour, the authority of one's chosen denomination (and its rituals), suffices for salvation and is the solution to all one's problems, in this world and the next.

Note that the cross itself is a solar symbol, with four rays radiating from a centre. In many cases, the cross is presented with a further four (or more) rays on the diagonals. Moreover, the auras of the saints can be seen as "little suns" radiating from their personae. An extreme manifestation of how solar Christianity is in its symbolism is the Throne of St. Peter in the Vatican, where clearly authority flows from St. Peter, and there are multiple solar motifs around where St. Peter's head would be (St. Peter was nominated by Jesus to found his church (Matthew 16:18)).

A second approach to illumination may be called the **lunar** approach. The idea is that over-illuminating an issue may "flatten" or oversimplify one's view. By this approach, the correct view of any matter is achieved by moderate illumination, as to not dazzle the observer's senses. This allows for more nuance and, therefore, a better appreciation of the complexities. Moreover, a strong light (with accompanying heat) might completely chase away the more subtle forces at work. The most prominent example of this lunar approach is Islam. Note the prominence of the moon on the flags of Muslim countries: for example, Turkey, Pakistan, and Algeria. Moreover, note that at the pinnacle of the dome of most mosques is a crescent, a depiction of the moon.

Note also that Christianity follows a solar calendar, and Islam follows a lunar calendar.

Science, having developed out of a Christian culture, is very much a solar enterprise. As we saw in the discussion of positivism, a driving myth of science is that one day it will be able to explain *all* phenomena using *one* scientific *system*. Physics researchers, for example, exert a large amount of effort on trying to unite quantum theory and relativity. The idea that there are two theories that are simultaneously correct makes scientists uneasy.

AI researchers to a large degree view themselves as scientists, so look for a "solar solution" to the problems of AI. Minsky is a glaring exception of a more lunar thinking (Minsky, 1987, 1991).

4.2.4 Polarisation of Knowledge and Doubt

The idea that we either know something completely or know nothing about it has been popular from Descartes until quite recently. Much of symbolic AI's work was predicated on things either being known or unknown (see especially expert systems). Most if not all appeals to (standard) logic also rely on this assumption.

4.3 Science

In every generation (presumably), people thought and had doubts about the then-prevailing system of thought. Often they thought they saw the world significantly better than others, and wrote books, but before the invention of the printing press (in the late 1400s), these books mostly had little impact. The church was largely successful in containing any alternatives to its world view. Following the invention of the printing press, it became possible to distribute the ideas widely, and the church in Rome lost its grip. This led people to believe that not only do they see the world better than any predecessors, but that they positively should set forth a programme for people's future thinking (often in book form) and get such a book printed and distributed widely.

On the 31st of October 1517, the protestant reform begun with Martin Luther nailing his 95 theses to a church door in Wittenberg. This led to an intellectual current in the west, lasting centuries, aimed at cleansing our thinking of the errors of the past, leaving behind only the now-clean truth.[4] This process starts with Luther at 1517, goes through the later protestant reformers, continues with the philosophers of the modern era (including Hume and Kant), and lives on in our current secular world view, to a large degree based on science. This scheme bequeaths us a few beliefs that need examination.

4.3.1 The Scientific Clean Sweep

There is a common belief in modern society (and amongst scientists) that there was a full revision of all knowledge as part of a "scientific revolution". This scientific clean sweep supposedly occurred in the 18th–19th centuries, and since then, we no longer believe in anything simply because we inherited that belief from previous generations. The rejected beliefs include most if not all superstitions, religions, and other "nonsense". Since this "clean sweep", goes this belief, we can trust all our knowledge to be "scientific", "sound", or at least to be a *bona fide* effort towards the one objective truth. This is seen as a result of "the enlightenment" or the "scientific

---

[4] Arguably the idea of cleansing our thinking of previous errors is a resurrection of a myth about Abraham destroying idols and founding monotheism (Freedman & Maurice, 1961, pp. 310–311).

revolution" (both terms invented in the 19th century, long after any underlying events) (Chapman, 2013).

This myth is patently false, in that no such events have been recorded, and science has semi-consciously inherited not only Thomas' assumptions that nature has knowable laws but more obviously Occam's preference of simplicity over complexity and many more scholastic assumptions. One of the real events that form the cultural–historical basis for this myth of a clean sweep is Francis Bacon's idea of the "great instauration" (Gower, 1996, Chapter 3). Another is Descartes' attempt at a clean sweep of knowledge in the first pages of "Meditations", from which he retreated back to Catholicism within a few pages (Descartes, 1952). Yet another real historical basis for the idea that science needs religion no more and can divorce it completely was Lyell's and mainly Darwin's sweeping away of any need for a creator in the western world view during the 19th century (P. Watson, 2006).

Sometimes, as sciences struggle for the truth, this "clean sweep" is seen as incomplete and needing just "one last push" as is evident in the writings of J.B. Watson. This is the main route through which these ideas influenced psychology, the cognitive sciences, and AI. Our present science (post-Darwin) is in this sense still a crusading science. It is a science that fights against all remnants of prejudice, against religion, against superstition, and against any "new age" or romantic nonsense. This is visibly a live and current concern of some cognitive scientists: Minsky, Dennet, and others fought the secular corner in their spare time when not engaged in cognitive science. Wheeler also celebrates the "muggle principle" (demanding that there be no magic involved) as one of his axioms (*Daniel Dennet Discussion with Marvin Minsky: The New Humanists 2/2*, 2012; Wheeler, 2005).

Herbert Simon quotes Watson extensively. Watson saw himself as cleaning up psychology from an incomprehensible reliance on introspection and calls for the use of methods as similar to physics and chemistry as possible (J.B. Watson, 1913). In some of his arguments, he explicitly accuses his opponents of being anti-Darwinian. Watson views his work as a continuation of the systematisation of science, and Simon continues in the same vein, most clearly in his debunking of the methodologies of existing schools of business administration and founding a more scientific and quantitative school of business studies in Carnegie-Mellon (Simon, 1996a).

4.3.2 Science Is Distinct from Magic or Religion

There is a deep-seated relationship in human societies between magic and authority (see Section 3.2.3). An example is how monotheistic religions established their authority using miracles: the burning bush, the splitting of the red sea, Mount Sinai, the bread and fish, raising the dead, etc. In modern times, physics has provided the world with miracles such as electricity and the atomic bomb, so its authority became established in the same tradition that gave authority to the earlier religions. If we don't want to be taken in by modern propaganda, we should be aware that the success of science in some fields does not guarantee its success in others. An entertaining example is economics calling itself (in a rare tradition of self-deprecation) "the dismal science" (Lucas, 2009).

In the last hundred and some years, we have a culture that is so impressed with mathematics, science, and technology, that it has (following the cultural habit of deification of the miracle worker) created a near religion of science. Note how policy makers never tire of saying that we need to emphasise in our education systems more "STEM subjects" (see Section 3.2.4) and how all organisational issues are frequently referred to consultants from some school of business or another. Contrast the frequency of consultation with business schools with the frequency of consultation with historians.

In principle, there should be no "great men" in science, any more that there should be prophets or messiahs. But humans love heroes (see Section 3.2.1). Darwin and Einstein certainly are treated with reverence, the first for doing away with the need for a story of creation, and the second for doing the ultimate act of sorcery – predicting an event in the night skies – a bending of light by gravity, no less (Sponsel, 2002). In popular imagination, Einstein also gets more credit than he actually deserves for atomic energy.

The cultural similarity between scientists and religious figures does not stop there. In an echo of the (mainly Christian) ascetic movements, many scientists and scholars relish the ascetic purity of tedious and boring work exploring minutiae, while half complaining and half congratulating themselves that their generation has to do the grunt work before anyone can do the more interesting "big picture" work. They humbly avoid big or interdisciplinary theories. A good example is how "large histories" (putting together the entire outline of human existence so far) such as "Guns Germs & Steel" and "Sapiens: a Brief History of Mankind" (Diamond, 1998; Harari, 2012) started appearing only quite recently, many decades after a systematic historiography began (Bloch, 1953). External, visible signs of science's relation to monasticism can be found in the special clothes worn by some professions, such as white robes in laboratories and much more ornate habits in major installations, like nuclear reactors. Additionally, in the context of the counter-intuitive epistemology of modern physics, scientists also sometimes attribute to themselves some special status, as illustrated by the thought experiment known as "Wigner's friend".

Some further religion-like characteristics of cognitive science are visible in how Simon relates to Watson, in how Watson was allowed to *abolish* introspection with his (1913) paper with evidence that (at least today) would be considered too flimsy for an undergraduate paper. Additionally, Chomsky's following may be smaller but is only slightly less cult-like than the cults of Freud or Jung. Entire theories were modified or abolished on Chomsky's say-so (Murakami, 1995; Shamdasani, 1998).

4.3.3 *The World Is Modular, Logical Atomism, Determinism*

The idea that the world is modular asserts that we can always separate (in the world) or analyse (in our mind) any non-atomic situation in terms of parts and that such an analysis would be useful. Note that this works very well in analysing artefacts (see Section 8.2.5), and this is also useful in many sciences. We have so far had no (technologically impressive) success with such analyses of the mind.

Logical atomism is the (related) idea that a finite amount of data can describe anything. It can be discerned in the writings of Plato, Hobbes, and Laplace. It owes much of its current popularity to the Cartesian coordinate system and to the associated idea that any point can be represented in hyperspace and that every object can be represented by a collection of points. As Winograd and Flores show the idea that the world can be divided into objects is part of the rationalistic tradition. Logical atomism is also widely attributed to Russell and Wittgenstein (Proops, 2017).

Determinism builds on atomism, the idea that not only is the world analysable in terms of parts but that these parts are ultimately analysable in terms of atomic sub-parts. Determinism adds the idea that "… given a specified way things are at a time t, the way things go thereafter is fixed as a matter of natural law" (Hoefer, 2003). This received one of its best-known expressions in Laplace's thought experiment, defining a demon who given the state of the world 100 years ago could predict all our actions.

These ideas (that everything is decomposable, can be seen as a machine, and would be replicable under mechanistic assumptions) are closely related, and are alluring, but (as far we can know) are utterly wrong. They (partially) worked for physics, but (so far) not for AI.

4.4 "Wooly" vs "Rigorous" Thinking

The AI community seems to think that there is "good thinking" (as done in the sciences, and especially in their own AI laboratories) and there is "bad thinking" as done by strange irrational people like philosophers that do not agree with the AI community and religious fanatics. Feigenbaum (a student of Simon) answered an interview question about the role of philosophy in AI as follows: "What artificial intelligence needs is a good Dreyfus…. And what does he offer us instead? Phenomenology! That ball of fluff! That cotton candy!" (McCorduck, 2004, pp. 229–230). Feigenbaum lives in an objective world and makes no attempt to understand subjectivity.

A brief tour of some aspects of this rejection is due.

4.4.1 *Secularisation*

Behaviourism was a smaller revolution than it was presented to be (Costall, 2006, p. 642). As mentioned, Watson's teacher insisted that "objectivism" would be a better term than "behaviourism". Behaviour has been studied before, but the fanaticism to exclude the subjective was new to psychology.

Watson's revolution can be seen as a radical form of secularisation – after we got rid of non-scientific notions such as god, angles, spirits, and the soul – maybe we should get rid of the mind too. The mind isn't amenable to scientific methods, so why not just abolish it as a subject of scientific enquiry? This was precisely what Watson did (see Section 1.5). This is not only a carrying forward of the scientific/secular revolution but also a continuation of the Protestant zeal to purify our world view, cleansing it from any corrupt traditions, accepting "only scripture". It is no accident that such protestant-like zeal took hold in the United States, specifically. This zeal to deprive ourselves of our humanity also carries an echo of asceticism. The less human we permit ourselves to be, the more pure we become (P. Watson, 2006).

Cognitive science is presented as a revolution against behaviourism, in that we are now allowed to discuss a "mind", as long as this mind is "cognitive", that is, computer-like and non-subjective (Costall, 2006). John Searle (1932–), one of the most prominent philosophers in this field, said we should "carve off and eliminate the subjective experience" (1992, p. 115). Much of this book stands in opposition to this stance, at least in terms of technology.

4.4.2 Philosophy Is Seen as Bad

Philosophy was founded (by Socrates) as a "stand-alone" discipline, perhaps even as the "mother of all" other disciplines. In the struggles to impose Christianity on the Roman and medieval-European worlds, philosophy was banned as a stand-alone discipline with its own claims of truth but survived as a "handmaiden of theology" – assisting theologians (who became the intellectual ruling class) in affairs of logic and abstract thought. Later, with the decline of theology and the ascent of science, philosophy also evolved ("for the changing market") to being the "handmaiden of science". As if this rebranding of philosophy as a servant of whichever ideology was ascendant were not bad enough, during the excesses of Marxism philosophy had to hide under the even more absurd facade of being a "handmaiden of ideology" (Evangeliou, 2008).

4.4.3 Especially, Continental Philosophy Is Seen Negatively

Immanuel Kant (1724–1804), a key philosopher, put paid to any notion that humans have direct access (information) about "things-in-themselves" (which he called noumena). According to Kant, all we see is phenomena, that is, appearances to us. So, we have no way of having truly objective knowledge nor is there any human endeavour that would lead us to a proof or disproof of the existence of god.

Very roughly speaking, there were two diametrically opposed reactions to this starting in the 19th century and continuing to this day.

One reaction, which grew organically in Germany via Hegel, Schopenhauer, etc., leading to today's phenomenologists, accepted Kant's verdict that there will never be any knowledge of the things-in-themselves. They hold that in such circumstances there is nothing left for philosophers and researchers to do but to investigate the phenomena as phenomena, and first amongst the phenomena of the world is the phenomenon of our own subjectivity and our own perception. This, in a sense, is the epistemological cousin of ontological idealism (Berkeley). Phenomenology investigates what it is like to be a (human) subject. The leading phenomenologist in the 20th century was Heidegger (see Section 2.1), and Dreyfus (the main critic of AI) was his student.

The other tradition, starting with Frege (in Germany) and continuing with Russell and the logical positivists (see Section 4.1) became Anglo-American thought (also known as analytical philosophy). They basically sidestepped Kant's observation, by arguing that what can be demonstrated in public repeatedly and reliably will henceforth be *defined* as objective reality and that this is what science should investigate. This stands over an established tradition (stretching back before Newton) of demonstrating scientific experiments in the Royal Society and hence takes its ultimate authority from the British royal family (ruling *by Divine Grace*). The fact that Kant ("with respect") sees an unbridgeable gap between the observed phenomenon and the thing-in-itself behind it is neither here nor there for this school of thought. One of the consequences of this thinking is that if there really were to be a deceptive evil daemon intent on confusing us, or if one were to be a brain-in-a-vat, or living in a simulation, etc., then one would be deceived by this intersubjective constitution of reality – in other words, a powerful enough external force would be successful in deceiving science.

In the last few decades (if not longer), there has been a disconnect, a mutual incomprehension between the analytical and the continental schools of philosophy. These schools differ in terms of subject matter, in that (broadly speaking) for the continental school the subjective point of view is considered secure, while the objective world is questionable. For the analytical philosophers, it is the other way around. To a large degree, analytical philosophy sees its trade as a handmaiden to science, as tidying up conceptual issues around the empirical work done by the scientists (see Section 4.4.2).

In the English-speaking world of science in general, and around (early) cognitive science in particular, the rejection of continental philosophy is total, so much so that it is not even seriously entertained. Simon, who makes no bones about rejecting continental philosophy and its messenger (Dreyfus), calls Phenomenology a "religion". Even thinkers like Brooks (the former director if MIT's AI laboratories) protest loudly that their work is unrelated to "German philosophy" and that is "based purely on engineering considerations". He explicitly distances himself: "In some circles much credence is given to Heidegger... our work was not so inspired" (Brooks, 1991). This fierce rejection of continental philosophy, and mainly its German phenomenology component, cannot be divorced (in terms of sentiment) from the rejection of German culture in general and specifically of German romanticism as a precursor to Nazism.

4.5 Humans and Minds

4.5.1 The Human Mind Is a Natural Kind

This may be seen as a strange claim to make and a strange claim to argue against: "The mind is a thing that can be studied". More technically (in philosophy) we would say "the mind is a *natural kind*". To say that a kind is *natural* is to say that it corresponds to a grouping that reflects the structure of the natural world rather than the interests and actions of human beings (Bird & Tobin, 2017).

This means it can be studied independently of any other human factor, like the human heart or lions. It also means that it is one thing and implies that it is amenable to one explanation, unlike a collection of diverse things. Moreover, it seems to imply that it has nothing to do with the soul or emotions.

The very term "mind" entered its current use through a centuries-long process (roughly 1500–1900) whereby people wanted to discuss (what we would now call) the mental world without associating it with the "soul". This is part of the ongoing attempt to "clean up" our language and make it more scientific. The evolution of the "mind" out of the "soul" involved philosophical and political concerns, not least concerns regarding the treatment of the deranged in mental asylums (Makari, 2016).

This assumption is also a prerequisite for some of the following assumptions.

4.5.2 Humans Are Like Computers

In every generation humans have conceived of themselves in terms of the latest technology: In ancient times, man was thought of as a "clay vessel with a divine spark", while later (including the times of Descartes) the prevailing metaphor was of clockwork. In the late 19th century, with the development of hydraulic and pneumatic technology, Freud describes the human psyche using terms such as repression and eruption. Today, a favourite metaphor of the mind or brain is as a *computer* (Bolter, 1984).

This idea, that the mind can be usefully thought of as being like a computer, is the central metaphor of the cognitive revolution. We encountered this quite forcefully in the debate between Dreyfus and Neisser (Section 2.2), but this is as open a secret as can be – the omnibus history of cognitive science is called "Mind as Machine" (and there is little doubt that the "machine" is a computer) (Boden, 2008). This metaphor reinforces older (Cartesian) clear and distinct on or off ideas that we either know things or we don't (like the computer's 0 or 1).

The assumption (widespread in cognitive science) that there is a level in which the mind can be usefully discussed that is computational will be further critiqued in Section 6.5.3. However, there is a further widespread attempt to simplify humans beyond what is warranted – the attempt to describe humans as having "lower" or "higher" faculties and as "rational animals".

4.5.3 Lower and Higher Human Functions

Humans have "lower" and "higher" faculties, and the "lower" can be ignored: Sex, humour, religion, and politics have nothing to do with thinking and cognition. Emotions, greed, and many other all too human aspects can, perhaps should, nay *must* be ignored.

Consider the number of entries in the following books' indexes for the following key words (Table 4.1).

The first two books deal with the entire history of research into psychology (Boring) and cognitive science (Boden). The last (McCorduck) deals with the history of AI. It is striking that all three books view humour and politics as irrelevant, while McCorduck, who is specifically interested in AI, correctly documents that AI has no interest in any of these terms. Sex gets a lone mention in the study by Boden (2008), as Darwinian "sexual selection". Even here sex is not seen as directly relevant to cognitive science, it is only an external influence.

4.5.4 Humans Are Rational

Some researchers in AI make the claim that humans are rational explicitly (Bringsjord, 2008), some by their actions: After making a clear distinction between human-like and rational behaviour, the main textbook of AI proceeds to teach rational AI for the rest of the 1,000-page volume (see Section 6.1). The historic paper titled "A logical calculus of the ideas immanent in nervous activity" (McCulloch & Pitts, 1943) speculates of a connection between the worlds of biological neurons and of Boolean logic. The very idea of "mind as machine" insinuates that humans are (at least partially) logical and hence rational. The rationality of economic agents is also a cornerstone of economics.

The idea that humans are rational has multiple sources: One is the creation of man "in the image of god" (Genesis 1) combined with the later attribution of perfection to this same god (notwithstanding his imputed human-emotional characteristics, like jealousy). There is an additional source for this idea in economics' notion of "rational man" that was introduced into AI mainly via Simon. Simon's greatest accomplishment (by his own evaluation and by the Nobel Prize committee (Nobelprize.org, 1978; Simon, 1996a)) was his idea of "bounded rationality". This idea represents both a limitation on human rationality (humans can be only as rational as they can be *within the bounds* of available information and time), but it also represents a reaffirmation that within the bounds of information and time, people *are indeed* rational. This faith in human rationality carries through in all of Simon's

Table 4.1 Number of Index Mentions of Selected Words in Histories of Cognitive Science

	Sex	Humour	Religion	Politics	Physics	Memory	logic	Subjectivity
A history of experimental psychology (Boring, 1929)	0	0	8	0	13	20	0	0
Man as machine (Boden, 2008)	1	0	27	0	7	22	84	9
Machines who think (McCorduck, 2004)	0	0	0	0	4	6	28	0

work. In AI, the notion of bounded rationality expresses itself in his notion of satis-ficing. Simon's influence on both computers (receiving the Turing prize) and across many of the social sciences can hardly be exaggerated. The rationality of humans has been abundantly refuted in every generation (Ariely, 2009; Tuchman, 1990), and yet (at least in cognitive science), this idea refuses to die (Bringsjord, 2008).

Our culture, and specifically cognitive science, reveres rationality to the point of denying other characteristics of human mental life. This is the main reason that AI research so far has been rooted in the biological and the rationalistic levels and not in the individual subjective level. Much more about that in chapters to come.

This idea that humans are rational sits well with the rationalistic tradition but is distinct:

- Thinking 1: The belief in human rationality is about how Mary thinks of her lamb. Mary is rational.
- Thinking 2: The rationalistic attitude is a good way for scientists to explore the human mind and for AI people to use in modelling it. We are all ratio-nal, and nature is rational, therefore rationality is the best way to go about research in psychology.

4.6 Other Worries about Religions

We can see the following **influence of religion** on AI: In just one AI paper, "What Hath Simon Wrought" (Feigenbaum, 1989), the author (apart from the faux-biblical title) used the following terms as names for eras in AI research: "Genesis", "Exodus", and "Leviticus" (three of the five books of Moses). This is not just flowery use of language. Feigenbaum also says: "in the beginning (also).... was a *credo*, shared by all and rarely articulated. It was later stated and named by Simon and Newell in their Turing Award lecture (Newell & Simon, 1976): The Physical Symbol System Hypothesis. ... It was.... an *article of faith*, a beacon. Believing in it was a *badge of belonging* to the AI science" (stress added). Lest it be thought that this religious thinking is Feigenbaum's own idiosyncratic proclivity, a review of public administration presented Herbert Simon as "a proper missionary" and as a "young Jesus in the temple". This report also described him as an "unrepentant knight of the enlightenment" (Augier & March, 2001).

The following two issues do not have a direct impact on our more explicit assumptions in doing AI – but they have a deep impact on our attitude to the whole project, on our enthusiasm and our fears.

4.6.1 Genesis

In discussing how we view our own intelligence, one should consider how we view our place in the world in the broadest sense. In this question, in our monotheistic/post-monotheistic world, it is impossible to ignore the book of Genesis.

The Genesis myth of creation not only reinforces the supremacy of the one god but also locates humans as the pinnacle of creation (Hasel, 1974). God created (in order) heaven and earth, plants, small animals, larger animals, and finally humans, "in our own form and image" (Genesis 1). This contributes to our sense that humans are superior to the rest of creation. But this story not only locates us above the rest of creation, it also says that god created us specifically in his own "form and image". This is an enigmatic but central point.

Later, in the story of the Garden of Eden (Genesis 2), Adam eats from the tree of knowledge. One of the reasons given (in exegesis) for the prohibition on eating from the tree of knowledge is that Adam would become knowledgeable like god. Adam eats from the fruit of the tree of knowledge and acquires the ability to distinguish good from bad, as god can. These stories establish the idea that mankind is both knowledgeable and like god. Later when the idea of rationality will be adopted by Christianity from the Greeks, man will be seen as rational by divine design.

This identification of humans' "form and image" with god's leaves us with a dilemma, since humans definitely are not like god, in that they cannot create worlds by just declaring them into being: "God said let there be light, and there was light". Humans have to toil and are managed by god. Humans are categorically inferior, and yet, we are told by these myths that we are like god. Moreover, monotheistic religions teach us to fear god as being a far superior being and not to forget our inferior nature. And yet our religions also tell us in the first couple of pages of scripture that we are like god, in both "form" and "image" – whatever these mean. This is (on its surface) a heresy right in the beginning of the bible or at least a serious problem.

Let's re-examine one aspect of this dichotomy. We cannot create light, stars, plants, or animals by speech alone. The highest (and final) achievement of god in creation is the creation of man – so if we were indeed like god, we would have been able to create not just stars and plants but also a new race of creatures, *in our own form and image*. This leaves us with the following situation: Until and unless we can create a new creature in *our* form and image, we are not finished with our development as humans, and in a sense, god is not finished either with *his* project of creating us in *his* own form and image. For as long as we cannot create a humanoid creature like us, we are not truly in god's "form and image".

So if we were successful in creating a fully-human robot, with a fully-human mind – we would not only graduate ourselves into being like god, we would also allow god's project of creating the world to complete indeed.

4.6.2 Heresies

Introspection, looking at the working of one's own mind, is (by the same idea of humans being "in the image of god") looking at god's soul, and one is not supposed to look at god's face, let alone god's soul or anything near it (Exodus 33). Moreover, when one introspects one peers into one's own soul, and the judgement of one's soul is reserved to god. That would also be heretical in the monotheistic context.

Looking at one's own subjectivity acknowledges subjectivity's existence, and in a sense (at least the subjective existence) of the soul. This is anathema to science because either science denies that the subjective exists at all, or science has no tools to deal with the subjective. In any case, the mere discussion of the subjective exposes science's shortcomings. Getting results in technology based on an observation of the subjective is the purpose of this volume. This would challenge science to explain how the non-existent or the non-scientific can be of benefit to mankind. In this book, we will not worry about these things. This is a book about technology. Being technologists, we want progress by whatever (legal) means.[5]

Note that science (as a social phenomenon) sometimes takes on monotheistic characteristics, including an aversion of any competition, dogmatism, and distaste for any discussion outside its own realm.

4.7 Prejudices Pertaining to AI: Summary

This chapter presented some assumptions that prevail in much of our society and specifically in much of AI research. Perhaps, some of these should be relaxed in order to expose new avenues for AI. In Part 2, I will give an example of what can become available to us if we overcome these presumptions: I will argue that introspection, long shunned in psychology, cognitive science, and AI, is recommended as a basis for AI development.

---

[5] Thanks to Ron Chrisley and Josh Weinstein for many discussions on these topics.

AN ALTERNATIVE:
AI, Subjectivity, and Introspection

Chapter 5

Central Argument Outline

This chapter presents the outline of the main thesis of this book, namely that "Introspection is recommended for developing Anthropic AI". This chapter includes the full argument with a finite list of holes. Subsequent chapters will fill in these holes and add detail. Part 3 of this volume will give some pragmatics and several working examples, and will discuss some consequences of this project.

There are four key terms that will be used, that are worth previewing here as a preliminary outline.

1. This thesis is about **human-like artificial intelligence (AI)**, as opposed to rational/idealised AI.
2. Within human-like AI, my focus is on **anthropic AI**, approximating the underlying mechanisms of humans as such, rather than the accomplishments of western, modern, well-trained adult people.
3. **Subjective methods** in AI have been relatively neglected though they give us some access to how we work, at a level that is practical to simulate, rather than (say) simulating every cell in a brain.
4. **Introspection** is how we can access subjectivity.

This chapter will start with some context for the argument, some issues relating to types of truth and will discuss in detail the middle term "is recommended for developing". The following two chapters will discuss the purpose, "anthropic AI" and the means, "introspection". The subsequent two chapters will prove the argument being made, that introspection is recommended for developing anthropic AI.

5.1 Context for Central Argument

5.1.1 Science vs Technology and Human-Like vs Rational

The following two distinctions are important to be born in mind while discussing AI, in terms of the type of motivation involved:

■ Some researchers build AI models in order to *scientifically understand* humans, mice, insects, neural functioning, or some other scientific question, while others build AI in order to solve problems of *technology*. Science is usually a long-term project, while technology is usually short term. This contrast between science and technology as to motivation should not be confused with the contrast between them as to the types of truth required, see Section 5.1.3.

■ Some researchers aim for human-like AI, and some aim for rational or ideal AI (see Section 6.1).

These two distinctions should be seen not as dichotomous but as continuous.

For example (referring to Illustration 5.1), see the technological motivation of chatbots, from Eliza to commercial chatbots and the entrants of the Loebner Prize (Mladenić & Bradeško, 2012; Weizenbaum, 1966). These aim for human-like performance here and now (technology), using any trick available. Meanwhile for cognitive simulations (or computational psychology), the aim is to simulate working models of human cognitive faculties for science (Sun, 2008). In sharp contrast, search engines (such as Google) aim at the best possible result regardless of how humans would fare at the same task, as do other machine learning implementations.

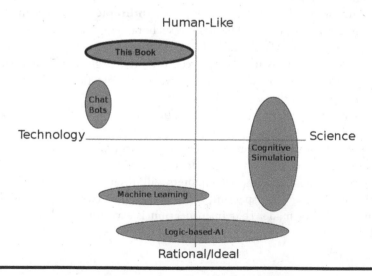

Illustration 5.1 Locating different AI efforts in key distinctions.

Most of the current "buzz" around AI is in this field, of machine learning. Logic-based AI is an attempt to explain humans scientifically using various types of logic (Bringsjord, 2008) and has also been the basis of much of ("good old fashioned") classic AI, including its large technological component (McCorduck, 2004).

Both these distinctions are a bit more complex than they seem, at least for AI: We *do*, at the end of the day, need to translate any human-like ideas into a formal computer language in order to make an AI system work – such is the nature of the technology available to us at the moment (see Section 10.3.5). More on what is meant by "human-like" and "anthropic" is found in Chapter 6.

The distinction between technology and science isn't sharp either – a working system demonstrates to science what can be achieved by the underlying mechanism, and conversely, scientific models (such as neural models) serve as the bases (or inspirations) for AI systems (see Sections 5.3 and 10.1.1). A demonstration of how seriously this link is taken by contemporary science could be seen (as noted above) in a note on Richard Feynman's blackboard at the time of his death, reading "what I cannot create, I do not understand"[1] (Feynman, 1988; Resnick, 1993). Another point to recall about the interaction between science and technology is that in every generation people conceive of humans in terms of the latest technology, for example Aristotle's "clay vessel with a divine spark", notions of the heart as a *furnace*, Freud's *hydraulic* models, and today's notions of the brain as a *computer* (Bolter, 1984).

So the project presented here is about human-like, technological AI. An important part of the methodology is keeping track of truth claims and what kinds of truth are being claimed.

5.1.2 Philosophy of AI

Much of this book discusses the *philosophy of AI*. Being a relatively small and obscure interest, this calls for a discussion of the very nature of the field.

One way of looking at philosophy in general (and the oldest) is as the all-encompassing love of wisdom.[2]

The specialised fields (physics, medicine, architecture) can be seen as spheres of knowledge from which philosophy as such has to a large degree retreated. Questions of the interaction of materials (for example) are no longer examined by philosophy, or even "natural philosophy", but are examined by chemistry and physics. So extending the graphic metaphor of "spheres" for a moment, philosophy (as a field) is left responsible for a "Swiss cheese" – all that is left of knowledge after the specialists took charge of their spheres – the areas between fields, and the areas far removed from any specialised field at all.

---

[1] Photo of blackboard: http://archives.caltech.edu/pictures/1.10-29.jpg.
[2] This is why researchers in all fields are granted a Doctorate in *philosophy* (Ph.D.) when they qualify to do research.

But this "subcontracting" of the specific spheres of knowledge to their respective experts is not total. Difficult questions such as those raised by quantum mechanics are discussed often by philosophers (Ismael, 2015). Philosophers also reserve the right to discuss the "meta" fields, such as philosophy of science and ethics in medicine. In fact, any questions that are seen as neglected within any of these specialised fields can be taken up by a philosopher. In the case of AI, Dreyfus (see Section 2.3) stands out as a philosopher who intervened forcefully in a field in which he was not part of the research community. Moreover, issues of methodology are often seen as "philosophical" even by practitioners of the specialised fields who would otherwise be disinterested or even hostile to philosophy as such.

The field of this book is the *methodology* of AI invention and development – *how AI researchers come up with their ideas.* Understanding this requires a bit of the intellectual history and philosophy of AI *as a technology.* This book will not deal with ethical issues (Bostrom, 2016).

AI may be viewed as "the intellectual core of orthodox cognitive science" (Wheeler, 2005, p. 68), or it may be viewed as a technological field (Russell & Norvig, 2013). This book is interested in AI as technology. Any technological models may optionally later inspire or form the basis for theories in psychology, but that is not the focus here.

It seems that "philosophy of AI" (at least AI as a technology, which is the concern here) would be a sub-field of "philosophy of technology". Again, this warrants a closer look.

5.1.3 Philosophy of Technology

A major difference between theories of technology is often their position on the question of whether technology is merely "applied science" or has some different inherent nature (Franssen et al., 2013, sec. 2.2).

On the side that technology is applied science, Franssen et al. quote Bunge saying that "technology is about action, but an action heavily underpinned by theory—that is what distinguishes technology from the arts and crafts and puts it on a par with science". Bunge seems to be stressing the distinction between the (old) crafts like carpentry and modern technology, with its heavy reliance on science (e.g. computers). Computers and many other enabling technologies of our current lifestyle would be impossible without quantum mechanics. This break between the old crafts and the (possibly threatening) new technology is important to ethicists who worry about new technologies, not least the later Heidegger (2009).

On the other side, we find both Skolimowski and Herbert Simon (see Section 1.6) who see continuity between the old crafts and modern technology. Skolimowski says that "science concerns itself with what is, whereas technology concerns itself with what is to be". On the other hand (an earlier version of), Simon (1996b) says that "the scientist is concerned with how things are but the engineer with how things ought to be" (Franssen et al., 2013). In terms of their characterisation of science, there is little difference between Skolimowski's "what is" and Simon's "how things are". In terms of technology, Skolimowski's "what is to be" is quite different from Simon's "how things ought to be", at least in terms of approach.

Skolimowski's position, if taken to mean "what it is to be" in terms of physics or metaphysics, seems far less interesting *in terms of technology* than if we read it as a call for a functional definition of artefacts: "What *would it take* for something to become X". A car *is* a horseless carriage in terms of the functions it aims to fulfil but not in terms of the internal materials and techniques involved. So by this (functional) reading of Skolimowski, he is saying that technology is about the internal functions that give rise to the overall functions, and presumably technologists are engaged in fulfilling these functions in whatever way feasible. Simon's definition ("how things ought to be") seems to be either teleological[3] or stressing the external functions of any contraption. Under the later reading, Simon is more interested in how a contraption functions *for us and our larger purposes* than in its internal mechanics. This is in line with Simon's interest in the social sciences, public and business administration, public policy, etc. So the difference between Simon and Skolimowski seems to be one of stress on the outer vs inner functioning of artefacts (respectively).

In these definitions, we see that the crux of the matter for technology is function rather than truth. Truth is for scientists, function is for technologists. This is a key point in this book.

As a consequence of this difference in relation to truth, there are also the following differences:

■ Science has an insatiable appetite for precision. Technology always has a practical limit to any obsession with precision – a "tolerance". Tolerances are often numerically specified, for example in mechanics and electrical engineering.
■ Science aspires to generalize and come up with a definitive theory of everything – one ultimate reality calls for one unified theory (see Section 4.2.2). Technology on the other hand deals with multiple perspectives: the perspectives of the various parts of a machine and the thermal, mechanical, and electric perspectives, etc. of each part and/or the whole.

A key example of the use I will make of the lower truth requirement in technology is in Sections 8.2.2 and 10.3.5.1: If, as (Nisbett & Wilson, 1977) have shown, introspection gives us only the outline of *what* is accomplished by the mind without the *how*, in AI programming (as a technology) we can substitute whatever technical trick we have (in our skills as programmers) to achieve something similar in a computer. In psychology, as a science, this of course would not do – scientists demand (ultimately) an explanation of mental processes in terms of the brain and physics.

---

[3] Concerned with purposes.

5.2 Notions of Truth

It is the aspiration of science to aim for the most accurate facts and to stick to the truth with great zeal. This commitment to strictly follow the best version of the truth leads, amongst other things, to disdain for the humanities or any of the "loose" sciences (see Section 4.4). In this sense, it is a main concern for psychology to move from the "loose" or "woolly" sciences nearer the more "proper" sciences (Costall, 2006; J. B. Watson, 1913). Mathematics, sometimes called "the queen of sciences", has little content *but* the demand to stick 100% to a well-defined notion of truth. This book will show that in technology not only are we not obliged to such a strict adherence to the truth but we are positively hindered by any notion of maximal truth. In a sense, a main methodology of this book is examining different types of truth claims about AI and keeping these truth types distinct and clear.

5.2.1 The Idea of a Single Truth

Many people believe that there is one truth. This idea originates in monotheism but has mutated into the scientific world, not least through positivism (see Sections 4.1 and 4.2.2).

Regardless of the origin of the idea, we can see in today's literature a commitment to a single truth, be it a scientific physicalist truth (Simon, see Section 1.6) or a phenomenological, idealist, or Heideggerian truth (Dreyfus, see Section 2.3). This yearning for a single truth is also expressed by attempts to solve the mind/brain problem once and for all, such as the Blue Brain project (Markram, 2006). I propose, for AI, a more short-term and practical alternative, using multiple and competing perspectives concurrently. This is similar to Minsky's "scruffy" notion (Minsky, 1991).

5.2.2 Perspectivism

For AI as a technology, the discussion in Section 5.1.3 of technology vs science brings us to consider perspectivism, which allows us to hold both horns in case of a dilemma, understand several contradictory aspects, and ascertain pragmatically what kind of truth is requisite in every particular case. In a sense, a central aim of this book is to show how wrong types of truth (wrong perspectives) were used in AI research and a way of rectifying that.

For now, let us look at perspectivism per se:

> Against positivism,[4] which halts at phenomena—"There are only facts"—I would say: No, facts is precisely what there is not, only

---

[4] Note that the positivism mentioned here is Comte's rather than the later Logical Positivism, see Section 4.1.

interpretations. We cannot establish any fact "in itself": perhaps it is folly to want to do such a thing [...]

In so far as the word "knowledge" has any meaning, the world is knowable; but it is interpretable otherwise, it has no meaning behind it, but countless meanings. –"Perspectivism."

It is our needs that interpret the world; our drives and their For and Against. Every drive is a kind of lust to rule; each one has its perspective that it would like to compel all the other drives to accept as a norm.

(Nietzsche, 1889, sec. 481)

As an example, consider a rather dated armchair found in the social room in the department of informatics at the University of Sussex. What is it? Which of the following is "The Truth", or "Reality"? It could be

- a chair, an armchair
- part of the equipment of the social room/the department/the university/the educational system/the United Kingdom/the west/humanity/an elitist plot to exclude the uneducated/etc.

But it can also be seen as

- a physical thing, a solid, with a location/certain weight and size/existing in time
- pieces of wood and cloth, arranged a certain way
- a large collection of dead (mainly plant) cells
- molecules, elements, atoms, subatomic particles
- quarks or whatever else the physicists will come up with in the future.[5]

But it is also:

- a coloured object, mostly greyish-blue, part of colour scheme, part of a setting
- old, discoloured, damaged, dangerous, a health and safety violation
- a disgrace to the department (and all other bodies up to humanity, see above)
- a relic from a bygone era.

And we could go on endlessly, describing every part in every context and from every perspective.

---

[5] It seems that (for some) the whole discussion of "what is", or "what is real" has, for the first time in the history of philosophy, been subcontracted out to some other discipline, namely physics. Even when we treat occasionally "atoms", "sub atomic particles", "quarks" or suchlike as the building blocks of the objective universe, we mostly agree that if physics found some new subdivision (below the current "standard model") from which all quarks, leptons, bosons, etc. are made, we would immediately accept any new scientific consensus as our new ontology.

This multitude of perspectives is visible in everything about us, and we choose which perspective to use, as appropriate, while we interpret the world. If we were to look at a person rather than a chair, the possibilities of interpretation would be even greater. Extremists might say that none of these perspectives is more true or real than any other – for our pragmatic purposes it suffices that each may be considered more appropriate for a given context or indeed, perspective.

Note that often people tell each other to "get real" or to discuss "the real world". But in what sense can we say that some perspective is more real than another? To return to our example: For a lawyer, the chair is a health and safety violation, a liability, a risk. For the biologist, it is dead organic matter. For me (on some days), it is ugly or (on other days) homely. How can we decide this? I propose that we *don't* and that we suspend[6] any discussion of one objective reality and treat any demand to "get real" as suspect, even violent attempt to impose a specific perspective (see the later part of Nietzsche's quote above).

5.2.3 Perspectives, Realities, Agendas, Occam

This particular section deals with motivations for different ways of thinking. Accepting or rejecting any of the statements here does not change the main argument. It is provided as a guide as to why many people reject perspectivism (in practise if not explicitly). There are two main motivations to collapsing a multi-perspective discussion into a single perspective:

■ The demand to narrow down a discussion to a single perspective is driven by an active agenda – if there were no agenda, there would be no need to focus. This is true both of the "calendar" meaning of the word "agenda" – "we need to get something done in limited time" and of the more sinister-sounding "political" agenda, where there is a group specifically interested in shutting down some discussion by making it "unreal". An example "close to home" is how Watson shut down introspection, see Section 8.2.1 and the end of Nietzsche's quote above.

■ The other motivation for collapsing a multi-perspective discussion into a single perspective is individual. Having a single perspective simplifies a discussion greatly and allows faster progress (at the cost of depth). Moreover, (looking also from a child's mentality) completely believing in a single truth gives one a sense of security and closure, as a child has once an adult tells them "everything is OK". Having such closure is consoling and allows us to function in a world that is inherently unpredictable and frightening (see Section 3.1.2).

---

[6] Let purer philosophers worry about this. Here we are doing philosophy-of-technology, with an eye towards technological results, not towards the deepest truths.

As we have seen, we often want one powerful truth, so we can become its loyal servants and always win, by this one truth winning. Occam's razor is the most prominent tool for reducing multiple truths into one, and not surprisingly is a rare relic from the centuries before the scientific revolution that is still revered as if the pope still instructs us as to what to believe.

So let us, for now, eschew any hard-and-fast discussion of any "one reality" and just examine perspectives. This of course brings up the question: In what perspective, in which sense, do I make the claims of this book?

5.2.4 In What Sense Is This Book True?

In publishing this book, I claim, at least in some sense, that it is true. But what kind of truth do I claim? I claim a pragmatic truth – as befits a book that is ultimately about technology. So why perspectivism? Because adopting different perspectives at different times *works*. Engineers do it all the time when they design modules – they design the interaction between the complete modules and also the internal structure of each module. They design the electronic characteristics of a system and then move to look at the thermal design and then the mechanical structure, moving between these distinct perspectives. In a sense, this book will promote perspectivism as a tool and pragmatism as value system (for technology development). Later (especially Chapters 7 and 10 and Section 8.7), I will discuss subjectivity and introspection, introducing many perspectives and claiming (some) validity for some of them. This book is about a method for developing ideas; ideas for AI. But ideas as such are not the bottom line – the bottom line (in technology) is letting what works win, without prejudice towards any particular perspectives.

So what needs to be shown are plausibly profitable avenues in anthropic-AI research. Further, we need to show how these profitable avenues of research are neglected by current conceptions, and why these avenues make promising starts at addressing interesting fields.

5.2.5 Notions of Truth: Summary

A central theme, perhaps the central method running throughout this book, is how different notions of truth are used in different contexts in AI research and how some of these may need to be re-examined. The demand for less truth than necessary will lead us to absurdities, but the demand for more precision than can be found constricts our ability to invent. As Aristotle had it:

> It is the mark of an educated man to look for precision in each class of things just so far as the nature of the subject admits.

(Aristotle, 2009)

5.3 Outline of "Is Recommended for Developing"

This book's main claim is that "introspection is recommended for developing anthropic AI". Subsequent chapters will deal with the main terms "introspection" and "anthropic AI". For now, let's look at the middle terms: "recommended for developing".

5.3.1 "Recommended"

Recommending something is not a guarantee that it would always work. It is an assurance that one has reason to believe that it would work (or be profitable) in enough of the cases to make it worth pursuing. In other words, though a recommendation is not a guarantee, it is also not vacuous.

Here is a summary of how this recommendation will be backed in detail in subsequent chapters: After introducing the terms in this chapter and in Chapters 6 and 7, in Chapter 8, I will show that using introspection for AI development is *permissible* (even though it was treated so far in the literature as illegitimate), and in Chapter 9, I will show that using introspection is a plausible way of gaining access to a description that in many cases suffices for the reproduction of human skills.

As detailed in Chapter 8, introspection was forbidden by Watson, as of 1913. Watson forbade introspection for psychology, as he wanted to strengthen psychology's claim to being a science and to make research into human behaviour contiguous with research in animal behaviour. This was motivated both by the prestige of the "hard" sciences and by a Darwinian effort to eliminate any special status of humans over the rest of the animal kingdom (Costall, 2004, 2006). Regardless of debates in philosophy and psychology about introspection in the last 100 years, not a single AI developer embraces introspection wholeheartedly and uses it to build working systems. This will be shown to be misguided since the type of truth required in technology development is quite different from the one required in science. Additionally (even if we were to assume a scientific discourse), the attitude of AI developers seems to ignore the distinction between the context of discovery and the context of justification. The conclusion of Chapter 8 is that introspection (even the worst type, discussed below in Section 7.3) is an *acceptable* basis from which to build AI. Even in cases in the past where introspection *was* partially used as such a basis that usage was done timidly and apologetically, as if "in sin".

As will be shown in detail in Chapter 9, introspection is the basis of most attempts to turn mental skills (knowledge how) into any sort of communicable form. Since some skills are transmitted in human culture for many thousands of years, the very survival of civilizations for more than one generation is a living testimony to the (at least frequent) success of introspection. Introspection and communication succeed in capturing enough of the essence of skills so that they can be communicated from one generation to the next. An argument can be made that the very (evolutionary) reason we have consciousness is to allow the communication of acquired skills from one individual to the next, including the young. This can lead to the interesting side of asking who is evolving, humans or civilisations, and who owns whom – do humans have cultures or do cultures possess humans? Conveniently, this is outside the scope of this volume. The conclusion of Chapter 9 is that introspection is a *plausible source of ideas* for anthropic AI.

One can recommend various processes for AI developers. One could recommend reading poetry, meditating, taking a walk, or sitting on a comfortable chair. One could even produce evidence that some of these recommendations do improve AI research. Here my recommendation is based on a more intrinsic link between introspection, skills, and anthropic AI. Having shown that introspection is both acceptable and plausible, details of my precise recommendations are found in Chapter 10 and examples are provided in Chapters 11 and 12.

One must bear in mind that at the moment no AI researcher is wholeheartedly embracing introspection *and* writing code.

5.3.2 *"For"*

This book recommends introspection for developing anthropic AI. So we are looking to make anthropic AI *based on* some introspection. The exact nature of this "based on" relationship and many examples of different types of AI and what these are based on will be found in Section 10.1. For now, suffice it to say that Y, a design for an AI system, is based on an observation X (that could be an introspective observation) iff:

A. There is a causal link from X to Y.
B. X is the dominant influence on the workings of Y, that is, there is as little pollution as is practically possible by some any other factor such as a prior theoretical commitment. In our case of AI based on introspection, this would require acceptance of introspection (X) as an acceptable source of ideas, not to be obfuscated or denied; minimisation of attachment to, or influence of any theoretical framework, such as mathematics, logic, or some theory in cognition, psychology, religion, or even phenomenological literature.
C. Corresponding functions are achieved in similar ways (data flows, data structures, temporal order, etc.).

A more detailed version of this definition and how it relates specifically to introspection is given in Section 10.1.1. Examples of similarities of process and data flow are given in Sections 10.1.2 and 10.1.3. For the detailed process of how introspection turns into code see Section 10.2.

5.3.3 *"Developing"*

This thesis concerns development of anthropic AI, specifically the "discovery" or "idea" phase, as opposed to the software development phase. In talking about the processes that go into developing AI, one would benefit from keeping a clear notion of five different minds (or "part-minds") that may be involved in the process and have different perspectives and concerns. Consider Illustration 5.2 on page:

- The **Basis** – This is the base idea or the inspiration used to build the AI design. It need not be a complete mind but probably has to be some kind of information-processing or "intentional" entity. Illustration 5.2 presents the examples of logic, mathematics, neural nets, honey bees, introspection, and externally observed behaviour.
- The **AI** program, the machine or robot being built.
- The **Practitioner** who uses the basis as a guide or model and builds the AI system. Examples (in the picture) are Trenchard More, John McCarthy, Marvin Minsky, Oliver Selfridge, and Ray Solomonoff (Knapp, 2008).
- The **Observer**, who may comment on the AI or the process of its development, but is not directly and actively engaged. Examples include Dreyfus, McCorduck, and Flores.
- The **King**, or administrator, or the research funding agency. This is "he who pays the piper" or "she who exerts control", explicitly or implicitly. A prime example from AI would be DARPA.[7]

In some cases, one and the same person can fulfil more than one role, for example Minsky was both a practitioner and an observer (Minsky, 1991).

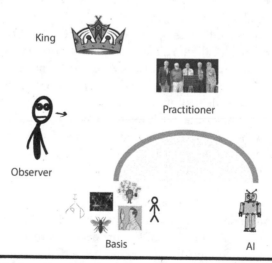

Illustration 5.2   Roles in AI development.

---

[7] The degree that AI specifically and computers in general were developed as military tools is an under-appreciated question (Edwards, 1997). The evidence in the terminology such as "commands" for instructions, etc. is suggestive. This point was made to me by Blay Whitby.

This volume, mainly from the position of an **observer**, will argue for the **practitioner** using introspection, which means taking both the role of **practitioner** and of **basis**. <u>This book is *not* about building **AI** systems that will introspect themselves</u>. It is about the AI **practitioner** using his own introspection as a **basis** for his designs. Schematically, this argument is a plea by an **observer** to the practitioners to use their own subjectivity as the **basis**, the inspiration, for novel **AI**; and also imploring the **kings** to fund such research. In Chapters 11 and 12, I will take also the position of the **practitioner** in order to provide working **AI** examples of what is recommended here, and in doing so, I will also introspect, so I will use my own mind also as the **basis**.

Perhaps it is worth reiterating what was underlined above – this volume is not directed at introspecting AI systems. This is not because those are a bad idea, quite the contrary. If we want to create truly human-like systems, such systems will most probably need the facility to reflect on their own actions, including their metal actions, and hence introspection would most probably be requisite. But at the moment, we do not have AI systems of a sophistication where such abilities are a reasonable next step. For the current stage of research, the urgent task is opening up introspection for the practitioner, that is, recommending the practitioner to use their own subjective experience of their own mind as a basis for AI development.

Some future ideas that would have to be completed before we ask for systems that *do* introspect themselves are discussed in Section 13.2.

5.4 Central Argument Outline – Summary

This chapter provided an overview of the main argument: *introspection is recommended for anthropic AI*. Two main terms remain undefined: "anthropic AI" and "introspection". These will be discussed next, followed by the arguments making up the recommendation in two subsequent chapters.

Chapter 6

Main Term: "Anthropic AI"

This book's thesis is that "introspection is recommended for developing anthropic AI". This chapter is about the aim, the purpose: "anthropic AI". Anthropic artificial intelligence (AI) will be defined as pursuing the computer implementation of (an approximation of) the base, minimal, human ability that *allows for* our culture but is independent of it. It will be contrasted with enculturated AI, specifically the prevalent AI that assumes as its target a western, modern, well-trained, and adult intelligence.

I will first discuss human-like vs rational/ideal AI and then will distinguish anthropic AI as a subtype of human-like AI.

6.1 Human vs Ideal/Rational

Russell and Norvig, in their canonical introduction to AI introduce a distinction between human-like AI and rational AI (Russell & Norvig, 2013, pp. 1–4). Most of the AI work in the past 60 years has been of the rational, idealised kind. Rational AI aims at correct, or best-possible, solutions. Human-like AI aims at imitating humans, with all their frailty and hopefully ingenuity. Russell and Norvig's distinction is a slight oversimplification. There are other actual existing non-optimal intelligences other than the human case. In cognitive science, there are bodies of work on insect and swarm intelligences and other animals' intelligence. This an active field of research both in industry (Raibert et al., 2008) and science (Baddeley et al., 2012), but these are not directly relevant in the short term to human-like AI and will therefore not be further discussed. Russell and Norvig also make a distinction between thinking and acting, which is not relevant here.

As a rule of thumb, if an AI system does not **make mistakes** or if you can prove meaningful theorems about it, it is rational AI. There is nothing wrong with rational AI, which is a thriving industry. But shunning the human-like because it is not mathematical enough, not neat enough, or because our scientific methodologies do not apply easily – that would be neglecting an area of research for no better reason than that it is difficult.

It is important to note that not only is human-like AI neglected in research, it is nearly entirely ignored in *teaching* AI, especially in computer-science settings. In page 5 of the aforementioned canonical textbook of AI, after discussing this distinction, the authors declare that their "text concentrates on general principles of rational agents and on components for constructing them" and proceed to use the rest of their 1,090 pages to teach rational AI alone, possibly misleading undergraduates into the impression that that is the only sort of AI that exists.[1] This is understandable for the authors, as human-like AI is now a fringe area, but ignoring it completely is alarming considering that their book is used by 1,293 schools in 116 countries (Russell & Norvig, 2016).

There is nothing wrong with rational AI. The only problem is that it is (by definition) *not* about humans as they *are*, but insofar as it is about humans at all, it is about how they *should be*. This distinction should be kept separate from the distinction between AI motivated by technology and AI motivated by science (Section 5.1.1 provides a two-dimensional map of some AI efforts so far).

There is an interesting parallel to human-like AI in human-like robot (hardware) construction. Nick Hockings aims to build human-like hands, using exact replicas of the human anatomy, down to the level of tendons. At the level of tendons, he switches abruptly from being committed to the human-like to implementing the tendons using whatever techniques and chemistry are available to build "tendons" as similar as possible to the natural. The idea is to *emulate* the natural, not recreate it, but to do it at a level as low as currently technically possible, feasibly (Hockings et al., 2014). In creating humanoid robots, we need to emulate the underlying mechanisms but only insofar as possible. There is a point where in the technological interest one must give up and go to modern plastics and 3-D printing (in robotics) or "just program" in AI (see Sections 6.5.4 and 10.3.5).

6.2 Motivations for Human-Like AI

6.2.1 Rational AI's Interaction Is "Clunky"

Motivations for developing rational or idealised AI are clear: Computer technology around us would be impossibly difficult to engineer if it were not deterministic, mathematical, and as fast as possible. Advances in machine learning, etc.

---

[1] An interesting question would be who reads introductions to 1,000-page engineering textbooks. I imagine that these pages are neglected by nearly all readers.

are ubiquitous and making tangible contributions to the lives of people (nearly) throughout the planet. Examples (just from smartphones use) include speech recognition, natural language interfaces and navigation systems that dynamically learn the maps and one-way systems of cities.

Regardless of all these advances, even the most fêted and expensively developed (rational/idealised) technologies today (such as Siri) are clunky, "robotic", etc. The idea, common in Japan, of using robots as companions or caregivers and companions to the elderly is greeted with much scepticism in the rest of the world because of this clunky behaviour (Robertson, 2007).

Other examples of existing AI's failure to capture the human way of doing things are its best-advertised achievements: IBM's "Watson"[2] cannot hold a conversation, and the various attempts at (the broad family of tests called) the Turing test are ultimately exposed as short-term "bags of tricks" with little expandability (more about bags of tricks in Section 6.8). Other attempts at human-like AI have been purely academic-scientific, in the field of cognitive simulation. In any role where genuine, practical understanding of the human way of doing things is required, robots and AI are so far rightly excluded.

Let's look at a couple of categories of motivations for human-like AI:

6.2.2 The Versatility of Human Intelligence

In the "Ode to Man" in Antigone, Sophocles expresses his wonder at the abilities of man:

> Wonders are many, and none is more wonderful than man; the power that crosses the white sea, driven by the stormy south-wind, making a path under surges that threaten to engulf him....
>
> And the light-hearted race of birds, and the tribes of savage beasts, and the sea-brood of the deep, he snares in the meshes of his woven toils, he leads captive, man excellent in wit....he tames the horse of shaggy mane... the tireless mountain bull.
>
> And speech, and wind-swift thought, and all the moods that mould a state, hath he taught himself; and how to flee the arrows of the frost, when 'tis hard lodging under the clear sky, and the arrows of the rushing rain; yea, he hath resource for all;...only against death shall he call for aid in vain; but from baffling maladies he hath devised escapes....

(Sophocles, 2009)

Human intelligence is interesting in its general-purpose nature, its ability to achieve such a diverse range of accomplishments. Human intelligence can learn and act in

---

[2] Named after the founder of IBM, no relation of JB Watson the psychologist or P Watson the historian.

ill-understood and uncertain circumstances, such as "crossing the white sea". Any system that tries to be human-like must therefore be a learning system. Humans not only learn all their lives (to varying degrees) but also make mistakes, so aiming at some mathematically correct behaviour may well miss much of what human intelligence is about.[3]

Possibly the most powerful motivation for human-like AI rather than rational-idealised AI is the fact that *humans invented rationality*, so we can expect human-like AI to be more flexible and have wider application (even if it may be less reliable and less optimal). This is of particular interest for the situation of generative AI, where AI will hopefully be employed to develop further AI (van der Zant et al., 2013).

Formal logic, as we know it today, is specifically a western invention, starting in ancient Greece. Even in the modern west, not everyone thinks logically, and even those who make a conscious effort towards the feat of thinking logically often fail (Ariely, 2009). None of us were born as logic machines, we were (at best) brought up to be skilled in logic. We were educated into and through logic. So there must be an underlying mechanism that *allows* for the emergence of logic. Some evidence that such a mechanism exists can be found in its malfunction in the case of fallacies. This was explored in detail in the case of algebraic mal-rules (Payne & Squibb, 1990).

6.2.3 Getting along with People

Human-like AI would be useful in areas where human-like behaviour would be better than rationally optimised behaviour – where the very essence of the job is to get along with people, where it is key that the computer be easily understood in human terms, and where it would also be useful for the AI system to understand the human way of doing things. Areas of applicability would include:

- Car driving: Driving cars by computer has made great strides in recent years but still has difficulty with pragmatics (Richtel & Dougherty, 2015). Pragmatics are often culture-dependent. What is done, for example with lanes, is different in different cultures: In Brazil, where politics has driven lanes to be narrower, the idea that a large lorry can take two or even three lanes in a motorway is considered normal. In Bangkok, lanes will form and dissolve on hard shoulders wherever possible.
- Delivery robots: As online shopping becomes the norm, the desire for fast delivery increases, and a demand is created for faster delivery (Amazon is developing a drone for the extreme version of this problem delivery in 30 min

---

[3] Much work in rational/idealised AI is done statistically, aiming (for example) to be "probably approximately correct" (Russell & Norvig, 2013, p. 725). This is idealised AI since it aims to get the probabilities *right*, and the approximations *optimal*.

("Amazon Prime Air", 2016)). A lightweight robot that can deliver packages to doorways would be invaluable. That would require navigating the addresses, negotiating spaces crowded with pedestrians, and understanding such human communications as handwritten notes saying "If I am not home please leave packages at flat 6".

A particularly interesting case is **care giving robots**. In rapidly ageing societies, there is a growing need for carers to keep elders company and to serve as interfaces to digital technology, which in turn can help in physical care (Broekens et al., 2009). Regardless of ethical issues (see Section 6.9), such technologies may become essential especially in societies (Japan stands out) where immigration of human caregivers is not a politically palatable solution (TheEconomist, 2013).

Humans have a tendency to anthropomorphise (treat as human) all entities, for example note Aristotle's idea that heavy objects "want to" go downwards. Regardless of efforts by educators to combat this tendency, humans are still predisposed to think that way. This predisposition is seen even in science where we say things like "the system obeys the laws of physics" or "light follows Maxwell's equations". There is no obedience or following going on – this is all "in our eyes", in *our* tendency to attribute human characteristics to inanimate things.

As robots become more ubiquitous, they will be operated by people with fewer skills. One cannot expect any training given to the patient/operator of a robot to reliably last, due to amplified forgetfulness and confusion in old age – so patients will revert to assuming that the robot *is* human-like.

In the case of elderly patients cared for by robots, this will be much worse (Sharkey & Sharkey, 2011). Patients will assume that robots can apply rules "reasonably" while rational-ideal AI systems have no idea of what "being reasonable" may mean. This can cause patients to trust robots to behave in ways that would be expected of a human but beyond the robot's preprogrammed ability or worse – against a clear preprogrammed prohibition. Since this expectation by the patients is unavoidable (and may be life-threatening), as technologists we need to rise to the challenge and make some robots as human-like as possible (perhaps within some hard outer boundaries).

6.3 Characteristics of Human-Like AI

Human-like AI would allow robots to form malleable habits, as opposed to rule-based systems (like driverless cars picking up the local driving culture). By thinking and acting in a human-like and culture-adjusted way, robots would be better understood by humans. Moreover, once this technology is advanced enough, a truly human-like technology would allow robots to form their own (speculative) understanding of human actors in their environment, to speculate about the human intentions, and cooperate with these humans.

Consider for a moment, how computers play chess or any other similar board game (see Section 1.2). They assume that the human would behave (more or less) according to the machine's own algorithm. The computer can understand the human and vice versa since they are playing the same game and can in sense simulate each other: "If I were in his position, I would do that...".

Generalising from board games to any other situation involving two of more players, a good way to understand another actor is to be able to simulate them and see how they would react in different situations. The advantage of human-like AI in understanding humans is therefore analogous to computer-chess algorithms' ability to understand a human playing the same game. For every system, it is easier to simulate (and to understand) a system similar to itself. It would be very difficult for a system that uses one thinking method to understand another system that thinks differently. As long as the domain of action is a formal domain, like chess, rational/ideal AI has the edge and wins against humans. Once we move into the human arena, we need human-like AI. This does not preclude integrating diverse technologies together (Minsky, 1991).

None of this is to say that human-understanding behaviour is *in-principle* impossible for any machine that is based on logical–rational principles. Obviously if we were ever to program a computer to behave like a human, the computer would still run on silicon chips, which implement a formal system (see below, and Sections 7.1.2 and 10.3.5).

6.4 Human-Like vs Anthropic

Let's examine the issue of whether we should want to simulate a fully-fledged, enculturated mind or whether it would be better to simulate the pre-culture, un-enculturated, naïve mind. If we had a good simulation of a fully cultured mind, it would animate robots that would work in *one* culture. If we go deeper and aim to simulate the un-enculturated mind, we would get the *ability* to get the AI system enculturated into *any* culture. Most of AI so far went for the first, enculturated option, in *anthropic* AI, we will aim for the later, un-enculturated option.

So why not use the term "human-like AI" as my target? Because behaving mathematically or logically is a *possibility* for humans and would therefore be *part* of a "human-like" concept, I specifically want to exclude such sophisticated highly trained thought: Being **western, modern, well-trained, and/or adult** – These may all be desirable qualities in terms of current culture and setting (this is a western, modern, book) – but none of these qualities is inherent to being human, and none of us (western, modern, well-trained adults) were born that way. We *learnt* (or *were trained*) to be that way. One could argue that being well cultured is good, but I argue that simulating our "best practices" is *not* what is needed currently in AI:

- Where "best practices" are clear, we can use normal programming or rational AI. We already have that.
- Where things are not clear, we need a system that can learn the complexities.
- A system may have a better chance of learning these complexities if it learns them in a way similar to how we learn them, that is, doing it the way we humans do it, which is more versatile and broader in scope than just "western, modern, well-educated adults".

Another important point to note is the question of who decides what precisely "western-modern well-trained adult", or "best practices" means. A learning system with fewer pre-judged commitments can better adapt to situations.

Distinguishing a human from their cultural or social context is not simple or easy. Probably this is not even completely possible. But we can try: One of the main questions in this approach is "what is it about *this animal* that allows it to participate in *any* society or culture, let alone our modern one?" It is generally accepted that this will include intelligence or the ability to learn skills and habits.

To get at this level we need to get under, or behind, or around, education, or training, as a person's training is a social phenomenon of the specific society in which that person was educated. This attempt to get beyond education is probably never completely possible but should remain an aspiration. How to go about doing this is the topic of Chapter 10.

I propose using the Greek for human, "Anthropos", to mean the untrained, basic human. This jives with the way that anthropology studies *all* humans, including the "primitive".

Anthropic AI aims at minimally human intelligence – without presupposing any of our cultural heritage (insofar as possible). Anthropic AI is **defined** as the base, minimal human ability that *allows for* our culture but is independent of it.

6.5 Perspectives and Levels in Human Modelling

Next, I will survey the different levels we can deal with or model the mind, both for psychological exploration and for AI technology development. But first we must slow down a bit.

6.5.1 Are There Really Levels or Layers in the Mind/Brain?

Caution is advised when discussing layers or levels in the human mind/brain. The idea that things are neatly arranged in layers comes from several sources. In engineering, it is useful to think in modules and layers, and in software design, not only do we have many layers, we even have a hierarchy (in the types of layers), where some layers are more important and get to be called "platforms" – like Microsoft's "Windows", the "Java Virtual Machine", "IP" (the internetworking protocol, as in

"TCP/IP"), etc. In software, the levels are usually very well defined, with the interfaces between layers called "APIs". The idea of the mind being *constructed in layers* is seductive but twice wrong: First, the mind is not *constructed* but is an evolved characteristic of the human animal. Second, we have no evidence that there is anything like *layers* inside humans.

It is far more likely that the mind is like the gold-bearing reefs of the Witwatersrand Basin in South Africa: Gold settled at the bottom of a primordial lake for millions of years, then the lake bed (arguably initially a layer) dried, deformed, and was partially eroded away. Next, most of the gold-bearing deposits were buried deep in the ground. Later, a large meteorite hit the ground, tearing and throwing up into the air a 300 km wide part of the earth's crust. As this mass of matter crashed in chaos, some of the gold-bearing formations were exposed, with no particular shape. It so happens that half the world's gold comes from these formations. There are no layers involved, just a lot of history (Safonov & Prokof'ev, 2006).

Coming back to the human mind, the brain's anatomy (its "architecture") is composed of multiple organs, which evolved in different eras. But that is also misleading, in that the older brain organs continued to evolve, and so, there is no ground to treating them as distinct modules or layers – these organs may be anatomically somewhat distinct, but they function together. It is doubtful we can even delineate distinct mechanisms – there are no clear and distinct "layers" or boundaries to be found nor is there a reason to believe we may find them in the future. The reason people search for such oversimplified models is that it would be very convenient for our western-modern mode of thinking if we could find such layers. Again, the human situation is more complex than the ideal/rational situation. Neglecting the human just because it is difficult may be a good way to get the first few AI systems going, but eventually, we need to tackle the human as it is, rather than the western, modern, formalised way we think that we *ought* to think.

Layers are how *we like* to think about machines, problems, etc. It is something we superimpose on the world in order to make sense of it, like a grid on a map (see the term "adhyasa" in Indian philosophy, Section 13.4.5).

6.5.2 Multiple Levels of Discussion

Having defined anthropic AI as the base, minimal, human ability that *allows for* our culture but is independent of it, we can turn to examining what the alternative approaches to human-like AI may be. Being part of the modern west, we cannot avoid some superimposing of distinctions at least in this meta-discussion – let's just bear in mind that any layers are part of the *analysis* and not of the human. We can identify several modes or "levels" or "layers" in which one could observe, discuss, and try to simulate humans, their behaviour, or their intelligence. Each of these levels takes multiple forms and can have AI approaches associated with it. I am not making any claim with this list, this is for purposes of clarification only.

1. **Atomic, molecular** (or lower)

    In terms of scientific purity, this may be the best level to simulate anything (that is not so small as to have subatomic effects). The problem is that we do not have the data (an atomic-level scan of a human) nor the computational capacity. So this is (currently) infeasible, regardless of the waves of optimism unleashed by the Human Genome Project in the early 2000s (Bower & Bolouri, 2001).

2. **Cellular** (see Dreyfus's "Biological assumption", Section 2.3)

    In a similar vein, simulating every cell or every neuron is a current goal, for the decades if not centuries to come (Markram, 2012). For *now*, it is infeasible. Moreover, if and when we have a full-brain simulation, there is no guarantee whatsoever that the mind inhabiting such a "brain" will be in any way normal and/or able or willing to communicate with us.

3. **Bio-functional** (cell assemblies)/neural networks

    This level simulates fewer individual neurons or (more accurately) neuron-like abstractions. With this kind of modelling, researchers are trying to simulate either small parts of the brain or entire systems using a (rather strong) assumption that whole cell assemblies behave somewhat like a neuron. Another motivation for this research is exploring what *can* be done with neural nets. These neural nets are also used in technology, unlike the previous perspectives.

4. **Cognitive theoretic** (see Dreyfus's "psychological assumption", Section 2.3)

    Cognitive models (such as SOAR) and classic symbolic AI propose a computational model for various faculties that underlie individual human activity (Laird & Rosenbloom, 1996; Sun, 2008). These models (when used as a scientific tool rather than for technology) are verified by comparing their performance to human performance in similar tasks. In technology, it is the basis for some of Good Old-Fashioned AI (GOFAI), especially heuristic and satisficing algorithms.

    The tasks achieved by these models mostly seem quite contrived and divorced from everyday life (Dreyfus, 1979, 2007). The cognitive models themselves tend to be parsimonious, like a small computer program. An example of how badly these systems fail at being human-like is that we still do not have an artificial controller for a human-like hand with any dexterity.

    I distinguish between these cognitive models that are based on psychological *theory* (in turn based on science, mathematics, computer models, etc.) and models based of *subjective descriptions* (point 6 below).

5. **Personal behaviouristic**

    This is the level of recreating external behaviour. A notable example is passive walking robots (Collins & Ruina, 2005).

6. **Personal-subjective** (see Dreyfus's "epistemological assumption", Section 2.3)

    This level is concerned with the individual humans, *as we see ourselves*, not as a natural phenomenon to be examined externally. Here, we are interested in the subjective (see Section 7.1), without prejudice to age, gender, race, culture, or historical time. It would include anything that pertains to *Homo sapiens sapiens as such,* without any cultural additions, such as anything which would be specifically western, modern, well trained, or adult. It would include the *facility* to learn any language and cooperate with others, to construct edifices and imagine worlds. This level excludes anything that is culture-specific, like literacy or any particular system of logic. Our favourite cultural artefacts, language and mathematics, are already amply explored in rational-idealised AI, in the points below. This level is this book's *ultimate* goal – anthropic AI. But since we do not have this yet, the current goal has to be making strides in this direction.

7. **Social-behavioural**

In this level, basic cultural artefacts, like language, are explored. This is where generative grammarians (like Chomsky) argue with other schools of linguistics, like statistical linguistics.

8. **Social-normative** (Logic, Bayesian)

This is the level of *normative* cultural artefacts, like logic, laws, etiquette, etc. Specific to the west are logic, mathematics, and science. Much of GOFAI is in this level, for example Simon's Logical Theorist (Newell & Simon, 1956).

One should recall that this level has positive and negative aspects: On the positive side, social norms give us science and technology, without which there is no AI (and so many other things). Moreover, without our western normative traditions, I could not write this – I would have no Latin alphabet, no computer, no web or email, and no readers. The western scientific tradition also gives us empirical methodologies that we need in any modern systematic pursuit, including technology or AI. On the negative side, our tradition gives us the drawbacks of the rationalistic views, as described by Winograd and Flores and as critiqued by Dreyfus. As Minsky had it, AI is stuck – and I suggest it is stuck at this and the biological levels (McHugh & Minsky, 2003).

Every level seems to require the levels before it in this list, but its existence is a contingent fact about the levels before. Not all functioning organisms have neural systems; not all neural systems we would want to attribute full-blown cognitive abilities to; not every cognitive mind need generate a subjective perspective; it is reasonable to assume that young children have phenomenal experiences even before they acquire any specific culture; and not all cultures developed logic as an articulated body of knowledge, a few developed mathematics, but science as we recognize it today was only developed in the west relatively recently.

These levels can be seen as all relevant simultaneously, as perspectives (see Section 5.2.3). However, as AI developers, we need to choose at which level to focus our efforts. So far, AI technology has mainly been at levels 8 (logic programming, Bayesian approaches, some of GOFAI), 4 (GOFAI, cognitive simulation), and 3 (neural nets). Some thinkers, unpopular with the majority (e.g. Dreyfus), would argue that the cognitive level (4) does not exist as such but is only an artefact of our present scientific fashions (level 8). This deserves some discussion.

6.5.3 The Cognitive Level Is Problematic

The term "mind" (or "mental") is used in the literature relevant to AI in two distinct senses. The first is the layperson's intuitive sense, as in "what is on my mind" – it is the subjective world of one's own experience (or consciousness), it is what is accessible by introspection. This is often called the "phenomenal mind". However, in the psychological (cognitive) literature, the term "mind" refers (often if not always) to imputed processes that go on inside a person in order to achieve the performance that people *empirically* achieve (Nisbett & Wilson, 1977, p. 232). For example, much of cognitive science would say things like "the mind is what the brain does" (Skinner, 1987) or "the mind involves top-down processes" or "the mind has short and long term memories". The first notion of the mind is subjective, while the second notion *aims* to be "objective" but is actually (at least for now) speculative, with some correlational backing. We call this second notion the "cognitive mind", but I beg to not make this usage a claim that these mechanisms exist other than as a level of analysis.

Another way that the cognitive mind is often defined as "the underlying mechanisms – the cognitive processes and structures – that give rise to ... effects" (Ericsson & Simon, 1981). One can only presume this includes the seemingly universal behaviour of reporting on the existence and content of a phenomenal mind. Miller says that "It is the *result* of thinking, not the process of thinking, that appears spontaneously in consciousness". So also the word "think" seems to also have this duality – here, Miller defines thinking as the *underlying* process that we do not experience, while in everyday speech (and introspection) we usually consider "think" to refer to things we can be conscious of, as in "I think that *this* path to the café is shorter" (Nisbett & Wilson, 1977).

Note the aim of psychology (as a science) is to make cognitive models that reflect accurately what is going on in the brain and therefore predict accurately not only externally observable behaviour but also subjective experience (Seth, 2010). I have no argument with this aim, but I must point out that we are probably at least decades away from any models that in any way predict human behaviour and experience outside of constrained laboratory situations. So for now, the "cognitive mind" of which psychologists talk is no more than a set of theoretical constructs, with *some* evidence. Therefore, treating the cognitive mind as reflecting any sort of system that we can usefully emulate in usable AI is only one option and one which has arguably already been exhausted in terms of AI technologies (see Sections 4.3 and 4.5). The main thrust of this book is promoting the use of the subjective mind as a source of ideas for AI, via introspection.

6.5.4 Simultaneous Multiple Levels in Computers

Unlike the human mind, where there are no levels to be found (see Section 6.5.1), in a computer, there *are* levels, since the computer was *designed* that way. And yet, the question of what a computer is doing is not clear-cut. One could say it is working, if the power supply is on. One could say that nearly all its electric power is dedicated to keeping 0s distinct from 1s (BC Smith, 2005). One could view it as a 64-bit processing machine, shuffling chunks of data that size. One could view it as running MS-Windows or Linux or as running some software package, say an "Oracle" database. One could also see it as running some application like a billing system or as "collecting debts". Less positively, one could see such a machine as perpetuating the injustices in society. While within a specific discourse such as "what operating system is being run", there are specific answers, that can be categorically true or false,[4] I can see no way of determining what is the "correct" description in general, perhaps except asking what was the intention of the person configuring the system in the particular way that it is configured at a particular moment. Even this definition may be incorrect, as a learning AI system may bear little resemblance to any intention by a human. My cat will always view a computer as a source of heat to sit on. Again, there is no "correct" way to view a computer (see Section 5.2.2).

So even when we say that a computer is running some non-rationalist AI system, at the same time we can see that the computer is keeping the 0s and 1s distinct, is checking various checksums, and is running like a very digital and logical computer. The level in which a computer would be running a non-rational system is at the level of *our intentions for it*. We could call that the "conceptual level" or D.C. Dennett's (1989) "design stance". Every algorithm can be implemented by any universal machine, and a universal machine can be built in many ways, so I may argue against Bayesian statistics or logic but still run my anthropic algorithm on a system that used Bayesian statistics (perhaps) and Boolean logic (for sure) at another level. This topic relates also to pan-computationalism (Müller, 2009), (see also Sections 10.3.5.3 and 10.3.5.4).

6.6 Anthropic AI so far

Less **effort** is being invested in human-like AI in comparison to other technologies, and very little effort in teaching this field (see Section 6.1), the main effort that *is* ongoing in creating human-like behaviour is chatterbots for commercial (Deryugina, 2010) and Turing test (Mladenić & Bradeško, 2012) purposes; this is human-like but not anthropic. Moreover, I am aware of no *technology-oriented* efforts to create AI that emulates any *subjectively experienced* mechanisms of the

---

[4] Though note the further layers of complexity introduced by virtual machines or various types, and nested configurations thereof.

mind (though Agre tried emulating Heidegger's phenomenology, see Section 8.3.2). On the borderlands between philosophy and science, machine consciousness is a vibrant conceptual effort (Gamez, 2008). Most efforts to create human-like technology apply tried and tested paradigms of the rational-idealised kind, such as machine learning. This mismatch of means and ends invites Dreyfus's (1979, p. 100) quip saying that AI is trying to get to the moon by climbing a tree.

An interesting point is that historically "cognitive anthropology was nipped in the bud in the early 1970s" (Boden, 2008, p. 32). Margaret Boden (1936–) has a whole chapter (8) entitled "the mystery of the missing discipline" about how anthropology is ignored in cognitive science. This absence of an anthropological angle to AI could speculatively be attributed to some general abhorrence of the primitive, as testified to by the observation that Herbert Simon (see Section 1.6) has contributed to "every social science discipline <u>except</u> anthropology" (stress added) (Augier & March, 2001).

Anthropic AI assumes a pragmatic distinction between the layer of intelligence that allows for human learning on the one hand and the content of such learnings (culture) on the other hand. I find only two AI efforts with a technological orientation that were made that are relevant to anthropic AI in that they share this assumption:

The first is CYC (Lenat et al., 1985), which was an attempt to give a computer the rules, or knowledge, underlying "common sense". These rules were done in the spirit of an expert system, and the goal of the project was to use this "common sense" to overcome the brittle nature of such expert systems. However, "Lenat predicted that in 10 years Cyc would cope with novelty by recognizing analogies and would then be able to teach itself by reading the newspapers. Time is up and he seems to have made no progress on this front" (Dreyfus, 1996). In a sense, there were *three* layers envisaged here: The innate expert system engine (pre-programmed), the rules to be fed in, and the culture to be accumulated after such rules started functioning.

Another attempt to do something comparable to anthropic AI was COG (Brooks et al., 1999). The idea was to build on Brooks's older insect-like intelligent system, by attaching a system of little more internal sophistication to "an upper-torso humanoid robot called Cog" and to train it over time by interaction with the environment, like human infants develop. Again, Dreyfus puts it in his accurate but cruel style: "the 'long term project' was short lived. Cog failed to achieve any of its goals and the original robot is already in a museum" (Dreyfus, 2007).

There is a distinction (key to debugging) between these efforts, which can also be applied to AI in general: COG, like neural nets, cannot explain its own behaviour in (reasonable length) language-like communicable form. On the other hand, CYC, being an expert system extension, can print out a trace of how a logical deduction was arrived at. This explicitness and clarity is important in two senses: Humans, at least once they acquire the sophistication of very few years of age, can articulate reasons for (at least some of) their actions, and as will be argued in

Section 9.2, these are not "noise". Additionally, having the ability to explain how some outcome was arrived at is invaluable in debugging (see Sections 7.1.1 and 12.6.3).

6.7 Knowing That vs Knowing How, and a Hint on Data Structure

Let's preliminarily look at the kinds of data structures involved in different approaches to AI. The main data type of AI systems often reflects a view or a perspective about what type of knowledge is most basic and should be the native data type of the AI software. A word is due about this and some other arguments in philosophy of mind: When these arguments are being conducted they are most usually about what is the *correct* way to *understand* humans, *scientifically*. However, as technologists, and even more so as technologists looking for ideas, we have no need for correctness, since we are not doing science (see Sections 8.2.4 and 8.2.5). We need perspectives, *ideas for technology*. So if in some scientific or philosophical argument scholars are adamantly arguing between two or three positions – in AI as technology, we can try each and every one in turn (more about this laissez-faire attitude in technology in Sections 5.1.3, 5.2, 8.2.4, 8.2.5, and 8.7).

We can distinguish three kinds of knowledge:

1. knowing how to do something – say, ride a bicycle. Call this "knowing how".
2. knowing a person – say, your best friend. Call this "familiarity".
3. knowing that some fact is true – say, that the Red Sox won the 2004 World Series. Call this "knowing that" (Fantl, 2014).

Following Fantl in ignoring (2), which seems to be mere recognition note that the psychological distinction between explicit and implicit knowledge is similar though not identical to the knowing that/how distinction. Bearing in mind our purpose of producing novel human-like AI, let us examine the possible positions on the relations between "knowing how" and "knowing that".

In terms of AI, the three positions have different implications for design. Considering one's stance on the basic knowledge type, we should also consider what would be the AI system's basic data structure.

1. **Intellectualism** is the position that all knowledge-how is based on (and reducible to) knowledge-that. This is the position reflected by Simon's General Problem Solver (GPS) and many other projects, including prolog, expert systems, and arguably the vast majority of classic (and statistical) AI (Dreyfus & Dreyfus, 1986, p. 146). When people design AI systems, they often discuss (explicit) knowledge about the state of affairs in the world, rather than skills.

This position is most explicit in symbolic AI (like expert systems) or more subtle in the statistical knowledge of learning systems.

Appropriately, the data structures found in classic AI are usually combinations of the following:

– Statements of facts and/or of rules, as in first-order predicate calculus.
– Statements of probabilities, in Bayesian and other statistical systems.

The "naked" expert system as such is like a prolog interpreter, an infrastructure for inferences, and a store of explicit "knowledge-that". A human "knowledge engineer" translates human knowledge into this format, sometimes even trying to grasp knowledge-how. Fuzzy logic (see Section 11.1) was introduced to help with the difficulty of formalizing skills.

2. **Anti-intellectualism** recognises the distinct existence and validity of both categories of knowledge. Perhaps the best expression of this position in AI is Minsky's call for a pragmatic mix of diverse of AI mechanisms (Minsky, 1991).

   Some might argue that both "knowledge-how" and "knowledge-that" are underpinned by some third terminology, but we have scant idea what that third terminology might be (short of simulating an entire brain), and this will surely be very complex. One could present intellectualism (above) as saying that the underlying uniting mechanism is some sort of "knowing that", while radical anti-intellectualism (below) can be presented as identifying this underlying mechanism as being sort of "knowledge how". This middle position does not specify what the underlying mechanism might be.

   Pragmatically, we have no such underlying concept which is readily implementable in technology, at a level that even aims at convincing human-like AI. The nearest attempts are vaguely based on brains (probably since brains are the only place we see an underlying mechanism for both types of knowledge).

   The data structures associated with this approach are brain-inspired, mainly:

   – Neural nets
   – Brook's emulation of multiple cooperating mechanisms (Brooks, 1991)

3. **Radical anti-intellectualism** arrests that all knowledge-that is based on knowledge-how, for example knowing that $2 + 2 = 4$ is seen as just a set of behaviours one can be skilled at, like the ability to say "two-plus-two-is-four" and to produce other behaviours that "apply this knowledge" in appropriate times (Fantl, 2014). This position has not been explored in AI yet and seems compatible with phenomenology and Dreyfus's works, especially the emphasis on skill as the basis for a more phenomenologically correct AI (Dreyfus & Dreyfus, 1986). One should note that this is a "road less travelled by" in AI. It may well be worthwhile remaining sympathetic to this position (see Sections 12.6.4 and 13.4.2).

A data type that would implement knowing-how needs to have less categorical elements than first-order predicate logic, so that skills can be implemented correctly not just in the canonical and clear situations but also in *similar* situations. Fuzzy logic (see Section 11.1) makes a start, and more advanced examples will be provided in the rest of Chapters 11 and 12.

Another reason to be sympathetic to knowledge-how as the basis for AI systems is found in noting (following Ryle) that knowledge-that is inert – it is like statements written on paper or stored in a computer. In order to *apply* knowledge-that, one needs to know *how*, but moreover, one needs to have a mechanism that not only *knows* how to implement such inert knowledge-that but actually *does* it – like a CPU not only "knows" how to run programs but actually *does it*. So knowledge-that just cannot function alone in the world, it needs an active mechanism with the right know-how, and an inclination to act.

Since we are here interested in *anthropic* AI, as distinct from the AI that imitates western, modern, well-trained adults, we can leave "knowledge that" to be developed in the enculturated, learned phase. We needn't focus on "knowledge that" directly at all, leaving us to focus on knowledge-how.

6.8 Metaphysical Non-problems

There are some debates that spring to mind at this point but that have no technological impact, and therefore, it is best to remain agnostic about these. These debates often overlap and are sometimes simply the computer science vs the philosophical names for similar if not identical issues. The main points of these debates can be summarized thus:

Some technologists would object that chatterbots are not "real AI", that their mechanism is just a "bag of tricks" that would not constitute "real intelligence" or "a mind" under any construal (Deryugina, 2010). As a programmer, it is difficult to read the source code for "Eliza" (a classic AI program that simulates a therapist) and come to any other conclusion. I would like to refrain from making a judgement that *all* bags of tricks are somehow categorically "not a mind", just because "Eliza's" bag is nearly empty. Who are we to assume that our native intelligence is anything *more* than a (larger) "bag of tricks"? In a sense, in anthropic systems, like in COG, we are trying to build a system with a base intelligence that will collect more skills as it learns and evolves – so to speak "filling up its bag" as it goes along. Eventually, the behaviour could be sophisticated, hopefully even human-like.

Searle (1980) defines "Strong" vs "Weak" AI. His argument against strong AI is based on the following assumption:

> Intentionality in human beings (and animals) is a product of causal features of the brain.

He proceeds to use his famous "Chinese room" argument[5] to show that

> Instantiating a computer program is never by itself a sufficient condition of intentionality.

Searle discusses several replies to his argument, one of them being the "other minds" reply. It argues that we have no way of knowing whether a *person* understands Chinese, other than by their behaviour. So if we attribute genuine understanding to people, we must attribute it also to machines that display similar behaviour. Searle says:

> This objection really is only worth a short reply. The problem in this discussion is not about how I know that other people have cognitive states, but rather what it is that I am attributing to them when I attribute cognitive states to them....

But for us as technologists, the last thing we care about is "what it is that I am attributing" or what the *true* meaning of cognitive states is. We care about machines that are fit for purpose, that work well enough. This is all that we will be attributing to our AI systems, and the way to verify the criterion of "fit for purpose" is empirically.

The philosophical or scientific question of what "true" intentionality or cognition is may take many decades to resolve. As technologists, we needn't wait for that. The problem of whether a mind is "real" or not is a question for philosophy, not for technology – and here we are interested in technology.

Once we have far more advanced anthropic AI systems, the question of how "real" an AI mind is could be rephrased in terms of the depth of similarity between the artificial and the natural-human intelligences. These days are far in the future.

6.9 Ethics

If and when we would have human-like AI, it would give rise to a bevy of philosophical problems. As mentioned above, the strong/weak AI argument is analogical to the "other minds" problem, which is unsolved, by most thinkers' reckoning (Hyslop, 2014). Moreover, a truly human-like AI would give rise to (at least) three types of ethical problems:

1. Should we treat the AI as an entity capable of *real* experience (for example suffering) and, therefore, an entity towards which we would have moral obligations?

---

[5] Let's imagine a room with a person inside, ignorant of the Chinese language. Image also that this person has a rulebook that instructs them to process squiggles on pieces of paper, and produce other squiggles on paper as output. The denizen of the room follows the rules diligently. Even if by a miracle the rule book makes the person in the room produce good answers (in Chinese writing) to questions in the Chinese language, Searle would like to say that the "Chinese room" (the system of the person + rulebook) does not understand Chinese.

2. Would such AI be dangerous, in that it could become aggressive or try to take over the world in some dangerous (to humans) way? (Bostrom, 2016)
3. Would it be fair to have humans relate humanly towards a machine and develop an emotional bond with such machines? (Whitby, 2011)

Since human-like AI is in such a pitiful state at the moment, I view it as morally safe to exclude any ethical worries from *this* book. This must be revisited if human-like AI becomes significantly more successful than it has been so far.

There is an opposite angle on human-like AI. The whole idea of making artificial humans is precisely in order to replace human labour. In a sense, we would like, if possible, to bring back slavery without any genuine human suffering. Slaves understood our language and customs and provided personalized service. However, the very mention of slavery is near taboo in our society: We no longer keep slaves explicitly, but we should broaden our view. Human-like AI would possibly alleviate a lot of the tedium of current workplaces, some of which (especially in poorer part of the globe) may seem to future generation as repugnant as full-blown slavery seems to us today.

So there are ethical risks but also possible benefits in human-like AI. Because of the pitiful state of the technology, none of these will be further discussed.

6.10 Anthropic AI: Summary

When I use the term "anthropic AI", I mean human-like, pre-cultural AI; aimed at technology. Not AI trying to be a western, modern, well trained, or adult, and not directly aimed at understanding humans *per se* (as in the science of psychology).

Human-like AI tries to simulate human intelligence. Once we remove the currently prevailing biases of the western image of what human intelligence consists of, we get anthropic AI.

Anthropic AI is in a sense human-like AI taken seriously. Humans are born immature and learn general and specific skills. The general skills can be seen as a maturation of the basic abilities, but the culture-specific skills are, as defined, specific to the environment of the individual. If we want human-like intelligence, then we need this ability to adapt. Most existing learning systems are rational/ideal, and the few systems that aim at human-like behaviour (like COG or CYC) are very far from achieving this purpose.

Chapter 7

Main Term: "Introspection"

This chapter aims to clarify (to the degree necessary) the very concept of introspection and to prepare the ground for Chapter 8, which argues that introspection can be legitimately used in some scientific and technological contexts. Chapter 9 will argue that introspection is a promising basis for anthropic AI. Chapter 10 will detail the kind(s) of introspection recommended for anthropic AI. Examples follow.

Introspection is a type of self-observation. Being the observation of one individual, it is subjective. Moreover, being an observation of one's own mental states/processes, it is inaccessible to others *in principle* and is therefore doubly subjective. Phenomenology (in contrast to introspection) is an attempt to study human experience in a controlled and peer-reviewed way (Gallagher & Zahavi, 2012, pp. 28–29). In a sense, it is an attempt to create an intersubjective literature based on human subjectivity, an "objective" description of the subjective human condition. Sometimes the phenomenological literature becomes quite difficult, but luckily we need not go that far into it for our technological purposes (see Section 2.1).

7.1 Studying Subjectivity

Subjectivity is not a favourite topic of science, for evident reasons: Few of science's methods (empirical repeatability, mathematics, induction, Occam's razor) work in the subjective realm. This area is so fraught for scientists that several attempts have been made (most prominently by the logical positivists and by Watson) to banish subjectivity from any discussion, that is, to *legislate* for systematically ignoring what is clearly always there, in each of our experiences (Seth, 2010).

7.1.1 Why Subjectivity?

As we saw (in Section 6.5.2), there are many levels in which we can discuss and/or simulate humans. Some of these are impractical (e.g. the atomic level). Some have already been tried repeatedly in AI (cognitive simulation, neural nets, mathematics, logic, probability theory). Strangely, the level most available to us as individuals, our own subjective experience of ourselves, has been neglected. Here are some of the reasons to choose this level (beyond just trying something different).

Since our concern is with a technology that aims specifically to behave in an anthropic manner, an intuitive preference could be to use **terminology and mechanisms** that people can readily relate to. Humans relate well to each other's subjective narrations about their internal mental states: Many conversations start with "How are you" – soliciting precisely this sort of narrative, and some continue with "How could I do X", soliciting instructions based on the respondent's internal understanding of herself (for an extended discussion of how humans instruct each other successfully using introspection see Section 9.2). Moreover, humans who have no language in common still assume the existence of phenomenal mental states in strangers in terms familiar to their own daily discourse. It is plausible that if we were to build systems based on our own subjective daily experience, such systems would have a good chance of being easier to relate to and hence more useful (eventually) as, for example, caregivers for the elderly (see Section 6.2.3).

People like anthropomorphising things, like "the tree wants the sun". In order to allow people to interact more smoothly with robots, we need to have some level in the robot that functions in a way similar to humans, so that both the robot can parse how people are behaving, and people can parse how the robot is behaving (see Sections 6.2 and 6.3).

A secondary reason to be interested in the subjective is that simulation of subjective processes would be easier to debug than lower level processes, since we have no intuitive understanding of lower levels such as our own neurons or neuron assemblies. Going any lower than subjectivity would complicate debugging.

Going to any higher, more formal levels (where cultural assumptions begin) leads us into methodologies that tend to be clunky and not truly human-like.

7.1.2 Locating Subjectivity

Most AI systems are implemented in software, on a computer platform. The computer platform is designed to implement a formal system (though being a physical object in the world any computer is subject to the whims of real world, such as power cuts) (B. C. Smith, 2005). On such a formal system, there is usually an operating system and many other pieces of software all making no attempt to break this formal structure. Actually, it would be in principle impossible to break out of a formal system: That is why we use *pseudo*-random number generators – there is nothing random in a formal system.[1] However, using software, one can try to simulate non-formal systems, such as the weather, to a certain resolution. Such is the type of AI promoted here: Using software for simulating the processes that we experience subjectively, the human thought process, which is not formal. However, a human can learn to think formally (e.g. in school), and so, in principle, human-like AI could also learn to use logic and mathematics, thus creating a three-layer "sandwich" – formal systems below and above and the mess of actual human thought in the middle (Goldie, 2012).

Consider these three levels in humans: The lower level, the hardware, which could be called the implementation level and is well understood in computers and is being painstakingly researched in humans by neuroscience. This level in humans is not accessible to consciousness and therefore is not readily available to the AI developer (Nisbett & Wilson, 1977). The middle layer, where we have the informal "mess", is available to our subjectivity on the human side and is called for in this book as software on the computer side. The upper cultured level is achieved by years of education in humans (imperfectly, since humans are fallible (Ariely, 2009)). We could try to train introspection-based AI systems to do formal tasks, but that may be a fool's errand – we can use existing formal systems for that.

The common argument against much of AI (Dreyfus, 2007) is that it tries to short circuit this sandwich and pretend that humans are rational through and through, this is most pronounced in logicism (Bringsjord, 2008) but is visible also in Simon's work, for example the General Problem Solver (Newell & Simon, 1961b). Some strands of cognitive science try to see the "mind as machine" (as per the title of (Boden, 2008)) ignoring the messy middle, at their peril. Other parts of the cognitive science community, such a Papert as quoted in Section 3.1.1, recognise this messy middle and very few if any have tried to simulate this technologically (see the nearest attempts in Section 6.6).

7.1.3 What Is Subjectivity

So what is subjectivity? It is the fact of how things look *for us* (Seth, 2010). For us collectively, and/or for each of us as an individual; in the present, and/or in general. The subjective world, a bit like the objective universe, seems **endlessly complex**, but worse, it seems that we can never agree on anything in the subjective realm, so no division of labour is possible, no proper gathering of data, no science, and possibly no systematic study at all. The subjective realm is not made of "moderate-sized specimens of dry goods" with which our mind is so adept (Austin & Warnock, 1964, p. 8). These difficulties are why it is often called "ineffable" and left to the poets.

---

[1] A truly random value can be obtained from outside the computer, either by using keyclick timings (as is done in many Linux systems) or inputting some quantum-value from a special device, obtaining a truly random value. In any case, the randomness is being imported from outside the formal system (Isensee, 2001).

The idea that studying subjectivity is difficult or impossible is the received view in most of the English-speaking academic world. Strangely, where science fails, many other professions succeed: Lawyers convict or clear criminals with arguments that discuss intent, feelings, etc. journalists discuss the emotional states of politicians, businesspeople, and other news makers, and novelists have little problem with discussing the subjective. Scientists will protest that their "findings" are non-repeatable, non-quantifiable, consist of "folk psychology" (Ravenscroft, 2010), etc., but that does not stop these professions from being *consistently* successful on their own terms. Moreover, there have been at least two major attempts to explore subjectivity systematically outside the English-speaking world. One was in **Indian** philosophy (Zimmer, 1951) which is outside the scope of this discussion (but surely should be explored in the context of AI elsewhere, see Section 13.4.5), and the other is **phenomenology** (Gallagher & Zahavi, 2012) (see Section 7.1.5).

Note again that in many academic discussions of subjectivity, the accepted nomenclature (which I will follow here) for the environment is either "physical *universe*" or "human *world*", to denote the objective and subjective perspectives, respectively.

7.1.4 Subjectivity Can Be Studied

An important part of subjectivity is its perspectival nature, (apparently) another is the qualia, or the what it is like to be a subject in a situation (Nagel, 1974). I take no stand on the anatomy of subjectivity – that is a philosophical discussion with little or no impact on technology (Mandik, 2001). This section shows that subjectivity *can* be explored, in technologically meaningful ways.

Some rudimentary starts on exploring subjectivity in cognitive science have already been made. Subjectivity seems endlessly complex, so one should be careful never to "tick the box" labelled "subjectivity" and consider any one example definitive. The following are all good starts:

- Any perceiving agent, even a camera, has its own *geometric point of view* and need not take a god-like objective perspective. So (for example) humans need not calculate (objective) motion equations in order to know how to catch a ball but can implement some preferences regarding the angle of sight *from their own point of view as a player* and catch a ball with minimal difficulty (McLeod et al., 2003).
- Every system that tries to make sense of a situation (rational or not) has a limited amount of information, computational resources, and time available to it – this is Simon's "bounded rationality" for which he got the Nobel Prize (Nobelprize.org, 1978; Simon, 1996a). We are "only human".
- All learning AI systems can be seen as subjective, in that every running specimen of a machine-learning algorithm is a product of its own training set, in a sense, a product of its own life experience. The field of machine learning is acutely aware of this in how it manages training sets.

As we see, subjectivity is not one thing but a target for a (possibly never ending) search. It is a search to be pursued (at least) for as long as the search is fruitful.

Another avenue to explore the subjective would be introspection. We all have a direct and relatively unhindered access to our subjectivity in introspection (Hyslop, 2014). Each and every one of us is a specimen of human subjectivity. Another way to study subjectivity is to read reports given by others (perhaps from the phenomenological tradition), but these are also based ultimately on someone's introspection.

7.1.5 Phenomenology, Hetero-Phenomenology

A study of subjectivity has been attempted before, in the phenomenology tradition. As we saw in Section 2.1, "Phenomenology is the study of structures of consciousness as experienced from the first-person point of view" and is arguably as old as Buddhism, but (at least in the west) it "came to full flower in Husserl" (D. W. Smith, 2013). Heidegger, Husserl's student, revolutionised the ontology implied by phenomenology – for Husserl and most of his students, questions of being or ontology were "bracketed" or set aside, leaving the phenomenologist with essentially an idealist ontology. Heidegger (see detailed introduction in Sections 2.4.2 and 2.5) argued that we cannot understand the human condition other than in the human's concerned involvement with the world, and this human interaction is Heidegger's new notion of an ontological foundation. In making this human condition the foundation, Heidegger points out that fundamental to a human's interaction with the world is interpretation – making sense of the situation, one is always already inside.

Phenomenology is the systematic and peer-reviewed study of experience (Gallagher & Zahavi, 2012, pp. 28–29), but it is also a literary tradition, including Husserl, Heidegger, and others. Some would argue that it is more akin to a sect, where Heidegger's musings are accepted as gospel, than to a truly peer-reviewed and debated discipline (Romano, 2009). Conveniently, we do not need to have a position on this matter, as we are *not* promoting a phenomenologically correct methodology for AI (like Dreyfus) but *individual* introspection by AI practitioners. Phenomenology *is* important to this book's argument because it is one of the main alternatives in the literature to cognitivism and it stresses the subjective. In an important sense, this whole book aims to pave a road about halfway between phenomenology's critique of AI and classic AI – agreeing with the phenomenologists that rationalism is limited, and we need subjectivity, but breaking with phenomenology and moving to the side of classic AI in demanding that software be written, regardless of how much violence that may do to our models of subjectivity. Elegantly constructed models, as phenomenology has (which are not programmable), are useless for us as technologists.

Hetero-phenomenology is a systematic attempt to explore the subjective "in the second person" using interview techniques, hence "hetero" – "other" (Dennett, 2003).

An interesting sub-case of hetero-phenomenology is Hurlburt's (2011) effort to explore "pristine experience" using scientifically valid practices and maximum care (Hurlburt et al., 2013). For example, in some experiments, subjects were asked to carry a buzzer and report on their experience when the buzzer goes off, immediately, so as to minimise pollution of the introspective input from later thinking. The focus of Hurlburt's work is understanding our actual experience, an illusive subject matter, with as much honesty and rigour as possible.

7.2 Defining Introspection

Much of the rest of this chapter will examine some definitions and delineations of introspection and discuss how they stack up.

This book deals only with introspection within the context of it being a plausible basis for AI development and so has little need to involve itself with the many debates about the nature of introspection itself.

Let's start with a definition and a characterisation of introspection:

Overgaard (2008) defines introspection as:

> an observation and, sometimes, a description of the contents of one's own consciousness.

I will assume in the rest of my discussion (with the bulk of the literature) that indeed consciousness is what is enumerated in the observation process known as introspection, so when you introspect you are looking at consciousness. This means that we also assume there is no other consciousness (non-introspectible) and no other introspection (which is not observing consciousness).

Schwitzgebel (2012) surveyed many definitions of introspection and gave six characterizations of introspection. Most definitions of introspection include the following criteria (abbreviated). Introspection is

1. About **mental** events, states, processes, etc.
2. About the **first person**
3. Simultaneous or in **temporal proximity** to the mental event, state, or process (not a medium or long-term memory).

By most definitions introspection also

4. Is **direct**, not involving (at least any complicated) inferences
5. Is detecting **pre-existing** mental events, states, processes, etc.
6. Requires an **effort**, not constant or automatic.

For building AI, the targets of introspection (at least initially) would be *processes that influence any operations on information* that can feasibly be replicated in a computer – as opposed to the vague ebb and flow of subtler emotions, levels of alertness, and other observable mental states and processes. These later elements may be of use in AI in the future, but that future is further away and does not concern us yet. Introspecting the fact that one feels cold or believes some peculiar fact would have no immediate utility for AI design. The "products of introspection" would be some reports on how information is processed that would be useful for AI development (see Section 10.2). An example of introspection is given in Section 7.4, with further examples in Chapters 11 and 12.

A word is due about the "effort" (point 6 above) required (by most thinkers) in introspection or even the idea of introspection being an action, represented by a verb. In one sense, introspection is one of the most passive actions possible, since the world of our own consciousness is available to us without much effort, just for the noticing. So "noticing" is required, as per point 6 above. But in a sense, we need to make a further effort when introspecting, to be authentic, to tell things as they are, and not as we may expect them to be (by our own criteria or by society's, see Sections 3.3 and 10.3.3). Also if the introspection is being expressed using words, there is the effort in speaking coherently, for example not mixing languages.

7.3 A Boundary between Introspection and Science Collapses

Strangely, even though introspection is presented by mainstream cognitive science as utterly wrong (Ericsson & Simon, 1993; Nisbett & Wilson, 1977; J. B. Watson, 1913, 1920), there are some similarities between "thinking aloud" (TA), promoted by both J.B. Watson and Simon and introspection (Ericsson & Simon, 1993; J. B. Watson, 1920). This discussion is important (1) since TA is a central technique in psychology, (2) since it presents an interesting boundary case for introspection, and (3) since one of the main characters here, Herbert A. Simon, is also a central pillar of the AI community (see Section 1.6). Note that Simon nowhere disagrees with Watson's TA technique, he sees himself as building on Watson's TA, further elaborating it.

The difference between TA and introspection seems to be that in (acceptable) TA the person reporting his thoughts is naïve, not a psychologist, and the content of the report is about some subject matter *other than* psychological mechanisms.

Further below, I will show that mainstream psychology's aversion to introspection and neo-introspectionists' concern for *correct* introspection both share a scientifically motivated aversion to unexamined inferences mixed into the data of any systematic study. However, further examination of this preference shows that it is naïve and unwarranted: All observation is interpretative, and "clean data" is a mythical creature.

7.3.1 "Thinking Aloud" (TA) Can Be Seen as Introspective

This section is not trying to *establish* that TA *is* introspective as a matter of fact, but just to show that a case can be made that it is introspective, or that it is *arguable* that TA is introspective. Later I will show how TA was distinguished from introspection.

TA as a technique was established by J.B. Watson (1920), and was discussed and expanded on most famously by Ericsson and Simon (1993). My concern is with the currently acceptable practise more than with Watson as a historical character.

Watson was the leader of the behaviourist revolution and it was he who largely abolished introspection as a legitimate technique in psychology (J. B. Watson, 1913). Considering that Watson was vehement in denying introspection any legitimate role, it would be very odd to find something similar to introspection mentioned positively in his writings, especially from the same years he was running his anti-introspectionist campaign (Costall, 2006).

However, Watson (1920) introduces an idea of "thinking aloud" (TA), *in contrast to introspection*, without clear definitions or references.[2] He states that for starting an experiment using TA "usually a request is sufficient" (J. B. Watson, 1920, p. 89). He adds that the subject has to enter into this experiment in "the proper spirit" without detailing what that may mean (Ibid., p. 92) and states that a "scientific man is quite willing to enter into the experiment with zest", again without leaving us any hint as to what is meant by this "scientific" subspecies of mankind (Ibid., p. 91). He does, however, give a few examples of such TA.

The most detailed example Watson quotes is of a colleague who came to stay in an apartment in which Watson "had rooms". He challenged the guest to figure out the use of some contraption belonging to the landlords, while TA. Here is the full protocol as recorded by Watson (round parentheses are Watson's notes in the original text):

> "The thing looks a little like an invalid's table, but it is not heavy, the pan is curved, it has side pieces and is attached with a ball and socket joint. It would never hold a tray full of dishes (cul de sac). The thing (return to starting point) looks like some of the failures of an inventor. I wonder if the landlord is an inventor. No, you told me he was a porter in one of the big banks down town. The fellow is as big as a house and looks more like a prize-fighter than a mechanician; those paws of his would never do the work demanded of an inventor" (blank wall again). This was as far as we got on the first day. On the second morning we got no nearer the solution. On the second night we talked over the way the porter and his wife lived, and the subject wondered how a man earning not more than $150 per month could live as our landlord did. I told him that the wife was a hairdresser and earned about eight dollars per day herself. Then I asked him if he did not see the sign 'Hair-Dresser'

---

[2] This style of writing was normal at the time.

on the door as we entered. The next morning after coming from his bath he said, "I saw that infernal thing again" (original starting point). "It must be something to use in washing or weighing the baby-but they have no baby (cul de sac again). The thing is curved at one end so that it would just fit a person's neck. Ah! I have it! The curve does fit the neck. The woman you say is a hair-dresser and the pan goes against the neck and the hair is spread out over it." This was the correct conclusion. Upon reaching it there was a smile, a sigh and an immediate turn to something else (the equivalent of obtaining food after search).

(J. B. Watson, 1920, p. 92)

Note that this "thinking aloud" is *not* a case of the "extended mind" (Clark & Chalmers, 1998) – not a case of thinking using external props (like doing arithmetic, saying out loud, or jotting down "carry 1"). Rather, it is a case of "letting one's thoughts escape through one's mouth" in the everyday process of trying to figure something out.

Alarmingly (for our attempt to understand introspection), this technique could be seen as being close to a case of introspection. Note however that the definitions we are now using are all recent, and Watson wrote 100 years ago, so any problem with current definitions does not reflect badly on Watson historically, but these problems are still problems *for us*. The argument that TA is a type of introspection would stress that *mental contents* are being verbally reported in TA. Recall the definitions of introspection quoted above (Section 7.2).

I believe there is a prima-facie case that TA *is* some variation of introspection, according to the definitions. But it is presented by Watson as an *alternative* to introspection – he says: "...a good deal more can be learned... by making subjects think aloud... than by trusting to the unscientific method of introspection" (J. B. Watson, 1920, p. 91). Note that, Simon, who continues Watson's work on TA (Ericsson & Simon, 1993), agrees that there is a possible confusion here: "The use of thinking-aloud protocols as data was sometimes misunderstood as an attempt to revive introspection" (Simon, 1996a, pp. 231–232), so this is no idle worry.

7.3.2 Two Distinctions between TA and Introspection

Watson's legacy in terms of the boundaries of introspection is problematic, as we have seen above. Further elaboration of TA was one of Herbert A. Simon's research agendas. Simon wrote that: "...no clear guidelines are provided [*by Watson*] to distinguish illegitimate 'introspection' from many forms of verbal output that are routinely treated as data..." (Ericsson & Simon, 1993, p. 3).

Let's try to examine what the two poles of Watson's (and Simon's) contrasting of TA with introspection are: What they prohibit is the psychologist introspecting in his armchair, coming up with pronouncements about how his own mind works, and generalizing them as a general scientific fact. The psychologist is assumed to be already invested in some course of research in psychology and therefore bound to be biased. On the other hand, the naïve person, whether a "subject" in an experiment or a scientist who is *not* a psychologist, is assumed to be neutral. If such a neutral person gives neutral reports, just observations, then his "verbal behaviour" is legitimate unbiased data.

Let me propose two distinctions:

1. The *contents* of TA are the *contents* of the thinking process – in the paradigmatic example of figuring out the contraption. The text reads "The thing looks a little like an invalid's table, but it is not heavy...". In "classical introspection", the contents of the report can be about the *mechanisms* that are used to do the thinking, rather than the content of the thoughts.
2. In the forbidden "classical introspection", it is the *psychologist*, a trained individual with a research agenda, who is making the report, while in TA, it is a *naïve* participant in an experimental setting.

It seems that these distinctions are supported by Watson and Simon:

For the **first distinction**, about the contents of the verbalisations, Ericsson and Simon analyse Watson as follows:

> It should be noted that the kind of questioning illustrated by [Watson's (1920) story about the golfer, pp. 100–101] does not refer to to the subject's memory of a specific instance, but to how he thinks he performs activities *in general* when he is asked about them. Watson made a clear distinction between analytic classical introspection, verbal questioning of a subject, and thinking aloud. His views on the veridicality of the later kind of verbal report were quite different from his views on the first two.

> **(Ericsson & Simon, 1993, p. 58, emphasis added)**

So Simon objects to the generalisations that the golfer makes, to the fact that the golfer tries to give non-naïve, analytical comments about his conduct in general. TA would allow him only to verbalise about the task at hand, in the present moment, with no elaborations or speculations.

Later Ericsson and Simon (1993, p. 247) mention approvingly previous research by Ohlsson who

> ... coded TA protocols to distinguish between heeded thoughts, on the one hand, and introspections, retrospective reports, and communications to the experimenter, on the other hand.... Reports were classified as introspections if the grammatical subject was the speaker (e.g. 'I,' 'my head'); if the verb was epistemic (e.g. 'remember,' 'feel,' 'know') and if the verbalization did not contain specific information about the current problem.

So any comments or speculation on the "meta" level and discussion of how the mind does it, are banned.

Another insight into Simon's position is provided by his quoting approvingly from Duncker, saying

> While the introspector makes himself as thinking the object of his attention, the subject who is thinking aloud remains immediately directed to the problem, so to speak allowing his activity to become verbal. When someone, while thinking, says to himself 'One ought to see if it isn't-,' or, 'It would be nice if one could show that-,' one would hardly call this introspection.

(Ericsson & Simon, 1993, p. 60)

So the distinguishing criterion seems to be being "immediately directed to the problem" – again a distinction of content.

Turning to the **second distinction**: Is the person doing the verbalisation a professional with an agenda or a neutral, naïve person? Here, most of the evidence comes straight from Watson. He says:

> ...a good deal more can be learned about the psychology of thinking by making subjects think aloud about definite problems, than by trusting to the unscientific method of introspection.

(J. B. Watson, 1920, p. 91)

His phrase "method of introspection" is clearly a reference to "the introspectionists" – the psychologists that have not yet been converted to his behaviourism. Later he says that

> The behaviourist... is engaged in studying the process of observing as it appears in others, where the activity is not complicated by the demands of introspection. ... the behaviourist is a natural scientist and makes his observations upon his fellow man rather than upon himself.

(J. B. Watson, 1920, p. 94)

These are actually two arguments – the role of data source needs to be separated for two reasons: The need to notice the data (the role of the scientist) distracts from the task at hand, and separation of the agenda-laden scientists from the experimental subject is just good scientific practise, minimising theoretical bias (see also Section 10.3.3).

7.3.3 Inferences and Confusion

But if we set the word "introspection" aside for a moment, we can see a commonality between Schwitzgebel's (2012) criterion No. 4 (above in Section 7.2), that introspection be direct and TA's requirements as discussed above, that the TA report be by a naïve person with no agenda and be about the contents of the problem at hand, not about the mechanisms of thought. The commonality is that they both do not want any inferences to be already embedded in the data.

Let's look at this once more: For Schwitzgebel, a neo-introspectionist, two characteristics of introspection are that it is immediate (3) and direct (4). If it is not direct then it becomes speculation, philosophy, psychology, or one of many other things, but it ceases to be pure introspection. *Introspection* is Schwitzgebel's term for "good" non-inferential reports.

For Watson, Simon, and other psychologists, TA is the thing *without* inferences, the "raw data". They call that which contains inferences, speculation, philosophy, or psychological theory "introspection", and that is a *bad* thing.

So it would seem that all we have here is a confusion in terminology. They both want the non-inferential, "pure" reports. It seems that we have the same word, "introspection", being used for the same thing, except for the inference part where the same word is being used with *opposite* meanings.

A reasonable step now would be to call Watson's introspection Intro-W, and Schwitzgebel's Intro-S, sort out the differences and make peace. However, such a peace would be predicated on joining the seeming consensus against inference in introspection. The question we must ask is "Is such a position tenable?" regrettably the answer is no.

7.3.4 Non-inferential Observation Is Impossible

The desire to separate observation from interpretation has been ruled impossible both in the analytic and the continental traditions. On the analytic side, Bogen (2014) quotes Norwood Hanson, Paul Feyerabend, and mainly Thomas Kuhn in showing that in normal scientific observation:

1. Which aspects of a scene are seen as **salient** and worth recording vary by the set of assumptions the observer is already committed to.
2. Observers conceptualize what they see in terms of their favoured **conceptual framework**. An everyday example would be how different people and different cultures carve up the palette of colours.
3. The very perception can be influenced by "top down" considerations that are not in the actual world. This is demonstrated by Bruner and Postman's research using playing cards with *black* hearts.

All these worries come from a discussion of external observations in the natural sciences. They would be double and triple as worrying in the more complex case of introspection, where the process is entirely subjective, and the very process of observation may impact the content of any observation much more than in the case of observing an external object.

There is another problem with trying to separate observation from interpretation (and eliminate inferences) similar but distinct from point 2 above: When a person who is conversant in more than one language introspects (or thinks aloud), their mental contents tend to appear in more than one language. Any attempt to communicate intelligibly with another person requires translating and organising one's thoughts into one coherent language. This process of regularising expression is inferential. Arguably, even monoglots have to regularize their language in a similar way.

On the continental side, one of hermeneutics' main points is that all observation includes some interpretation. One quick way to make that point from the continental side is to recall the hermeneutic circle: We make sense of the whole only because we have a sense of the parts, but we also make sense of the parts only since we already have a sense of the whole (see Section 2.5).

Like Schwitzgebel's (2012) introspection and Watson's/Simon's "thinking aloud", hetero-phenomenology (Section 7.1.5) is also an attempt to get at the "raw data" of subjectivity.

7.3.5 A Boundary between Introspection and Science Collapses: Conclusion

Though they come from different apparent traditions, both cognitivists and the new introspectionists view themselves as being within the scientific tradition and want the "raw data". They want to have "data" so they can then work on the "mechanisms" in an open, peer-reviewable way. The idea is to reach some scientific *truth*. However, for AI, we don't need (or want to wait for) such objective, singular truths about intelligence. The scientific/cognitive understanding of intelligence is a long way in the future, and the continental candidate we have for such an "objective" or well-received "truth" is the phenomenology of Heidegger (see Section 7.1.5), and we saw that Heidegger is not readily programmable (Dreyfus, 2007). AI as technology cannot wait for these debates to be resolved nor is such a wait necessary.

As we saw above (Section 7.3.3), the attempt to separate the "good" from the "bad" observations of mental states has hit an impasse. Without prejudice to the efforts being made in this direction (Gallagher & Zahavi, 2012; Jack & Roepstorff, 2003, 2004), for the current purposes (technological AI), this effort must be abandoned – at the price of stating the following at its starkest: This book is promoting introspection, of the *bad* type: Whatever it was that was forbidden, in its broadest form – I am promoting *precisely* that, that is, self-reflective introspection, about mechanism, by theory-laden individuals, with inferences. Consider even that *some* introspectors may be self-conscious and evil charlatans – this possibility has to be carried forward into the rest of the argument. However, I will show in Chapter 8 that for our purposes here, even "bad" introspection is a legitimate source of ideas, and in Chapter 9 that at least much of introspection is plausible as a basis for anthropic AI. I will return to making distinctions between better and worse forms of introspection in Chapter 10.

7.4 What Kind of Introspection Is Recommended

This section is to a large degree a summary of Chapter 10, where the arguments are given in detail. An example of relevant introspection follows.

As we have seen, this book's argument does *not* insist on the introspection being particularly refined, correct, or exact, since it is not at all clear if that is possible, and in the context of technology, it is unnecessary.

Leaving aside any commitment to "correct" or "uninterpreted" introspection, unlike various thinkers about introspection in philosophy and psychology, in AI, we need to have a commitment to the sort of concrete and clear details that are needed in computer programming. We must try to describe the mental states and processes pragmatically, in terms that may be programmable. These descriptions will most certainly be partial, and we should never pretend that the description is exhaustive, or near-exhaustive. We may also relinquish any search for a quick and efficient way of distinguishing between "good" and "bad" introspective reports, not so much because such gradations are not possible but because over-attachment to correctness and precision has rendered most previous attempts at subjectively informed AI sterile in terms of producing actual testable systems (Dreyfus, 2007). The sort of introspection we should aim for is **mid-depth**: Roughly halfway between Simon (with his positive commitment to programmability) and the phenomenologists with their commitment to observing subjectivity as it appears, rather than as it should be. Note also that in Sections 8.5 and 9.3, I will speculate that all programming is introspective. In that specific case, the introspection is restricted by the limitations of the programming environment (e.g. python, i386 machine) to a small structured palette. In introspecting for AI, we look at the mind as it operates freely and only later formalise.

A "piece of introspection" *useful for AI* would describe some sort of interaction with the environment that would ultimately be programmable. Any introspective observations that have no impact on external interaction or are not programmable would be "epi-phenomenal"[3] and have no *technological* significance.

Consider the following example introspective report:

> How do I do long division? Damn – it's been a while – it was that tall teacher that taught that, right? OK, let's see – you take the number to be divided and put it here near the top of the page, and then there was that angle thing you draw... I used to like that angle! [...*non verbal recollection of the pleasant "liking"*...] Now where do we put the other number – di-vi-sor, was it, or di-vi-dor? Here? That doesn't look right...... what was that teacher's name? I really need to get this done before Jim comes in....

---

[3] In the mind/body problem, some would say that the body is wholly physical and explains all behaviour, yet nonetheless there is a mind, only it had to causal powers. Existing without having any causal powers is termed "epi-phenomenal".

It shows how irrelevant thoughts (and non-verbal reminiscence) such as "I liked..." intrude. It shows how fears and reminiscence drift in and out of consciousness, and how shaky one's real grasp on issues often is, behind any pretence of being logical. In all these respects, this example is more realistic than (say) Simon's claim that he "thinks in mathematics". I here assume that Simon also has human concerns, as does the example above. But note also that this example is not as clean and refined as Heidegger's descriptions of interacting with a nail using a hammer. The above shows us something about how we *actually* do things, as far as *we* are concerned and as Papert's said in the interview (see Sections 3.1 and 7.1.2).

Humans can view the same situation from multiple perspectives (see Section 5.2.2). Can we program these perspectives? Can we program their multiplicity? If one were a scientist sworn to tell the truth, the answer should be "no", since humans' subjectivity is too complex. But as technologists, this is not a question but a challenge to be answered by *action*, not philosophical discourse. Surely the challenge of multiple perspectives, and generally the challenge of **pragmatic approximations** of subjective perspectives is easier than Dreyfus's (2007) pedantic challenge of programming something as nebulous as the sum total of Heidegger's work. We can do this step by step. The phenomenologists may protest that it is "not Heideggerian enough" (Dreyfus, 2007), but Rome was not built in a day, and the worst enemy of the good is a nebulous idea of the perfect. How precisely such research can be done will be the subject of Chapter 10.

7.5 Main Term: "Introspection": Summary

We have examined (in Chapter 5) the overall argument of this volume that "introspection is recommended for developing anthropic AI". In Chapter 6, we defined anthropic AI as a subtype of technological human-like AI. In this chapter, we discussed the other main term, "Introspection", and some of its complexities. We saw that "clean" or "good" introspection may well be impossible and so resigned ourselves to using "poor" or "bad" introspection. Many readers may be scandalised: This outrageous neglect of quality will have to be justified.

We now turn to the crux of the matter: That introspection is *recommended* for AI. Before I show that using introspection is probably a good idea in Chapter 9, we must discuss one problem in great detail: The consensus in cognitive science is that introspection is illegitimate. That needs thorough debunking, especially since my argument promotes "bad" introspection.

Chapter 8

Introspection Is Legitimate

This book argues for introspection as a basis for developing anthropic artificial intelligence (AI). Having defined some of the terminology in this claim above (Chapters 6 and 7), this chapter will argue that introspection is a legitimate source of designs in AI. Those who hold the prevailing view, believing this is a non-scientific approach, have misunderstood the different relations of science and technology to truth, those who believe it has already been done are granting themselves full credit for half a step, and those who take great steps into introspection produce no concrete AI systems.

The possible attitudes to the status of introspection for AI that will be surveyed are that it is:

1. *Impossible*: Comte and other thinkers considered introspection impossible. These (by now uncommon) positions will be briefly discussed (and dispensed with) in Section 8.1.
2. *Forbidden*: Herbert Simon and the mainstream of cognitive science object to introspection quite dogmatically, based on Watson's (1913) paper. I will show that their objections do not hold under the modern analysis of the context of discovery vs justification, especially not in a technological context (Section 8.2).
3. *Commonplace*: Solomonoff (1968) and others admit that much of AI *was* done introspectively and therefore may consider my main point to be trivial. I will show that so far AI researchers only used introspection in a *shallow* manner, timidly, as if it were illegitimate (Section 8.3).
4. *Desirable*: Dreyfus (1979, 2007) and others are all for introspection (at least within the context of phenomenology), but they do not generally do much programming. This is the main "dissident" group from AI (Section 8.4).

5. *Unavoidable*: A preliminary case can be made that inventing AI without introspection would be impossible, if only because programming requires introspection under a specific role (Section 8.5). This (novel) discussion is delayed to Section 9.3.
6. *A hybrid position*: Introspection may *already* be seen as a "commonplace" in the context of discovery and "forbidden" in the context of justification (explained below). A case can be made that I have said nothing new so far. I examine what the consequences of this supposedly established practise would be if this description were true (Section 8.6).

Section 8.7 surveys various positions regarding the types of truth available in principle through introspection.

The purpose of this chapter is only to show that my position (encouraging introspection as a basis for designing AI systems) is novel and legitimate. The next chapter will argue why one positively should *expect* introspection to be a *good* basis for anthropic AI. The following chapters will show some details and examples and will discuss some consequences.

In traversing and analysing the various positions scholars have had towards introspection for AI, this chapter also provides a more fine-grained and clearly categorized view of the state-of-the-art than was possible in Chapter 1. Though the main thrust of the argument is against those who oppose introspection, this chapter will also contrast my argument's position within the field by critiquing other scholars, not least sympathetic ones such as Dreyfus and Agre.

Throughout this chapter, it is important to bear in mind that I am not yet arguing for the *benefit* or profitability of using introspection for AI. The main thrust of this chapter is debunking those who would shout down any mention of introspection, those who argue that using introspection is illegitimate, unscientific, or in any other way disallowed. In passing this chapter will also demonstrate that this rehabilitation is necessary, since no AI researcher uses introspection as such without compunction.

8.1 Introspection as "Impossible"

As Overgaard has it

> Brentano argued that a paradox exists [*in introspection*] in the relation between observations of 'inner' mental states and 'outer' objects. In order to observe and know about, say, an experience of a red apple, one must turn one's attention from that outer object which was cause to the sensation. This should logically make the relevant experience cease to exist, thus also the attempted introspection. ... Comte's first objection was that one cannot have an identity between the observer and the object of observation in science. He argued that the observer cannot be

'split in two' so that one part observes the other, and, thus, observation of one's own inner experiences is an impossible project.

(Overgaard, 2006)

Later thinkers such as Wundt resolve this problem by saying that introspection is based on a "change of focus" from the outer to the inner, and that in introspection, the vision is to a large degree a memory, a recollection of the mental experience rather than a direct report.

These objections are of ongoing philosophical interest (Schwitzgebel, 2012) but can be sidestepped for this argument: We can assume with Wundt that introspection is only a memory; here, we are interested only in inputs for technology design and not in some absolute or even scientific truths (see Sections 5.1.3 and 5.2.2). The content of introspections exists as a matter of fact regardless of any qualms we can have regarding their temporal status or admissibility in any of philosophy, science, or technology. The notion that we are dealing with particularly precise information in introspecting for technology has already been put to rest in Section 7.3.4. The idea that introspection is inadmissible is the topic of the next section.

8.2 Introspection as "Forbidden"

Practical objections to introspection also have a pre-20th-century pedigree. For example, Comte (again) argued that introspection "will generate unreliable and conflicting data" (Overgaard, 2006, p. 630). However, in terms of impact on current thinking, by far, the most influential prohibition on the use of introspection is Watson's.

8.2.1 Watson

John B. Watson (1878–1958) is the most oft-quoted scholar for objecting to introspection and was most vehement in his objections (see Section 1.5 for a full introduction). He does not mince words in criticising his opponents, to whom he refers collectively as "the introspectionists": "To make the data obtained by the language method virtually the whole of behavior … is putting the cart before the horse with a vengeance" (J. B. Watson, 1913, p. 172n), "It is hopeless for me to get his introspective report" (J. B. Watson, 1913, p. 172). Watson was forceful in his revolutionary talk, threatening psychology with a schism if his world view were not accepted: "… either psychology must change its viewpoint so as to take in facts of behavior, whether or not they have bearings upon the problems of 'consciousness'; or else behavior must stand alone as a wholly separate and independent science" (J. B. Watson, 1913, p. 159).

Watson saw himself as pushing for better **scientific practise** in psychology (viz. "control experiments" (J. B. Watson, 1913, p. 171)). He contrasts "the behaviourist" (an epithet he uses for himself) with the (old-style) psychologists:

> ... questions arise which I may phrase in two ways: I may choose the psychological way and say 'does the animal see these two lights as I do, i.e., as two distinct colors, or does he see them as two grays differing in brightness, as does the totally color blind?' Phrased by the behaviorist, it would read as follows: 'Is my animal responding upon the basis of the difference in intensity between the two stimuli, or upon the difference in wave-lengths?' He nowhere thinks of the animal's response in terms of his own experiences of colors and grays.
>
> **(J. B. Watson, 1913, pp. 170–171)**

Note how "color" is replaced by "wavelength" – not only more scientific but also closer to physics, the most prestigious of all sciences.

To maintain the unity of psychology and the coherence of the scientific programme (in a way that is compatible with the overall scientific program as understood at the time): "behaviourism... was an attempt to do one thing – to apply to the experimental study of man the same kind of procedure and the same language ... [*as*] ... in the study of animals lower than man" (J. B. Watson, 1931, p. ix). Also "the behaviourist attempts to get a unitary scheme of animal response. He recognises no dividing line between man and brute" (J. B. Watson, 1914, p. 1). Since animals have no consciousness that can be readily accessed (even by the introspectionists' lights), we should not even attempt the same with humans.

Within his programme of improving psychology's scientific credentials, his most direct attacks are on introspection and say that the content of introspection is "obscure" (J. B. Watson, 1931, p. x), the technique of introspection is unclear and imposes self-contradictory demands (J. B. Watson, 1913, p. 163), its terminology is incoherent even in simple distinctions of sensations (Ibid. p. 164), and (switching to personal attacks) its practitioners are effete (Costall, 2006, p. 646) and "insufferably prolix" (J. B. Watson, 1920, p. 97).

Like many thinkers, Watson is often remembered by simplistic slogans, such as "introspection is unscientific". His actual position was both more subtle and more strident than that – but that makes little difference to his eventual influence on AI (amongst other disciplines). What has influence is his somewhat-flattened memory, more than the living, breathing, complex person he was.

I will respond to these and other objections to AI based on introspection in Sections 8.2.4 and 8.2.5.

8.2.2 Cognitive Psychology's Attitude to Introspection

"Telling more than we can know: Verbal reports on mental processes" (Nisbett & Wilson, 1977) is one of the most cited papers "in the recent history of consciousness studies" (Johansson et al., 2006). Nisbett and Wilson complain that there is "... little or no direct introspective access to ... cognitive processes". They define cognitive processes as being "the processes mediating the effects of a stimulus on a response".

They contrast the cognitive, "real"[1] level with the contents of introspection, which "is the *result* of thinking, not the process of thinking that appears spontaneously in consciousness" (stress in the original). The amount of evidence that Nisbett and Wilson marshal is formidable, contributing to the canonical status of the paper.

As long as one agrees with their assumptions, that paper stands very well. However, the moment one tries to examine some of the underlying assumptions, it becomes less stable. Note that the authors are writing as psychologists, for psychologists, and see themselves as scientists, like when they conclude that their paper truly "buries" introspection as an element of psychological discourse:

> The accuracy of subjective reports is so poor as to suggest that any introspective access that may exist is not sufficient to produce generally correct or reliable reports.

From a scientific perspective, that is enough to damn introspection as a source of truth. But does that damn it as a source of models for technology? Note that they demand "generally correct" reports. Is that the correct level of truth to demand for developing AI? This will be discussed in Section 8.2.4.

They complain that subjective reports are often caused by a priori theories, rather than by some genuine observation. True to scientific purity, they abstain from any discussion of whether the data of subjective reports may be a mixture of genuine observation *plus* culturally accepted theories. Their austere conclusion is that these reports should be ignored.

One could worry, together with Dreyfus (1979) (see Sections 2.2 and 2.3) that the cognitive level is invented (see Section 6.5.3), and therefore Nisbett and Wilson's (1977) definition of the cognitive level as the "real" level would be alarming. But we can let that issue rest and accept multiple perspectives: Perhaps the "real" level is cognitive, perhaps neural, and perhaps phenomenal. My only comment on this is that those who hold these different perspectives all seem to be united in believing that there is only *one real truth*, and that all others are utterly mistaken (see Section 4.2.2 about this dogma). This may perhaps be a reasonable stance in science, but I argue (in Section 5.1.3) that it is counterproductive in technology. Below I will present arguments that deal conclusively with any worries to do with the validity of introspection for our technological purposes.

There is a somewhat entertaining point that will become relevant in Section 8.3.3: Having given ample evidence that introspection is of little value in terms of the "actual" cognitive processes, Nisbett and Wilson move on to speculate on the causes of people's (misguided) confidence in their introspective interpretations of their own thought processes. The authors discuss the "conditions that give rise to introspective certainty ... Confidence should be high when the causal candidates are (a) few in number, (b)... (e) ... In fact we appeal to introspection to support this view" (Nisbett & Wilson, 1977, p. 255). Fascinatingly, they appeal to

---

[1] "Real" by Nisbett and Wilson's (1977) lights, but recall the usage of "real", Section 5.2.3.

introspection as their source of evidence for this list, so perhaps even they are not as averse to introspection as they claim to be.

The authors introduce a distinction between "intermediate output" that *is* available to introspection and the actual process, which is not. As an example of how the intermediate results are the contents of the introspection, they quote a person describing how he recalled his mother's maiden name by recalling his uncle's surname (Nisbett & Wilson, 1977, pp. 255–256). This, again, will be relevant in Section 10.3.5.1. Let's preview the main point from there, as it shows how we gain crucial "cash value" from the distinction between science and technology (Section 5.1.3): If we know only the outline of *what* is accomplished without the *how* (as the authors complain), in AI programming, we can substitute whatever technical trick we have (in our skills as programmers) to achieve something similar in a computer. AI is not science (but technology), the trick we use need not be the same trick that the brain (or cognitive system) uses.

Nisbett and Wilson speculate on various reasons why people believe in their own introspections. The last reason they suggest, to sum up their paper, is that it may just be insufferably "frightening" to think that we know nothing of our own mind. I would retort that following Watson (mainly 1913), it had become fashionable in psychology to be harsh on any subjectivity (Costall, 2006). Only recently is scientific psychology recovering from this bias (Seth, 2010).

See also my analysis of "thinking aloud" (TA) and how it relates to introspection, in Section 7.3.

8.2.3 Other Objections

Herbert Simon (in his AI research, and also in papers on other topics, not least psychology) continues Watson's objections to introspection, though his case is a bit more complex (see Sections 1.6 and 8.3.3).

If my discussions with members of the university of Sussex are any indication, the main reason that people in cognitive science object to introspection is various versions of the worry that introspection is not objective, it is impossible to know who is right in an argument, and it is not even internally consistent in that the same person can come up with contradicting reports. I now turn to deal with these and the above (Sections 8.2.1 and 8.2.2) objections.

As a reminder, this chapter aims to convince the reader that using introspection as a basis for developing AI is *legitimate*, that is, it needn't be forbidden. The following chapter will argue that introspection should positively be pursued for anthropic AI.

8.2.4 Contexts of Discovery and Justification

There is a distinction (in philosophy of science) between the "context of discovery" where scientists get their ideas and the "context of justification" where scientists should provide evidence to support their claims (Schickore, 2014). In the context of discovery, Newton was permitted to take inspiration from falling apples when discovering the theory of gravity, and Kekulé was right to dream (while dozing) about snakes eating their own tail, giving him the idea of circular molecules (Rothenberg, 1995). The scientists have to produce their evidence for their equations or models later in the context of justification, but in the inspiration of their discovery, they are *entirely free*. Why then should AI researchers not be free, when inventing new AI designs, to use introspection? Before we claim that the new designs are good, we would have to test them as software, so we can be assured that no harm is done to empirical integrity. I am not arguing for letting introspection into the holy of holies of scientific fact (Watson and Simon would rightly shudder), only into foyer of scientific ideas. Moreover, for the purposes of AI, we need even less, just let introspection provide *technological* ideas.

So in principle, all inspirations and sources of ideas are allowed, in the context of discovery. But there is a seeming problem here, and a subtlety to be noticed. The seeming problem is that this argument trivialises introspection and supposedly says that recommending introspection is as good as recommending taking a long walk or drinking some juice to improve creativity in AI. The crude response would be "so be it", in this section, I am only combating the notion that introspection is *forbidden*, and if I have shown that it is as legitimate as taking a walk, then my work is done. A convincing argument that introspection is positively good for AI is supplied in Chapter 9, so we can leave it for now here.

However, note the three examples above: Newton's falling apple, Kekulé's dream of a snake eating its own tail, and taking a walk for AI. These examples, though all fine in principle within the context of discovery, are quite different. Newton was exploring *gravity*, and so a falling apple is directly relevant to the content of his research. One could speculate that he was considering the motion of the planets when he saw the apple drop and, therefore, could put the two together and come up with his unifying theory of gravity, valid both in the heavens and on earth. This example is one where the idea came from something *relevant* – gravity. Kekulé's dream of a snake eating its tail hinted towards *circularity*. Before Kekulé, the possibility of molecules' overall structure being circular was not considered, and hence, the structure of the Benzene molecule was a conundrum. So the dream of the snake gave him the *form* of the molecule. Taking a walk has little to do with AI as such. But introspection, as we will see in Chapter 9 and specifically in Section 9.2, is of great relevance to AI.

See Section 8.6 for an answer to any protests that the above is trivial and already understood throughout the AI community.

8.2.5 Truth in Science vs Technology

The focus of the literature condemning subjectivity and introspection (foremost J.B. Watson (1913, 1920)) is in the *science* of psychology, that is, the development and assessment of knowledge and models about the natural facts about human behaviour. The case of AI as a *technology* is different (Franssen et al., 2013; Simon, 1981), in that the ultimate criteria for the finished AI machine is not "is it true?" or "does it give good predictions?" but "does it work?", "is it useful?", or even ultimately "does the product sell?" (see Section 5.1.3).

In science, there is great concern for keeping inaccurate or wrong "facts" out of the body of accepted knowledge. This has several motivations:

- A mistake would produce wrong predictions.
- A contradiction may imply anything.
- In principle, it can be very difficult *logically* to pinpoint any problem once it has entered "the body of knowledge". For an extreme example, see the notion of logical holism (Quine, 1976).
- In practice, it can take a very long time to locate and root out any mistaken "fact" – for example, the geocentric view in astronomy held for well over a millennium. The story of overcoming this model plays an important part in teaching science (Matthews, 1994, p. 165) and, hence, forms a primary source of the scientific community's fear of errors.

In technology, the worry about "wrong facts" is much less pressing. If we have a wrong, misguided, or inaccurate assumption or model, then the products using the technology would likely not work, or at least be worse than the alternatives, and would be abandoned within weeks (if not minutes), rather than years, decades, or centuries. This is based on technology having a short life cycle, being pragmatic, and being *designed*.

When we are faced with a natural phenomenon that we do not understand, our ability to investigate it is limited by every conceivable complication: The system may have subtle interactions within it, may not be isolated from the rest of the world (Reutlinger et al., 2014), and may have yet undiscovered physics operating in it. Moreover, in science, the unexplained phenomenon itself may be holistic – unyielding to our (usually modular) analysis. On the other hand, in technology, we have an *intended* design, often modular, with a well-understood *intended* chain of causation. In the event of a problem, we can therefore at least localise which link broke in this *intended* chain of causation. That does not mean that any problem in technology is easily fixed, just that it is easier to recognise a malfunction, localise it, and isolate the "suspect" module, assuming (again) a modular structure with a clear intended causal scheme.

In highly complex systems, like a fully loaded modern personal computer, there could be tens or hundreds of millions of lines of source code involved, and no one person nor even a team that can be gathered in a room can understand what is going on. Moreover, some software is so old that no living person understands how it works. This complexity can create a *seeming* mystery, in that the intended chains of causation (that may malfunction) are not even known, in practise. This does not detract from the fact that in principle, technology can be easily debugged.

The difference between principle and practise can involve thousands of programmer years, but it is still only a management decision to devote the resources to truly debug a system.

A possible retort is that any real artefact outstrips its design and is a phenomenon in its own right that may present strange effects in as many ways as a natural phenomenon (an example would be Radium's impact on photographic plates (Mould, 1998)). There are two possible answers: The first one could accept the criticism and appeal to common practise, which shows that technological artefacts developing truly unexplained behaviour are much rarer than in the case of natural phenomena. The second reply (and a decisive one in this case) is that in the topic under discussion here, we have ideas (of variable quality) eventually to be expressed as software. Software is run using computers, a well-established technology that is specifically designed to behave digitally and deterministically (B. C. Smith, 2005). And so, as long as the hardware platform does not seriously malfunction, the behaviour of software is deterministic and clear or at least clear in principle, as discussed above.

Moreover, if a technology works, the typical attitude is "who cares" about any inherent truth values. Utility is the be-all and end-all of technology. A further point regarding technology with an "interesting" malfunction is that such a technology turns the conversation over to science. An example of both points is the placebo effect. Placebo drugs "shouldn't" work but they do. Insofar as a medical practitioner is acting as an engineer fixing patients, they will use placebo treatments pragmatically. In parallel, the placebo effect is a vibrant area of research in science. It seems to be in the essence of the engineering professions to not be interested in the seriously difficult issues – leaving these to science. Another example is that animal cloning is often successful and can be seen as a technology. However, often the cloned animals described in the literature did not have the same longevity as naturally bred animals. This anomaly became a subject of research in science (Klotzko, 2001).[2]

So our anxiety to preserve truth from being polluted by falsehood should be much smaller in technology than in science (see also Section 5.1.3).

8.2.6 Example and Summary of "Introspection Is Forbidden"

An example of how truth or lack thereof worked out well specifically in AI is the impact of the paper "A logical calculus of the ideas immanent in nervous activity" (McCulloch & Pitts, 1943). It inspired, over time, the notions of finite automata, integrated logic design (the core of computer electronics), and made a crucial contribution to our AI notion of neural nets (Piccinini, 2004, p. 175). This was all done notwithstanding the fact that the paper assumed

---

[2] Specific thanks are due to Josh Weinstein for discussions about these ideas.

... that mental states can be analysed in terms of mental atoms endowed with propositional content, the psychons, and that the neural correlates of mental phenomena correspond to precise configurations of neuronal pulses: individual pulses correspond to individual psychons, and causal relations among pulses correspond to inferential relations among psychons.

(Piccinini, 2004, p. 205)

These assumptions are in retrospect false but nonetheless caused great advances in computer and AI technology.

Introspection is legitimate as a basis for AI designs because it would be used in the context of discovery, where ideas are born. Any idea so formed would have to be tested empirically later. And even if somehow some piece of "wrongness" creeps from introspection into the final "findings" of the technological research, it would be weeded out quickly because the life cycle of concepts in technology (especially computer technology) is much shorter than of concepts in science. We definitely do not need "generally correct [*and*] reliable reports" for AI. Recall that is specifically what Nisbett and Wilson (1977, p. 233) were complaining about (see Section 8.2.2).

8.3 Introspection as "Commonplace"

So far I have discussed a mainstream bias of cognitive science – that introspection is "wrong" and hence forbidden. We now turn to two less dominant groups, first, and less distinct, are the "admitters". These people admit to using introspection, notwithstanding the bias against it. Surprisingly, some of the worst detractors of introspection also used introspection (e.g. Herbert Simon, see Sections 8.3.3 and 1.6); very occasionally they even admitted to it more or less openly. In Section 8.4, I will discuss the introspection enthusiasts, mainly Dreyfus. The question of whether AI researchers can do anything *other* than introspection will be discussed in Sections 8.5, 9.3, and 10.1.4.

This section surveys the evidence both for introspection being used and for introspection *simultaneously* being frowned upon. This later point is crucial for answering any objection that my argument is vacuous, in that AI researchers already use introspection freely and fully (handled in Section 8.6).

8.3.1 Sweeping Testimony

The most sweeping testimony that we have for using introspection are the least specific and the least personal:

The first and only direct testimony I found from a founding member of the AI community about the overall field of AI is from **Ray Solomonoff** (1926–2009) who was the founder of algorithmic information theory and one of the participants of the

1956 AI conference in Dartmouth (McCorduck, 2004, Chapter 5). He writes (in a sadly neglected paper[3]):

> *Almost all* of the artificial-intelligence work on problems of sufficient complexity... [*that are*] successful frequently enough to warrant trying them... are *usually* obtained by *introspection*; the experimenter is modelling part of *his own mind* within the machine.

(R. J. Solomonoff, 1968, stress added)

As we will see throughout this section, the testimonies do not specify what kind of introspection was used. This is an indication that introspection was frowned upon in the AI community – for these scholars are not stingy in detail in other matters. For example, we do not see here any explanation about whether the AI work was based on direct perception of mechanism or was the mechanism inferred? (see Section 7.3.2).

Sherry Turkle (1948–), a sociologist, relays the testimonies of some principal AI practitioners she interviewed: **Roger Schank** (1946–), the father of Case-Based Reasoning (CBR), said "There's only one place to get such ideas about intelligence, and that's from thinking about myself". And such thinking, we are safe to suppose, was based on self-observation – otherwise why would he be thinking of his *self* rather than some other concrete example. Schank is an extreme example of using introspection but denying it. CBR (to be discussed in detail in Section 11.2) seems to be derived from introspection, but I have found not a single mention of introspection in Schank's published works discussing AI. In a personal interview with Turkle, he admits to what he had concealed – see the quote above.

Turkle relays also **Donald Norman** (1935–) saying "In the end I have just [*observing*] myself, and if it feels right that's what I have to trust". **Marvin Minsky** (1927–2016) engaged (amongst many other projects) in building AI for jazz improvisation because he himself was involved with jazz. Minsky explicitly forbade any "psychological data" in his laboratory – so they used introspection. Minsky explains: "What you had to do was something like what Freud did. Tom Evans and I asked ourselves, in depth, what we did to solve problems like this and that seemed to work out pretty well" (Turkle, 1984, pp. 265–267).

Turkle explains that this was not seen as the dreaded "introspection" for two reasons: "First, they say that trying to capture one's thought processes in the form of a program forces you to confront objectively your initial idea of how you think you think. ... you can work towards closer and closer approximations". The researchers look for methods that would "both 'feel right' and 'run' – that will produce the right results". Second, she suggests that the conceptual world of computer programs somehow provides a better vocabulary than "naïve introspection"

---

[3] To the best of my knowledge, this paper was previously quoted only by myself (Freed, 2013, 2017) and in a retrospective recounting *all* of Solomonoff's work (Dowe, 2013).

for understanding what we see in mental self-observation (Turkle, 1984, p. 267). This idea that one first "captures one's thought" and later experiments with software based on the mechanism of such a thought is the closest precursor I found for my arguments on the contexts of discovery and justification (Sections 8.2 and 8.6).

8.3.2 Specific Apparent Cases

This section discusses apparent cases of the use of introspection in AI research, but the word "apparent" plays two different roles here: AI researchers admit to using introspection in specific cases – explicitly, and hence "apparently" in the "clear" sense of that word. However, in other cases, the use of introspection can only be inferred, or even speculated, since the prevalent compunctions prevent researchers from admitting to using introspection. These are "apparent" cases in the sense of "probable" or "suspected" uses of introspection. The purpose of this section is twofold: To show specific cases where introspection *was* used in AI and to show how researchers distance themselves from such usages.

A bridging case, both a survey of other people using introspection and a personal specific testimony, is the case of **Phil Agre** who says:

> ... I began by filling my notebook with exhaustively detailed stories from my own everyday life. By this time I had grown preoccupied with planning research, so I decided to gather some examples of real-life planning. In doing so, I was following an AI tradition of introspection that has been described aptly, if unsympathetically, by Turkle [quoted above, section 8.3.1]. Many early AI researchers were clearly attempting, at one level or another, to reproduce their own psyches on computers, and many of them drew on introspection to motivate their programs. Introspection as a formal research method in psychology, of course, had been comprehensively discredited decades earlier. But AI people have not regarded introspection as evidence but as inspiration; because the functionality of their computer systems provides a fully adequate criterion of the success of their research, they believe, it does not matter what experiences might have motivated the systems' design. And introspection is close at hand. But my own practice was different from introspection in one important respect: whereas introspection attempts to observe and describe mental processes under specially controlled conditions, I was trying to remember and recount episodes of concrete activity that took place in my own everyday life.

> **(Agre, 1997, p. 145)**

Agre's understanding of introspection is quite restricted – he says that it is usually done in controlled conditions – as a psychological technique that was mostly true (in the time before Watson), but there is nothing in the definitions of introspection as such to require this (see Section 7.2). Agre's description of introspection as "inspiration" is in a sense a precursor of my analysis in terms of the contexts of discovery vs justification (see Section 8.2.4), and in that sense, he is my "nearest neighbour". Agre ended up writing "Pengi" – which was *not* based on his own introspection but rather on Heidegger's philosophy (Dreyfus, 2007). So it seems that Agre has based his work on three things: (1) His self-reports on his everyday life, (2) introspection by pre-Watson psychologists, and (3) the tenets of the Heideggerian tradition. Even with Agre, we see an effort to distance himself from full-blooded introspection – "my own practice was different from introspection in one important respect...". This book *recommends* introspection as a conscious and unabashed basis for AI development. Note that Agre was interested in "planning research" – this is a fairly sophisticated attitude, while my interest here is in uncovering and programming underlying (anthropic) mechanisms rather than the "western, modern, well trained, and adult" or "correct" thinking that most of AI aims at (see Chapter 6).

For all his personal research and writing of "detailed stories" of his everyday life, Agre ended up writing his software based on Heideggerian philosophy, even based on a significantly simplified version of it (Dreyfus, 2007). It would not be much of a speculation to say the following: Agre ended up preferring the "respectable" and "correct" scholarly source over the frowned upon or forbidden personal introspection. This preference is unnecessary (in the context of discovery) and is what I refer to when I say that researchers "shy away" from introspection and refuse to engage with it in a "full blooded" way – and Agre was the bravest researcher that I have found, in terms of explicitly using introspection.

Consider **Alan Turing**'s (1912–1954) work on chess in the 1940s–50s:

> If I were to sum up the *weakness* of the above system in a few words, I would describe it as a caricature of my own play. It was in fact *based on an introspective analysis* of my thought processes when playing, with considerable simplifications. It makes oversights which are very similar to those which I make myself, and which may in both cases be ascribed to the considerable moves being inappropriately chosen.

> **(Turing, 1953, emphasis added)**

Note that Turing views his using introspection as a basis for a model as a "weakness". It is doubtful whether he is influenced here by Watson, since he was less of a psychologist than other AI developers, but the reservations he had about this usage is clear. Note that he does point out that making similar mistakes would be evidence of being based on a model of a natural mind.

There are two cases where we have some basis to believe that introspection was used though it was not admitted to. The case of **Roger Schank** erasing any mention of introspection in his research publications while admitting to it in an interview was discussed in Section 8.3.1. The case of fuzzy logic is more speculative.

The field of fuzzy logic originated with **Lotfi Zadeh**'s (1921–2017) paper "fuzzy sets" (1965). This paper gives no hint as to how these ideas originally occurred to Zadeh, other than that he was thinking about how people think rather than computers. The logical possibilities are that Zadeh was considering how concepts, categories, and set membership work for either himself or other people. The first will be a case of introspection (using his own mind as the basis of his design), while the second would be a case of third-person research into how people operate (or speculation). McNeill and Freiberger (1994, p. 15) provide the nearest text we have to a biography of Zadeh or to a historical account of the "fuzzy" idea. They say

> ... he had promised to work at the RAND Corporation later that month and had not yet chosen a research topic. So he lay down on a bed, his preferred posture for cogitation, and contemplated complex systems. And the notion of fuzzy sets struck him....

Since on that bed in July 1964 (as far as we know) he was not engaged in any interaction with psychological research about humans in general, it would probably not be a great misrepresentation to assume that he was introspecting when he invented the idea of fuzzy sets, and consequentially fuzzy logic (see also Sections 11.1 and 10.1.4, pt 4).

Note that regardless of whether we accept the speculation that Zadeh was indeed introspecting, his new and unusual notion based on "how humans think" (subjectively) was immediately couched in respectable mathematical terms, be they "set theory" or "logic". The pressure of researchers to be "scientific" seems to disallow a full-blooded acceptance of introspection even in the context of discovery. This is a philosophical error but should not reflect badly on any of the above scholars, as they are not philosophers. It is, however, the role of philosophy to point out that such shyness in using introspection in the context of discovery is unwarranted and probably hinders exploration of novel ideas.

8.3.3 Mainstream Cognitive Science Uses Introspection

Herbert Simon continued Watson's objections to introspection and took part in bringing much of behaviourism's heritage into the cognitive fold (Costall, 2006). However, while developing the Logical Theorist, at RAND in 1955, he testifies: "I was doing a lot of introspecting on my own problem-solving processes, so I tried to solve some problems from the Principia... I pondered as I walked about how one solves geometry problems... suddenly I had a clear conviction..." (McCorduck, 2004, pp. 161–162).

Simon, as we saw in Section 7.3, explicitly pushed for a continuation of Watson's "thinking aloud" and wrote extensively about the use of "thinking aloud protocols", culminating in his book "Protocol Analysis" (Ericsson & Simon, 1993). I have shown that the distinction between TA (encouraged by the Watson–Simon orthodoxy) and introspection (forbidden by the same orthodoxy) is:

1. The contents of TA are the *contents* of the thinking process. In "classical introspection", the contents of the report are about the **mechanisms** that were used to do the thinking, rather than the **content**.
2. In the forbidden "classical introspection" it is the **psychologist**, a trained individual with a research agenda, who is making the report, while in TA, it is a **naïve** participant in an experiment.

Simon used some TA protocols to develop his AI. In developing the General Problem Solver (GPS), he had to bend the rules a bit:

> But the most massive set of examples of the experimental strategy of 'just looking' is to be found in human problem solving. Density of data was the name of the game, and protocol analysis the way of playing it. Both Al Newell and I agree that the core of GPS was extracted directly from a particular protocol that we can identify. ... The GPS theory was extracted by direct induction from the thinking-aloud protocol of a [*single*] laboratory subject, without benefit of an experimental and a control condition

> **(Simon, 1996a, pp. 384–385)**

In using a single protocol from a single subject, he is giving up some of his scientific rectitude. Also, in using a specific protocol, he seems to be breaking one of the two distinctions that separate the forbidden introspection from TA – he is indeed using a naïve experimental subject, but he is using a subject not for the *content* of his thinking but for garnering information about mechanism. This is arguably introspection by proxy.

Nisbett and Wilson (though not directly engaged in AI) argue against introspection in one of the most oft-quoted papers in cognitive science (see Section 8.2.2). Still, they cannot avoid introspection completely and admit to it readily. As we saw above, after rounding up much data to show that introspection is wrong, they turn to speculate on the causes of the subjective certainty that people have regarding their own introspections. They present their theory that "Confidence should be high when the causal candidates are (a) few in number, (b).... In fact, we appeal to *introspection* to support this view" (Nisbett & Wilson, 1977, p. 255, emphasis added).

8.3.4 Introspection Is "Commonplace": Summary

So regardless of the engrained, sometimes visceral objection to introspection within the AI community (Section 8.2), introspection is somehow permissible (at least sometimes), "frequently enough" successful (Section 8.3.1), and has been used before in a widespread manner. This statement is not to fuse different thinkers' positions into one alleged chimera-like position but to point out the accepted overall conduct of the AI research community as such.

Introspection was often tainted (see Section 10.3.3) by prejudice in favour of mathematics in that the researchers described their method of solving problems (for example chess) not in a neutral, human-like way but in an idealised manner; as if humans give equal attention to all areas of the chess board (Turing) and never make mistakes (within the limits of the search depth – Simon) – as if we were all rational in all our thoughts (see Section 4.5.4).

Moreover, it seems that though many cognitive scientists and AI researchers do introspect and many even admit to it, they are still shy, timid, and apologetic about doing so. I argue in this chapter that introspection is permissible (so they can relax). In Chapter 9, I argue that it is actually a good and plausible basis for anthropic AI (and by implication maybe also for other fields in cognitive science). My problem with all the above scholars using introspection is that they do it too timidly. For a detailed discussion of how introspection could be done more fruitfully, see Chapter 10.

8.4 Introspection as "Desirable"

To recoup: This chapter is about how previous AI scholars related to introspection. Most scholars objected to introspection, near universally quoting Watson (1913). We have already seen that since we are here dealing with the context of discovery in technology, these objections do not hold. Further we have seen that even some of the same people who denigrated introspection used it informally. For completeness sake, let's discuss here Dreyfus's position (Dreyfus, 1979, 2007; Dreyfus & Dreyfus, 1986), who *indirectly* supports introspection enthusiastically (see Section 2.3).

8.4.1 Introspection and Phenomenology

Phenomenology is a branch of philosophy (written mainly in German) which attempts peer-reviewed reporting on experience, as available through introspection. Some of the main names in this tradition are Husserl, Heidegger, Merleau-Ponty, Gadamer, Habermas, and Dreyfus. Dreyfus is a persistent proponent of phenomenology in the field of AI, but he has not made any technological contribution and hence is considered by many to be outside the field of AI. Wheeler (2005) tries to integrate phenomenology into the mainstream of cognitive science using dynamical systems, action-oriented representations, and other concepts.

Just as the history of AI is intertwined with that of cognitive science, so is Dreyfus's critique of AI intertwined with his critique of cognitivism (Boden, 2008). Note, however, that Dreyfus does not distinguish human-like AI from the rational type nor does he distinguish technological from scientific AI (see Sections 6.1 and 6.4).

8.4.2 The Neisser–Dreyfus Debate

Recall the debate between Dreyfus and Neisser, a founder of cognitive psychology, in Section 2.2.

On the surface, Dreyfus and Neisser are on opposing sides – the first is an idealist and the second is a reductionist physicalist, the first is interested in subjectivity and the second in objectivity. Arguably they talk completely past each other and have nothing in common. But they do share this trait: They each argue that *their own* perspective is true, constitutes *reality*, and should be pursued to the exclusion of other positions. This idea of "one truth" or "reality" that should lord over all others is dogmatic and unnecessary (see Sections 4.2.2 and 5.2.2). It may be the purpose of science to arrive at a singular truth (though neither Popper nor Kuhn nor any other philosopher of science I can recall would agree), but it surely is *not* the purpose of technology to arrive at a singular truth (see Section 8.2.5). The purpose of technology is to make (and sell) products that people will find useful (and will buy again). So using different perspectives pragmatically is not only an option but a (technological and economic) imperative.

8.4.3 Introspection vs Phenomenology

The main problem with phenomenology as a basis for AI is that it is very difficult, if not impossible, to write software based on the refined but somewhat vague and sometimes flowery language of the phenomenologists (see Ed Feigenbaum's reaction to phenomenology in Section 4.4 and McCorduck (2004, pp. 229–230)). The phenomenologists are so advanced into researching what it is like to be human that there is no way to roll back 100 years or so and ask them to produce simpler models that make sense in terms of data structures and algorithms. Nor would it be fair to impose such a restriction on their field. Hence, I suggest introspection (rather than phenomenology) as the basis for human-like AI: introspection by the individual AI practitioners, as a basis for new designs in AI.

There have been several recent attempts to make phenomenology (and introspection) more accurate, more scientific, and more respectable (Jack & Roepstorff, 2003, 2004). These approaches, like Hurlburt's version of hetero-phenomenology (see Section 7.1.5), seem to be motivated by making introspection better in the sense of being more accurate, which is commendable but is in the spirit of science and/ or scholarly study rather than in the spirit of developing practical technology. Like Dreyfus – phenomenological "correctness" here trumps technological feasibility. Purity trumps technology – and with all due respect for these efforts they take us further away from implementable technology, so they are currently less relevant to AI.

8.5 Introspection as "Unavoidable"

I will only provide here a sketch of an idea that will be further developed in Section 9.3, once some more concepts have been introduced. This idea is novel, and I do not necessarily hold it as true (this is an open project). All I do here is present this position as another defensible position regarding the role of introspection in AI.

The vast majority if not all of AI, nearly by definition, takes the form of software. And in developing software, one has two options (or a combination of the two), either to use already existing code or algorithms, in which case nothing is novel or conjuring up something new. And how does a programmer conjure up some new way of achieving a task? This requires them to bear in mind the problem to be solved and imagine themselves in a sense to be (or be inside) a python interpreter, or an Intel processor, or some such software environment, and ask themselves how they would achieve the task at hand. The code would then be a log of the instructions that the programmer imagined that they would perform in order to carry out the task. So in this sense, all original programming requires one to project oneself, like a stage actor, into the world of a software environment, and to write a log of all the instructions that one would perform in such a world in order to achieve the task at hand. More detail will be given in Section 9.3.2.

If this argument is successful, this considerably weakens any position that seeks to disallow or denigrate introspection in the context of AI as a software-based pursuit. If introspection is inherent to *all* programming, a demand that we write software while not introspecting would be self-contradictory.

A possible counterargument could be that this position regarding the need for introspection for programming is orthogonal to the rest of the discussion about introspection as a source of ideas for even defining the requirements for a programmer. As with the main body of this specific argument, I remain agnostic and include this point as a contribution to the completeness of the discussion about the legitimacy of a role for introspection in AI research.

8.6 A Hybrid Position

Having discussed all these positions, one more (compound) possibility arises. Maybe several of the abovementioned researches (without saying so explicitly) hold a position similar to mine: That introspection is legitimate in the context of discovery and that in the context of justification it isn't. That could be the reason that several researchers' names appear both in Section 8.2 (introspection is forbidden) and also in Section 8.3 (introspection is commonplace). This position is speculative, since I have found no mention of these concepts in AI literature. But as quoted in Section 8.3.1, Turkle offers the explanation that using introspection within AI research was seen as legitimate for two reasons: "First, they say that trying to capture one's thought processes in the form of a program forces you to confront objectively your initial idea of how you think you think. ... you can work towards closer and closer approximations of something that will both 'feel right' and 'run' – that will produce the right results". Second, she suggests that the conceptual world of computer programs somehow provides a better vocabulary than "naïve introspection" for understanding what we see in mental self-observation (Turkle, 1984, p. 267).

One could now careen into a deeper analysis of which types of scientific method seem to be on each thinker's mind – but that would be highly speculative. The fact remains that no AI researcher has given a justification for accepting introspection for ideas while still rejecting it for evidence. We simply have no textual account with which to clarify the situation any further. So let us now assume (in the spirit of charity) that these AI researchers foresaw our present analysis in terms of contexts of discovery and justification, and therefore, we have (in this chapter so far) at most reformulated the received wisdom. Unfortunately, this analysis cannot stand because if indeed they thought they could use introspection freely in the context of discovery, they would indeed use it *freely*. However, as we have seen (Section 8.3), and we will see further in Section 10.1, the use of introspection so far has always been minimized, insofar as it existed at all. Zadeh (see Sections 8.3.2 and 11.1), for example, comes up with the fuzzy edges of concepts, and then avoids any further "suspect conduct", and retreats to the safety of mathematics. Introspection is always used as sparingly as possible, like a chef using some potent but frowned-upon ingredient: sparingly, timidly, with minimal fanfare – knowing that the dish will be bland without it but still hiding it as much as possible from the clientèle. One can only speculate as to why this is so (I give some background for such speculations in Chapters 3 and 4). It is no coincidence that Turkle, the sociologist, got nearest to this point: AI researchers view themselves as scientists and want to be seen as only using good scientific methods. This stands out in Simon's protestations that his deviation from scientific method is OK (see Section 8.3.3) and is foretold by Watson's talk of "the scientific man" (J. B. Watson, 1920), see also Costall (2006). Recall also Papert's point that we disown our natural thought processes and pretend to think logically (Section 3.1.1).

The only example of people using introspection freely are Dreyfus and his followers (ignoring for the moment the difference between individual introspection and systematic phenomenology). But hardly any of these free introspectors write any code. Agre, who indeed introspected and also tried to program some Heideggerian concepts, got condemned for not being "Heideggerian enough" (Dreyfus, 2007). (Why Agre is not celebrated by Dreyfus as a "first step" in the right direction probably has to do with Dreyfus's own puritanism and derision of the "first-step fallacy" (Bar-Hillel, 2003; Dreyfus, 2012).) So we have AI researchers that introspect very sparingly, not really capturing much of the benefit of introspection, and we have serious introspectors/phenomenologists who are "too grand" to write any actual software, resulting in a dialogue of the deaf – few people in the AI community listen to Dreyfus (McCorduck, 2004, Chapter 9). Agre, the only person who got anywhere near the conscious and open use of introspection as advocated here, got chased out of the profession, by both sides of the argument.

So the conclusion of the discussion so far is that the liberal use of introspection in the context of discovery should be allowed but without allowing the introspective process to get out of control, in the sense of becoming either an end in itself or simply so refined that programming the models becomes pragmatically impossible. However, some would worry that we still do not know what kind of information introspection would yield.

8.7 Types of Truth in Introspection

What does introspection give us? It would have been nice if we had direct access to guaranteed truths or at least clear observations like we have when dealing with everyday objects in the objective world. This is not the case. Let us survey what the worries and positions are. In what senses should we expect introspective reports to be true? This survey does not lead to a satisfying conclusion, like other discussions about introspection (see Section 7.3.4). There is a way forward though, as will be shown in Chapter 9.

1. Introspection cannot be scientific. In cognitive science we are steeped in the rationalistic tradition (see Section 2.4). One of its main tenets is that we "characterise the situation is terms of identifiable objects with well-defined properties" (Winograd & Flores, 1986, p. 15). We find this attitude natural in science, technology, law, trade, and many other pursuits that are public (external) in nature. However, once we go into the realm of the subjective, there are precious few "clear and distinct" (Descartes, 1952) identifiable "objects" in our subjective experience. Even the *categories* of "events", "objects", and "processes" (that Schwitzgebel (2012) uses in his characterisation of introspection) do not necessarily apply. Few "events" or "processes" in our mind have a clear beginning, and even fewer have a clear end (When did I *stop* being afraid of X?). **Mental processes are not "moderate-sized specimens of dry-goods"** (Austin & Warnock, 1964, p. 8).

2. Is introspection a good source of information? Introspection can reflect (or not) some objective reality. Many analytical philosophy positions (influenced by positivism, see Section 4.1) take reality to be one, *external*, and objective. Introspection does not give us any correct observations, by definition, since it observes things that are neither external nor public nor directly verifiable by others. However, an idealist position such as Berkeley's would say that there is no external reality other than our impressions of such a reality, and that external, objective reality is merely constituted in intersubjectivity. Even for

such an idealist position, though, it is difficult to show how a single person's introspection establishes any *public* "truth" or "correctness". **Introspection is often wrong about objective matters** (barring solipsism, where there is no objectivity separate from individual subjectivity).

3. The internal "introspective vision" could see correctly or not what is going on *for us* (bearing in mind that the use of the term "vision" is metaphoric). It is doubtful, therefore, that one can say that there is such a thing as a "wrong vision". The vision is what it is – it is what was experienced by the individual, either introspecting or reporting on some events. So we can say that introspective reports are incorrigible in objective terms (Schwitzgebel, 2012). This is not to say infallible – infallible would be about the objective universe, but introspection is about a specific person's subjective world. And how, on what basis, can we question someone else's subjective experience? We have no access to it! **Introspection is incorrigible about subjective matters.** Nothing here guarantees against introspectors falsifying their reports (consciously or not).

4. In describing *any* vision, having some experience or skill in the matter can be of use. Having a broader vocabulary of colours and shapes allows for a better textual report of a sunset, and there is no reason to believe that introspective verbalisation would not benefit from analogous acquired skills. Also, akin to describing a sunset, once the broader "strokes" of the vision are already described, there is room for more detail, if one has the patience for it. So at this level, there are better and worse introspections, though it is impossible to pass external judgement on their contents and even more difficult to have objective justifications for such judgements. We can assess and appreciate the level of detail as such. **Introspection can often be improved** (see Chapter 10). Whether such skill in introspection changes the *experience* itself or just the description is possibly an unsolvable problem. That, again, is a big worry for science but not for technology (see Section 7.3.5).

5. However, even in seeing a vision, there is a good chance that one's ability to even *see* things (also internally) will be impacted by one's **value systems** (see also discussion in Section 7.3.4 about the difficulties with neutral observations). This is an internalised (if you will a "cognitive", top-down) form of the following concern.

6. In *reporting* the content of one's introspective vision, one might not tell the entire truth because it may be embarrassing or show them up as transgressing on some value system. Admitting to having frequent sexual thoughts or any other socially objectionable contents may not be advantageous, so reports may be skewed (Byers et al., 1998). Also reports may be skewed by theoretical commitments, for example a well-trained scientist may claim to be thinking logically and mathematically when that is not actually what is going on. **Introspection can often be polluted by other considerations** (avoiding such pollution will be discussed in Section 10.3.3).

7. But, there is a seeming **contradiction**: How can I simultaneously say that introspection is "incorrigible" and then say it is may be "polluted"? In *principle*, introspection is incorrigible, and anyone engaged in introspection for AI may by all means go ahead and try designs based on their introspection and see what contribution they may make – let a thousand flowers bloom.[4] However, if someone were to say that all their thoughts look to them like flamingos, or alternately claim that all their thoughts are mathematical (as Simon (1996a) and many others in our field seem to do), or claim infallibility, one may reserve the right to have doubts about these introspections and about the utility that AI might garner from them. These doubts are based on the assumption that as humans we share some of our subjective world, similar to sharing walking using two legs. Some people will be different but not *that* different. But that would just be an opinion.

Gallagher and Zahavi (2012, pp. 28–29) define phenomenology to be introspection refined by the consensus of the phenomenological community. One could wager that introspections that are in line with established phenomenology would fare better than outliers (flamingos) as AI algorithms. The problem we have had so far was not so much with obtaining good introspections or phenomenology (Gadamer, 1979; Heidegger, 1962), but with programming these insights, see Dreyfus's failure to code *anything* and his continuing complaint that none of AI is "Heideggerian *enough*" (Dreyfus, 2007) and Section 8.4.3.

But, still some would worry, isn't introspection messy? There are entire lines of argument saying that introspection, as a process, necessarily interferes with the phenomena that is being observed (Schwitzgebel, 2012), that introspection may not be a process of self-observation, but of self-definition (Byrne, 2005), and that introspection, like other observations, is theory-laden (Bogen, 2014). Again, if I were seeking to show that introspection is *correct generally* (objectively), then each of these would be a significant blow – and collectively one can see why most researchers simply dismiss introspection, referring to Watson (1913). But here we do not claim *truth*, but ***plausible utility*** for AI. This chapter's aim (and this section's aim in a different way) is only to show the legitimacy, not the plausibility of introspection. Plausibility is the work of Chapter 9.

---

[4] I use this expression with great reservations. The original saying, by Mao Tse-Tung, was "let a hundred flowers bloom". It was used in 1956 in his opening speech for a campaign pretending to canvass the opinions of the Chinese intelligentsia about how the new Chinese state should be run. Whether initially sincere or not, the result of the "hundred flowers campaign" was that once "*the snakes were enticed out of their caves*" many of these intellectuals were killed or imprisoned. I use this expression here in its innocent connotation (Brown, 2010, pp. 313–318).

8.8 Introspection Is Legitimate: Summary

Introspection was considered suspect in philosophy (Section 8.1) and forbidden in science (Section 8.2). However, in the context of discovery, there should be no restriction on what ideas can be considered, and moreover, the level of worry about possible errors interposing themselves as truths is lower in technology than in science. So we have seen that introspection is legitimate as a source of ideas, and some developers of AI would (half-heartedly) agree (Section 8.3). The problem with the researchers that practise introspection is precisely that they do so half-heartedly and admit to it rarely. In being ashamed of using introspection, they can hardly reap the benefits that introspection may offer fully.

Dreyfus and others considered phenomenology (a close relative of introspection) a promising field of enquiry for AI (Section 8.4) but have produced no tangible examples of working designs. A speculative argument was provided saying that AI *without* introspection is impossible (Section 8.5), to be further developed in Section 9.3. A further discussion of a hybrid approach, assuming that the AI community already accepts the point about the contexts of discovery/justification produced a recommendation for allowing the *far more liberal* use of introspection in the context of discovery, while restricting any introspection to programmable models.

For anyone worrying about what kinds of truth can be produced by introspection, an argument about the logical status of introspection was given in Section 8.7. This culminated in a dual view of introspection: In principle, it is incorrigible, allowing any introspection the chance to be used as a basis for AI designs. In practice, it was conceded that there may be better or worse introspections, and these may have some bearing on the resultant AI. Conveniently, in technology, there is no harm in letting "a thousand flowers bloom".

The argument of this book is for using introspection wholeheartedly but without losing sight of the need to produce code (details on how this can be done are in Chapter 10).

If introspection is legitimate, we still need to figure out whether we *want* to use it – do we have indications that introspection would be a fecund source of good ideas? This is the topic of Chapter 9.

Chapter 9

Introspection Is Likely to Be Profitable

The argument of this book is that "**introspection is recommended for developing anthropic AI**". After covering a lot of the background in previous chapters, the last chapter showed that introspection is a legitimate method for inventing artificial intelligence (AI) systems. But being legitimate and permissible is not enough for being recommended: This chapter will argue why one positively should expect introspection to be a good basis for anthropic AI. Recall that recommendation is not a guarantee, what needs to be shown here is that introspection will plausibly be a good basis for AI inventions.

This chapter will include the following arguments:

1. Consciousness is inherent to all normally intelligent humans, and forgoing an examination of consciousness in the quest for AI would be as odd as forgoing the examination of horse carriages when trying to develop the horseless carriage (as the car was originally called).
2. If teachers use introspection to teach mental skills to their students, then the very survival of civilisations over multiple generations is testimony to the validity of introspection.
3. A case can be made that all software programming is introspection-based, and therefore, we have already plenty of evidence that introspection is often useful.

The next chapter will go into more detail on how to develop such AI (and which pitfalls to avoid), and Chapters 11 and 12 will give some concrete working examples.

9.1 Conceptual Arguments

One could present several a priori arguments for introspection for AI design but not everyone would be convinced by purely conceptual arguments (software engineers are notoriously suspicious, even of their own code). Moreover, one of the most convincing conceptual arguments I have in this context would require assuming idealism, which many would refuse. Instead, I will let Section 9.2 do the heavy lifting of giving a compelling argument. Here, at the conceptual stage, I will only make one argument, and move on.

The main model we have for intelligence is natural human intelligence. This is by definition the intelligence we want to emulate in *human*-like AI. Specifically in this volume, we are looking for anthropic AI, which is the un-enculturated intelligence, prior to any moulding of a particular mind to a particular environment or society. This is contrasted with the "western, modern, well-trained, and adult" mind that much of existing AI aims at. *AI is an attempt to functionally duplicate* intelligence, like artificial leather is an attempt to functionally duplicate leather or an artificial limb is an attempt to functionally duplicate a limb. One of the most basic things we expect an engineer to do when developing an **artificial X** is to examine the *natural* X as much as is needed, to glean ideas for their artefact from the natural X.

Every human mind is subjective (Seth, 2010), and hence, subjectivity is a matter of fact inherent to the human mind – the main specimen of intelligence we have available for examination. But most AI practitioners would have us construct intelligence *without subjectivity*. We have no natural example of such an intelligence, and so building AI without subjectivity would be building artificial X while excluding in principle one of X's most salient characteristics – indeed a bit rather like climbing a tree trying to get to the moon, as Dreyfus (1979) had it. I suspect this is the reason why AI has become moribund in the last few decades – why the initial optimism led to such meagre results (Langley, 2006; McHugh & Minsky, 2003).

9.2 An Argument from Education[1]

This section will discuss a specific, rather common type of education – the conscious teaching and learning of skills. This is not to detract from all other types of education or other aspects of human existence and development, such as emotions, mood, motivation, and countless others.

The argument outline is as follows: When *teaching skills*, the teacher needs to self-observe in order to know how the teacher himself does X, so that he can teach how to do X. In the case where X is a mental skill, then mental self-observation

---

[1] This argument was considerably sharpened by separate discussions with Joshua Weinstein and Simon McGreggor.

is required. Mental self-observation is introspection. The success human cultures have in transferring their mental skills from one generation to the next is testimony that introspection is neither noise nor nonsense but is sufficiently useful to allow the new generation to acquire the skills that are characteristic of that culture. If the words used by teachers who introspected help or cause the young to become skilful and people do not acquire the same skills spontaneously, it is safe to assume that the words derived from the introspection efficaciously contain useful information for reproducing the skill (in a healthy human). If information useful for human skill acquisition is in the introspective text, then: (1) Introspection is neither noise nor nonsense, and (2) introspection is a plausible source of information about the skill under discussion. The rest of this section details this argument.

9.2.1 Skill Questions

This argument focuses on teaching skills, rather than formal knowledge – on knowing-how rather than knowing-that. This is partially motivated by the previous conclusion (Section 6.7) that we should look more at knowledge-how than at knowledge-that. Partially, it is simply the best field in which to demonstrate that introspection contains useful information. Even if this argument has no validity outside the "teaching skills" arena, the conclusion that at least in this arena introspection is positively useful – this finding shifts the burden of argument to the other side who might argue that introspection is restricted *only* to that field. Note that the radical anti-intellectual position says that there is no knowledge *other* than skills.

Let's examine how we communicate knowledge-how, specifically how we answer questions about such knowledge. The issue of how we answer questions of knowledge-that is pretty well explored in AI (e.g. SHRLDU (Winograd, 1971)). We also have a raging theoretical debate on whether there are any representations involved in knowledge-that (Dreyfus, 2007; Shanon, 2008; Wheeler, 2005). The issue of knowledge-how and how we answer questions about it requires some discussion.

Note that when one asks a person a seemingly straightforward question, such as "Do you know how to ride a bike?", there are three different conversations that may ensue:

1. Most people hear it as: "Can you ride a bike", which would mean "Do you believe that you could ride a bike at will".
2. A teacher may also hear this same string of words as "Can you teach how to ride a bike?", and that in turn can be construed either as a request for a yes/no answer or as a request for teaching.
3. A scientist (perhaps a caricature of a scientific psychologist) may hear it as: "Do you know, in detail, what strategies humans deploy to ride bicycles?"

These are very different questions, but the answer to (3) includes an answer to (2). Consider a slightly different how-to question: "How can I get to London by train?"

Most people, including teachers, would see that as a request for directions and tell you which turns to take to walk to a railway station and suggest a train line from the selection available at that station, perhaps with some transfers. The caricature scientist's version of this question would be much longer but will include also the teacher's version. When asking how humans would navigate to London using trains, after answering all the scientific questions, ultimately the scientist will also need information about station locations, train routes, and schedules. So *both* answers will include train stations, routes, and timetables.

In a sense, in order to maintain scientific rigour, scientists *set aside* what they already know as they step into their scientific role (see Section 9.3.1 about roles). This is because scientists see their role as asking the fundamental questions and demanding detailed objective answers. For technology, perhaps that is a less-than-optimal attitude: a case of allowing the better, more detailed information to get in the way of the good, workable technique. In technology, the everyday human way of doing something is a good first stab at how to accomplish the task at hand. How to fill the gaps between the coarse details of the simpler explanation will be discussed in Section 10.3.5.1. Scientists want a whole and fully objective truth, technologists just want something that will work better than the previous technology: Wheels are far superior to beasts of burden in terms of carrying things around, but the idea of using beasts of burden was a huge technological evolution for humans over carrying loads themselves. Everyday people, and technologists, want to get the job done, not to get it done in the best possible way.

9.2.2 Teaching Skills

I have found three ways to teach skills (there may be more): explicit instruction, imitation, and "reverse imitation". One can learn skills by oneself (see Section 9.2.6), but here we are discussing *teaching*. These learning methods can be combined:

1. Instruction is when a teacher explicitly uses language to describe how to do something. A good example is a recipe.
2. Imitation is when the teacher provides a demonstration for the student to copy, by observation. Copying by observation may require repeated experimentation by the student and possibly repeated demonstrations by the teacher. This need not be formally orchestrated – learning by imitation (especially children from parents) happens in the everyday course of life. When a chef puts a video clip on the internet showing how they make some dish, this allows the viewer/student to imitate their method in more detail than a shorthand recipe. Watching the video even without the recipe (perhaps more times) would also allow a willing student to learn enough about how to prepare the dish to write out a recipe themselves.
3. "Reverse imitation" is when the teacher (say) stands behind a student, holds (say) their arms, and shows them the correct motion *using the student's own*

body. This is done in training beginners in crafts, music playing, and sports such as tennis. In a sense, the teacher sculpts a moving functioning skilful person out of the body of a novice.

The first method, "instruction" is fully explicit in that the skills are transferred using language, while the latter methods are at least partially implicit. However, one may object that the textual needs interpretation, while the embodied demonstration is the *more* explicit. This disagreement revolves around one's understanding of the word "explicit", but makes no difference to the main argument here.

Not all skills can be acquired by explicit-language teaching. For example, control of one's own limbs is developed by trial and error, in infancy (O'Regan, 2011). Even explicit instructions like "add a tablespoon of oil" depend on these basic motor skills which cannot be taught. The AI implications of this point will be discussed in Section 10.3.5.1.

Fascinating as some of these aspects are, we must concentrate on explicit-language instruction, since we will eventually need to write very explicit AI software. We must focus on how teaching begins, in the case of the explicit use of language in teaching. Our first concern is how the instructions come into existence, in the teachers.

9.2.3 Self-Observations

In the case of explicit instruction by words (the recipe of point 1 above), the teacher has to utter (or write) some text that will communicate the skill to be learnt. Where could this text come from? Maybe the teacher gets the exact text from a book – but then the question is begged, how does the author of the book come up with the text for teaching skill X?

1. The text could be remembered verbatim from the time when the teacher/author herself learnt the skill. This is unlikely for two reasons: First, it would require word-perfect memory over decades. Second, this would lead to infinite regress, the instructions had to come from *somewhere*, and unless we believe something like a God giving all instructions to mankind at some stage (on Mount Sinai?), we have to accept that the instructions on how to perform skill X have come from some human developing or "coming up with" them.
   A variant of this would be formal teaching from textbooks.
2. The teacher/author may be flailing in the dark, coming up with various nonsensical instructions, testing which of them work, and using those. This idea is a bit like Darwinian evolution. This is unlikely in that we see very few cases of nonsensical instructions being "tried out".
3. The teacher/author may be trying out doing X for themselves (either actually, or in their imagination), while self-observing to see what it is that they are doing. There is some evidence for this in the fact that a student would often

ask their teacher (as in the examples above) something like "How would *you* do X"? "You" here is the teacher. The student asks the teacher to observe themselves and tell how X is done. Doing X while observing oneself would also include imagining doing X and imagining doing X using various options, or recalling a procedure, "playing it out in one's mind", observing *that* and verbalising it, etc. As long as there is an action by the teacher being observed and verbalised, real, remembered, or imagined, there is some version of self-observation going on.[2]

A simple example of self-observation would be, when teaching how to ride a bike,[3] the teacher self-observes that in order to get onto the bike and start pedalling, he needs to tilt the bike towards his own body so that his first push down on the far pedal will not cause the bike to fall over to the far side. The teacher will also observe his habits in other areas, such as where he aims to move the bulk of his body, what angle he points the handlebar at, etc. All these are observations of the preparation to mount the bike – and the more of them can be made explicit, the more of an advantage the teacher can give their student. Learning to ride a bike can be done by imitation alone – but with instructions, it is learnt more quickly (and less painfully).

9.2.4 Mental Self-Observation Is Introspection

Some of the skills civilisations possess and pass from generation to generation are mental skills – skills like using nouns to refer to things, skills like deciphering alphabets (as you are doing now, we usually call it "reading") or deciphering pictograms, doing mental maths, and many more. As we have seen above, teaching a skill X requires the teacher to self-observe and communicate how the teacher herself does skill X. If this skill is purely mental, in that there is no external behaviour that can be observed, there are two important consequences:

1. Any option of the learning happening by demonstration and imitation becomes unlikely, as there is little for **the student** to observe. Possible exceptions to this are the bootstrapping of very basic skills like using one's limbs (O'Regan, 2011) and bootstrapping language, a special skill according to Chomsky (Cowie, 2010).
2. **The teacher** also has nothing external to observe in themselves when they perform a mental skill (no "tilting the bike").

---

[2] The "simulation theory of cognition" holds that the same mechanisms are used to perform, imagine preforming, and recalling performing any interaction with the environment. This theory is backed with neuroscientific data (Hesslow, 2012).

[3] The discussion about teaching one how to cycle is somewhat autobiographical. Thanks go to Gabriel Elizedek for teaching me how to ride a bike in my 20s (!).

To teach a mental skill, the teacher must therefore glean the information about how they themselves do X by *mental* self-observation. Now recall some definitions of introspection:

> Introspection refers to an observation and, sometimes, a description of the contents of one's own consciousness.
>
> **(Overgaard, 2008)**

> Introspection, as the term is used in contemporary philosophy of mind, is a means of learning about one's own currently ongoing, or perhaps very recently past, mental states or processes.
>
> **(Schwitzgebel, 2014)**

Recall also Schwitzgebel's six characterisations of introspection, in Section 7.2.

One may object that the teacher may be *imagining themselves* or *recalling* doing the task and not *actually* doing it. So they are not actually engaged in mental self-observation (introspection) in real time, therefore, violating Schwitzgebel's condition No. 3, "temporal proximity". How to tell the difference between "imagining oneself", "recalling", and actually exercising a mental skill is hard to define, even using neuro-imaging (Hesslow, 2012). However, these difficulties make little difference to my main point here, that the only way one can teach a mental skill to others is by looking at one's own practise – regardless of the degree to which Schwitzgebel's condition No. 3 of "temporal proximity" is fulfilled and regardless of whether the skill is being exercised "for real" rather than imagined.

9.2.5 Examples of Mental Skills Being Transmitted by Introspection

1. Consider mnemonic tricks for remembering words in a foreign language: In Hebrew, the word for house is "Bayit". So people like Breuer and Shavit (2014) invent tricks like the sentence "What a lovely *house*, I think I will *buy it*." ("Buy it" sounds like "Bayit") to help people remember the word. How do they know that they have a good sentence if not by playing it out "in their mind" and seeing (introspecting!) if it "works"?

2. Consider the game of "mental chess". It is like normal chess, only there is no physical chess set and one has to memorise the board and tell the opponent one's moves using words. This game is quite difficult, and one may come up with some tricks, such as clustering using various groupings, that help one remember the board positions. Again, to share such a trick with another person, the inventor of the trick must introspect.

3. Consider the case of remembering sequences, such as telephone numbers. We know that short-term memory can handle only 7 ± 2 units

(Miller, 1956). However, people can remember significantly longer sequences, using "chunking". For example, people could spell very long words well before scientific psychology started. Whoever came up with the mnemonic device of chunking saw that it worked in their own mind *before* they explained it to others. Similarly, other mnemonic tricks were invented inside people's minds first and then explained publicly using words. Consider the idea of being introduced to a new person called "Ben", and trying to vividly imagine them enjoying themselves with all the other "Bens" that one knows, in the hope that that image will stick in one's mind and help in the recall of the new acquaintance's name.

4. Consider this commonplace trick for handling anxiety: One should imagine the worst possible scenario, and imagine how one would cope in such an eventuality. Having sketched out how one would deal with the worst eventuality, the sense of danger and hence the anxiety subside.

A possible objection here could be that these are all cultural artefacts, and we are looking for anthropic AI, which we defined as being the substructure that allows for culture without including any of the contingent culture. There are two possible responses, one conservative and the other daring.

1. The conservative response is that this observation is correct, but what is shown here is that introspection carries useful information about our mental processes overall. The question of how to distil the un-enculturated anthropic layer is left to Chapter 10, with concrete examples given in Chapters 11 and 12. The short version of how this will be overcome is that we should *aim* in introspection for as low a level as possible, and that we should use introspection iteratively so as to refine the models used for AI. Recall we are not doing science here, and if we do not get something 100% correct that is not a catastrophe – technology is by far more tolerant of errors that science is (see Sections 5.1.3 and 5.2).

2. The more daring response adds that mental skills, as exposed by introspection, are *very* near the anthropic line. Consider that the examples above contain not only very high-level[4] skills, like "mental chess" but also some low-level skills like dealing with anxiety – an emotion (example 4 above). Anthropic AI was defined as aiming at the innate mechanisms that enables our culture without being part of any contingent culture. So looking at basic skills, as basic and infantile as possible, brings us near the elusive boundary between the cultured and the pre-cultured. We may venture to use some implications and speculations to reach an even closer approximation (recall Section 7.4) – let

---

[4] Note the use of "high level" and "low level" to describe different things that humans do. This tradition goes back as far as Plato, but has shaky foundations. I use it here in the accepted "intuitive" sense, with reservations.

a thousand flowers bloom. Recall again that we needn't reach the "true" "precise" boundary, since we are not looking for scientific or philosophical absolute truth, we are looking for a technological approximation.

A more pragmatic discussion of this point is found in Section 10.3.4.

9.2.6 Skills Only Part-Acquired by Explicit Instruction

If one were to examine skill acquisition more closely, as did Dreyfus and Dreyfus (1986), one sees that there are stages in the acquisition of skills, including for example reading (for the current purpose I will limit the discussion to English). In explicit teaching by an instructor, only a very basic and slow level of the skill is picked up. A simplified communicable "base" skill (involving deciphering every letter individually) is explicitly taught, with the intent of the student eventually discovering for themselves the "higher" variant of the skill which is superior but difficult to communicate, perhaps partially because of a limited vocabulary, perhaps because we need some experience with the "base" skill before we can discover the "higher" skill. Only after a lot of experience do we have the fluency that allows us to read entire words (often not noticing systematically jumbled text (Rayner et al., 2006)).

Does this have any effect on our argument on AI?

First, the main thrust of Section 9.2 is that skills are taught by teachers practising self-observation in order to generate their speech. At no time did I claim that *all* skills are taught. All that was argued is that *some* skills are taught, and that this teaching requires self-observation on the part of the teacher, and mental self-observation is introspection, so introspection is key to the transfer of mental skills between generations.

Second, this issue demonstrates that some skills are acquired without instruction, and therefore, maybe the "true" key for learning human skills is *not* introspective. This possible critique misses the mark in terms of this book's argument that "introspection is recommended for developing anthropic AI". This book does not claim that introspection will be key to *all* future AI development – that would be the sort of "one truth" dogmatism diametrically opposed to the perspectivist attitude here, see Section 5.2.

9.2.7 An Argument from Education: Summary

If person A invents some mental skill and they teach it to person B, they must be using introspection in order to describe what it is they are doing internally. They cannot directly describe neural or cognitive processes that are not conscious, since they not only do not know their own "scientific" states, they also cannot communicate to the student which correct "scientific" processes the student must adopt (their brain or "metal scape" might be different). Later when person B teaches person C, and C teaches D, etc., they all use introspection to tell each other how the skill is performed. The case is even stronger in that even if people teach what they are taught using verbatim memory, they must use introspection to describe their own innovations and improvements of mental skills.

These skills (that *work*, somehow, in the real world, using wet neurons) are transferred (and improved) from one generation to the next, by little other than introspective-based narrative.

In teaching, the text "take that digit, and then add it to the other one" is a description of what the teacher thinks (or introspects) she is doing. It can't be mere repetition because that would not account for innovation. If introspection were noise, no student could pick up a skill by this normal method of teaching, but we all do, ergo introspection may be inaccurate, may not descriptively reflect neural reality, but still **reflect enough of *some* reality** to allow the transfer of skills and culture over many generations (reliably enough for us to read texts from millennia ago).

So (at least some forms of) the contents of introspection have some validity, in a pragmatic ("it works") sense.

9.3 Programming Impossible without Introspection

This idea has already been sketched out in Section 8.5, here I will discuss it in more detail in order to show that introspection is not only plausible and recommended for AI but arguably necessary for *any* programming. But there is a pitfall: One might argue that if indeed all software development is introspective, what is the novelty in this entire argument? I will discuss this objection towards the end of this section.

This is a speculative position,[5] which I here only claim is *defensible*, not necessarily true. Arguing properly for this position is outside the scope of the current project, and the main thrust of the book's argument does not depend on it.

9.3.1 Role-Playing

Consider this famous quote:

> Life's but a walking Shadow, a poore Player,
> That struts and frets his houre vpon the Stage,
> And then is heard no more. It is a Tale
> Told by an Ideot, full of sound and fury
> Signifying nothing

(Shakespeare, n.d.)

---

[5] This argument appears as a separate paper (Freed, 2018).

When acting and communicating, humans assume a certain role (or "frame of mind"), usually depending on the social context. The classic example is the way people take on their "work persona" as they start their work day. This "work persona" is in the main similar to the job description the organisation would advertise to fill that role if it were to fall vacant.

> Administration is not unlike play-acting. The task of the good actor is to know and play his role, although different roles may differ greatly in content. The effectiveness of the performance will depend on the effectiveness of the play and the effectiveness in which it is played. The effectiveness of the administrative process will vary with the effectiveness of the organisation and the effectiveness with which its members play their parts.

> **(Simon, 1976, p. 252, 1996b, p. xii)**

Another example of people semi-automatically fulfilling a socially constructed role is that a bilingual person will usually speak only one language at a time.

There seems to be no such thing as the mind operating (in a way that could be relevant for action) outside of some cultural context even if it is the context of running amok (Carr, 1985; Wittgenstein, 2001a). This fact of the individual's behaviour being constructed in (usually) socially accepted roles is transparent to us in daily life but has been the subject of much research, see, for example, the acclaimed book "The presentation of the self in everyday life" (Goffman, 1971).

One of the roles one can adopt is the role of being cooperative with some scientific programme, such as Watson's (and later Simon's) "thinking aloud" (see Section 7.3.1), requiring that a "scientific man" take on such a role as thinking aloud "in the proper spirit" and possibly even "with zest" (J. B. Watson, 1920, p. 91).

These roles that we adopt come with certain prejudices in interpreting our environment. Again to take an example from bilingual people, the same utterance (the same series of phonemes) may be interpreted completely differently in the context of one language or another: "me" in English is the first-person accusative pronoun, in Hebrew the same sound (מ) is the personal interrogative, meaning "who?" Also, the same event (say the firing of a pistol by an assassin) could be interpreted differently by the same person, depending on whether they are acting in their capacity as a citizen of a polity or in their capacity as a scientist. In one case, one would present the events as an assassination, and in the other, one would explain the chemistry of gunpowder and the mechanics of the revolver.

This observation (that humans usually act within a context of a role) is not entirely alien to the field of AI. Note that the above quote is from Herbert Simon (albeit from his work in public administration, not AI). Note also the connection with hermeneutics (see Section 2.5).

9.3.2 Programming Is Introspective

In writing new code (not debugging or reusing existing code), phenomenologically a programmer projects herself, as an actor would project himself into a character, into an imaginary world where she is inside a world consisting of (say) the python instruction set, or of an "Intel" architecture, and asks herself how she could use the tools available (variables, arrays, loops, libraries, etc.) in order to achieve a task such as calculating VAT[6] or whatever the programming task is. There is a lot of "first-person thinking" going on, as in "how could **I** do this", "this could give **me** *that*", etc. The programmer's output, the code that is supposed to do the task, is a formalization into python (or "Intel") *instructions* by the programmer introspecting inside this "world of python". Where else could the code come from? I can find no evidence (or testimony) that there is anything like a tree search of possibilities as GOFAI[7] would have it. Note also the language that is used for the text that the programmer writes in order to invoke a feature of python: It is a "command" or "instruction". These words, outside the context of computers, are used in education in management, telling people *how* to do some bigger task by giving them details of the component tasks in simple language (see Section 9.2).

Moreover, in debugging, a similar thing happens. In the exercise known as "a dry run", the programmer projects herself, like an actor, into the role of a python interpreter and acts (in her mind, perhaps using pencil and paper) on the code and the data as a python interpreter would, always keeping half an eye on the intended result to see where the actual result deviates from the intended result. When such a deviation is found, the programmer would say that she found a bug (recall the "intended chain of causation" in Section 5.1.3).

Conversely, a programmer copying an algorithm from a book is not introspective.

9.3.3 If So, What Is the Point of This Book?

In the beginning of Section 9.3, a worry was presented that if indeed all programming is introspective, than what is the point of this book's argument? There are three retorts:

1. The distinction is subtle but clear-cut: In programming, one projects oneself into a formal system (python/Intel instructions) and tries to achieve a task (say VAT calculation) inside that formal world. Conversely, the method promoted by this volume to get to human-like AI would require us to observe our thought processes in their *natural informal form*, to describe them as best we can (see Section 10.2), and only *later* to formalise them as code.

---

[6] A sales tax common in Europe.
[7] Good, old-fashioned AI

The difference is whether we do the introspecting inside or outside of the formalised world of programming.

2. Another retort could be that if introspection is indeed so widespread and accepted, then why is it so often denied and obfuscated? This may have to do also with the next point.
3. There is a distinction between something being ontically novel, as in a novel entity, vs being notionally novel – the phenomena were around for a while, but we never noticed. As a bare minimum, the idea of introspection for AI is notionally novel (Chrisley, 2003).

9.4 Introspection Is Likely to Be Profitable: Summary

This chapter deals with why one should positively expect introspection to be a good basis for AI development.

Section 9.1 argued conceptually that in developing an artificial X one should not shy away from examining *all* aspects of X – so in developing an *AI* system one would be wise to examine all aspects of our natural human intelligence, including the subjective introspective.

Section 9.2 argued that introspection is neither nonsense nor noise, even using the worst-case notion of introspection (see Section 7.4). Rather, it is already used to allow know-how to pass from person to person, inducing across generations. Perhaps, this very ability of humans (to introspect) evolved specifically to allow the transfer of know-how from one generation to the next, allowing civilisations to survive by accumulated wisdom.

Section 9.3 tentatively argued that *all* programming is introspective and showed that that does not trivialise the overall argument. Being tentative, this argument is not necessary for the overall argument and was included for completeness.

As we have seen there is no point in looking for "truth values" as such in introspection for AI. This volume promotes using introspection as a source of *ideas* for anthropic AI as a technology, and that is justified by three moves:

1. The requirement for "truth" is shown to be secondary in technology to the requirement for utility, and the costs of a factual mistake are shown to be lower in technology than in science, at least as far as software is concerned (see Sections 5.1.3 and 5.2).
2. The argument from the "context of discovery" allows for *any* source of ideas, thereby making introspection as legitimate as any other source of ideas (see Sections 8.2.4 and 8.2.5). This may be seen as too weak, as by a similar token one could argue for taking a walk in the park before thinking about AI, but in principle, this is enough because of (*inter alia*) the next point.

3. The argument for the validity of introspection for education (Section 9.2) shows that introspection is not only better than noise but arguably the foundation of many of human culture's successes. It is therefore expected to be a positively *good* source of ideas for AI.

This is also supported historically, in that some of the more open practitioners of AI admitted to using introspection as the basis for their AI (see Section 8.3), even though they were acutely aware that introspection had a bad reputation in psychology. They however never used introspection in the wholehearted manner that is recommended here.

The argument of this book is that AI based on introspection would produce better anthropic AI. There is no hard-and-fast logical guarantee that introspection would always produce a good design, but it produces, as a minimum, "a sketch of a sketch" as Simon had it (McCorduck, 2004, p. 246), a basis for an idea for a design (see examples in Chapters 11 and 12). The resultant designs must later be evaluated experimentally, possibly improving the design by iterative introspection and coding.

Let's look at how this is done in detail.

GETTING PRACTICAL

Chapter 10

Details and How to Use Introspection for Artificial Intelligence

This chapter describes how to approach developing introspection-based artificial intelligence (AI). It also answers several questions that remain outstanding about the recommended approach, and how to go about doing introspection more "correctly" than some past researchers have done. This chapter and the examples following use a new notation: <u>Underlined text designates introspective reports</u>.

There is a seeming tension in the argument so far, which is about to get worse. On the one hand I promote a liberal approach to the possible bases of (or inspirations for) designs in AI: "let a thousand flowers bloom" (Section 8.7, point 7), while on the other hand this chapter will prescribe "correct" ways to do such introspection. My position is that all types of introspection are legitimate sources of ideas for AI, and some types are recommended as such sources. This chapter again *recommends* certain avenues as being more plausible, more "correct" than others, and gives some arguments. These recommendations here do not detract from the generality of the argument in previous chapters.

There are a few other points that may need re-emphasising:

- Human-like AI is not better than rational AI, it is just different, and what this volume is about, and hence is our focus here (see Section 6.2 for motivations).
- Any inspiration or basis may be used to develop any type of AI. In the extreme, this is a form of the argument that monkeys typing randomly for eternity would produce the entire British Museum's library (Borges, 2001). Therefore, from

173

looking at an algorithm, we can never deduce with cast-iron certainty its provenance in terms of inspiration or basis (or the species of the designer). The rest of this chapter will say things such as "neural nets are based on biology" as shorthand for something like "it is most probable that the AI method of neural nets was inspired by (a grossly simplified version of) real life, wet, biological neurons".

■ It seems that so far the vast majority of AI has been based on either mathematics (broadly construed), biological inspirations, or on cognitive models (Langley, 2006). These approaches have been so successful that often when developing new AI many researchers tended to "look under the lamp" in one of these three areas. This book is about broadening the search and recommending direction(s) to explore within the multitude of neglected possibilities.

10.1 Definitions and Delineations

This section will clarify what is meant by AI "*based on* introspection" and contrast the recommended methodology with existing approaches to AI. This contrasting with existing approaches will clarify what this book is promoting and how that is a new and exciting approach.

In delineating the different AI efforts so far, one should look at the following aspects:

■ What type of AI is being aimed at (human/insect/rational)?
■ What were the principal inspirations or bases for the technology?
■ How successful the effort was, empirically?
■ Especially in case of failure, does the result call into question the qualities of the entire approach or inspiration, or only the circumstances of the specific experiment?

The first section will set out some definitions as to what precisely is being recommended. Later sections will compare and contrast this with how other approaches seem to work.

In contrasting the proposed view of how to develop AI in detail with previous approaches, this chapter will also answer in detail any objection that there is little novelty in this approach to introspection for AI (see Section 8.6). The below survey does not claim to be complete but to present an extensive sample of how AI systems were based on various models.

10.1.1 Definition for "AI Based on Introspection"

As the idea of "an AI design based on introspection" is key to this book's argument, let's define it and look at some examples that fall outside and inside this definition (for definitions of introspection, see Section 7.2).

Y is Based on X

In this context Y, a design for an AI system, is based on an observation X (that could be an introspective observation) iff:

A. There is a causal link from X to Y.
B. X is the dominant influence on the workings of Y, that is, there is as little pollution by some any other factor (such as a prior theoretical commitment) as is practically possible. In our case, of AI based on introspection, this would require acceptance of introspection (X) as legitimate, not to be obfuscated or denied; minimisation of attachment to or influence of any theoretical framework, such as mathematics, logic, or some theory in cognition, psychology, religion, or phenomenology.
C. Corresponding functions are achieved in similar ways (processes, data flows, data structures, temporal order, etc.).
   Introspection (as a basis for AI) further requires:
D. Introspecting, that is, "looking" at or "listening" to one's own *untrained* mental processes (see Section 6.4 for an argument for untrained thought).
E. Proficiency in conceptualising and expressing the contents of this introspective "vision", in text, diagrams, algorithms, or suchlike.
F. Fidelity, that later could be judged (possibly externally) as credibility. Introspection is a type of witness account. The fidelity/credibility of witness accounts in general is discussed in historiography (see Section 10.3.1). For example, a design that never makes a mistake is not credible (as a human model), since humans make mistakes. Another example: A design that fits some theory too well might well be a result of theoretical pollution, see (B) above.

Let's survey the ways this can fail or (just another way of looking at it) how AI development has happened so far, and how these scenarios differ from the above:

10.1.2 Non-human-Like Inspirations

Some algorithms have clear inspirations, which are *not* human, let alone introspective. There is no specific reason to believe these would be good at producing human-like behaviour.

10.1.2.1 Genetic Algorithms (Twice)

The idea of the genetic algorithm (**itself**) has a clear inspiration – a (somewhat naïve) scientific model of biological inheritance and evolution (usually in a sexually reproducing population). This is based on biology (and fulfils A–C), but biology is not introspection (and does not fulfil D–F).

A genetic algorithm can be used to generate an **output**, any information entity for which there is an "objective function". In a specific case, a genetic algorithm can be made to evolve software for any purpose implied by the objective function. Such a successfully evolved design, since it was not made by any person, can be said to not be based on anything. That is not to say that it was not based in some way on the objective function (it was), but the loops and variables inherent in the code produced by the quasi-random processes of a genetic algorithm are bereft of any human design or inspiration at all. This obviously does not fulfil any of A–F.

10.1.2.2 Neural Nets

Similar to the case of the genetic algorithm itself, neural nets are based on biology, so likewise it fulfils A–C, only regarding biology, not introspection.

One could argue that introspectively it "feels like" our mind functions in a manner similar to a neural net in that there are alternating phases of chaos and stability, thereby fulfilling the criteria (D–F) for our experience as revealed by introspection, but

- The neural net's data structure and data flows are not visible to us humans internally, therefore, are not introspective but originate in scientific external observation and simplification of neurons (not output of introspection) – this violates C (Piccinini, 2004).
- The observation that the end result of two processes is similar is not the same as observing the process that produces these end results. Such an observation would be introspection and is lacking here (see more about similar results in Section 10.3.5).

Again, neural nets are based on biology (and fulfil A–C), but biology is not introspection (and does not fulfil D, E–F are debatable).

10.1.3 Human-Like Inspirations (Non-introspective)[1]

Behaviour: An example of building an AI system or robot that was based solely on externally observable human behaviour would be hominid robots in general, and a more specific example would be bipedal walking robots. This approach is scientifically unassailable, as it is based on hardcore observable facts (humans have two legs, knees, etc.) and is reminiscent of behaviourism. The disadvantage is that the behaviours produced by following this inspiration are not sophisticated. Any level of sophistication would require having some sort of mental processing (this was Chomsky's cognitivist argument in his critique of behaviourism (Chomsky, 1959)). Mental processing breaks the behaviouristic framework and has to be based on something other than behaviour as such.

---

[1] See also Section 6.5.

This example fulfils A–C for behaviour, not introspection, and therefore, does not fulfil D–F.

External analysis of human behaviour: One could create a far more sophisticated *model*, like (in natural language) a grammar, and try to base the machine's behaviour on such a model. This is only as good as the underlying model. Our ability, thus far, to model humans is limited. Alternately, one could have models or theories of how the (maybe even entire) human mind works, as researchers attempt in cognitive simulation (Sun, 2008). A–C hold for the abstracted models, D–F do not hold.

Substructure: Some would simulate the brain in its entirety, either at cellular or atomic levels. This approach is currently not feasible. Again, one could have a more abstract theory or how the mind is constituted, like logic, statistical inference, other mathematics, or some form of symbol processing (classic AI). A–C hold for the idealised model (or the entire brain), D–F do not hold. Newell and Simon's (1961a) insistence that their subjects think in "rules" can be construed as an example of this (see Section 10.3.3). A more brazen example is logic-based AI.

10.1.4 Types of Introspection for AI

Within the field of AI, there are several variants of introspection used (moving from the existing to the recommended and beyond).

1. Taking a literal view of sentences of the type to be discussed, and a somewhat idealist metaphysical stance, one could see every conscious human observation as arguably introspective. Saying "*I* see red" or "the measurement shows *me* 97" is introspective. Such **trivial introspection** does not lead to software designs, so there is no "based on" relationship (no A–C).

2. **Programming** is introspective: As we saw in Section 9.3, arguably all programming is introspective – it requires the programmer to imagine themselves as living in world of (say) python features and asking themselves "what would I do", etc.

   This introspection while "putting yourself in the computer's shoes" is introspection on *learnt* skills, the skill of thinking like a computer, a fundamental skill of programming. One cannot introspect in this way unless one knows how to think in terms of code. This specifically violates D's requirement for *untrained* mental processes, and it is not consciously based on introspection at all (A–C, D–F).

   The difference between my advocacy for introspection and this model of programming is subtle, yet clear-cut: Programmers *first* adopt the technological role of "being inside a computer" and then ask "how would I solve that if I were a program", while I advocate asking "how do *I, as I am*, solve that", and only later turning that fully human introspection into technical code.

3. A more general case is introspecting artefacts of culture – "I think **logically**", "I think using words", or even "I think in python" (as above). The general case is "I think using P" where P is a construct found in a certain culture. Though used often in AI, this approach would be the epitome of what this book is *not* aiming for – the terms of the introspections would be western, modern, well trained, and adult rather than anthropic.

Case-Based Reasoning (see Section 11.2) can be seen as an example of AI based on such introspection, in that it operates like a western well-trained administrator, using the best solution for any given problem. Again, this violates D's requirement for introspecting *untrained* mental processes. The problem with trained mental processes is that it gives us information about how *our culture* thinks (or how our culture thinks one *should* think) rather than how we *actually* think.

4. I argue for introspection on *natural* mental processes, not enculturated ones (see Section 6.4). This can be done minimally, by taking a **particular element** of how we think, such as the fuzzy edges of concepts, and building an AI concept around it. This is good as far as it goes, but often is then used again within some well-understood mathematical scheme, such as fuzzy *logic*. The novel idea here (fuzzy concepts) fulfils A–C and D–F, but it is then embedded in a logical-mathematical framework with all its non-anthropic characteristics (one cheer for fuzzy logic, see Section 11.1).

5. I further argue below (in Section 10.3.6) for introspecting **multiple novel elements**, for a more complete model of how our subjective mind works. These elements can be added gradually, interspersed with experimentation for feedback on how each step of the development of the AI design works, and allowing further introspection at each stage, looking at how our own thought processes differ from the model.

6. Note that I am *not* aiming for "Heideggerian correctness". Unlike Dreyfus, one can be agnostic about the correctness (or usefulness for AI) of any particular volume of phenomenological literature. Unlike Dreyfus, I argue that AI practitioners must remain committed to pragmatism, to programmability. So there are two things here: One is that the recommended technique is not married to the idea of "correctness", "precision", or "truth" in general, and the second is that I remain agnostic specifically as to the truth or lack thereof in the phenomenological literature.

So subjectivity is not only necessary for any conscious human activity as suggested by point 1 above but is needed for all programming and has been used by several if not all AI programmers before. But so far, AI researchers have been subjective and did introspection in a bashful "under cover" way (see Sections 8.3 and 8.6). It may well be time to do it consciously and properly, rather than coyly as if hiding from Watson's or Simon's wrath. We surely cannot hope to excel at developing human-like AI while actively pretending *not* to be human, as in cases where the inspiration or basis for the design is non-human or an idealised human.

10.2 The Process of Introspection for AI

In approaching the process of introspecting for AI, one should have an intention to perform the introspection in the spirit recommended here: Not polluting with theories, looking for processes rather than beliefs, etc. Details and examples follow below. For now let's look at the *structure* of the introspection for AI process.

Consider Illustration 10.1, starting at the top (bold terms refer to labels in the diagram). **Human mental activity**, as seen subjectively, is a process, symbolised

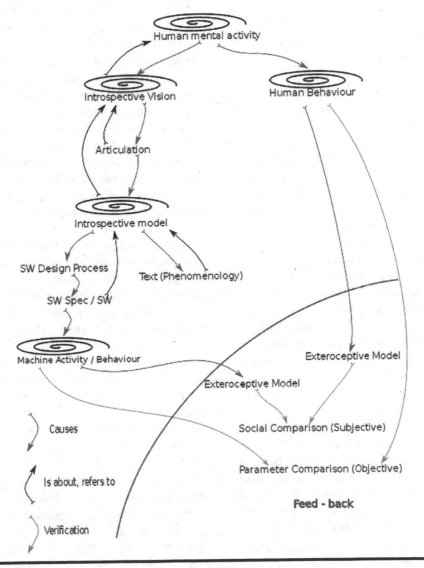

Illustration 10.1   Process of introspection for AI.

here as a spiral, that determines **human behaviour** (red arrows signify causation). **Human mental activity** can be observed by an **introspective vision** (bearing in mind that the use of the term "vision" is metaphoric), which at least partially mirrors the process of the **human mental activity** (hence the spiral here). In this stage, of the "vision", the issue of "looking for" comes to bear, see below.

Next, there is a process of **articulation** that does *not*, in a sense, mirror the original mental process but rather moves away from it – forcing the vision into a more communicable form. Here is where "pollution" is a danger. The process of articulation may be iterative, with the vision being further and better understood with additional attempts at articulation. The **introspective vision** refers to (black arrow) the **human mental activity**. **Articulation** produces an **introspective model** – some concrete idea of how the **human mental activity** appears to work. This model can be explained or expressed using **text**, which would be a phenomenological *report* about the **human mental activity**. We should keep this distinct in our mind from the philosophical tradition of phenomenology. Note that a text is just a string of letters – it is not a machine or a mind or a brain that can carry out a process (hence no spiral). The **introspective model** can also be used by a **software (SW) design process**, involving approximating and digitising, that will produce a **software specification** and ultimately **software**. This software, when run, creates machine behaviour, which hopefully in some approximate sense reproduces the original **human mental process** or at least the **introspective vision** (hence the spiral).

The output of this entire process can later be compared for feedback purposes to actual **human behaviour** in two ways (see area under blue arc). One alternative is objective **parameter comparison** – observed directly (perhaps even mechanically) in **human behaviour** and the **machine activity**. A second feedback method can involve people observing both the human and machine activity, and producing their **exteroceptive models** of the two activities, and compare them subjectively. Such a process is similar to (most construals of) the Turing test.

Note that there is no necessity for one person to be involved in the entire process. One person can have the **introspective vision**, do the **articulation**, and express his **introspective model** as **text** (written or spoken), and another person (or several) can engage in the **software design process**, etc.

Note also that the entire process can be an iterative process (not just the articulation), where refinements of AI designs are made by further introspection, modelling, etc. Introspection can be refined in the sense of adding details, sometimes even changing the fundamentals of the picture. For example, a trivial (non-AI-related) introspection could be "I think it will rain today". A deeper observation of a similar situation can yield something like "By my experience these clouds don't mean much either way, so I can't really say, but I fear being caught out and getting wet, and even more I fear being blamed by my friends for not saying it would rain. So I say it will rain even though I don't know". Notice that the underlying dominant influence has shifted from *thinking* (that it will rain) to being socially *afraid*.

Another way that introspection can be refined is by the development of terminology. Once one is versed in terminology (in any field, I see no reason why introspection should be an exception), one can describe more using less words. This ability to economise and increase precision in language, useful in any case of description, is of particular importance in introspection because the observation happens in the same mind where the phenomena being observed are occurring, and the danger of interference between the two processes is ever-present (and to a degree unavoidable) (Schwitzgebel, 2012).

10.3 Comments on the Process of Introspection for AI

10.3.1 Introspection Is a Witness Account

When one reports on one's introspection, one gives a testimony about what one had "seen". There is every reason to expect that any known issues of reliability in testimony would arise in the case of introspection, so it is worth summarising one of the canonical sources on the technique of writing history, "The Historian's Craft" (Bloch, 1953). Bloch observed that believing everything that is presented as evidence is naïve, but also *mis*trusting *all* evidence from a source willy-nilly just because some of the evidence presented by that source is questionable – would also be equally naïve. Often fashionable inaccuracies are accepted as truth, and one must especially be careful with "common sense", since first common sense is nothing other than the fashionable prejudices of a certain society, and moreover, common sense changes over time, usually with no fanfare. Often convenient rumours are not denied because they suit some agenda.

The notion of "sincerity" has a very broad and dangerous meaning, it can incorporate many of the above prejudices – "many witnesses deceive themselves in all good faith" (Ibid.). People are often unaware of the simplest things around them, such as the number of windows in a familiar room. In our case, introspectors may need to practise in order to see the obvious about their actual thought processes, since they are so familiar.

In history, the determination of the precise cause of an event is difficult in the extreme, but that is also the case in chemistry: We do not know which molecule in the mixture made the whole thing explode. We can only describe the antecedent conditions, not the exact cause. Also, no witness's testimony is equally reliable on all matters but, in our case of introspection, for *technology*, the *precise* truth is of less consequence.

Witness accounts vary by the societal context. But even errors or forgeries, once detected, can tell us much about the society that produced them. Ideas that prevail in a society have great impact, like the belief in German cunning in First World War France that led to an overestimation of their intelligence capabilities. Likewise, if you look at the naïve introspection of the pioneers of AI (see Section 8.3.1), you will see that they attest that they think mathematically. This confabulation in itself is a testimony to the mathematical prejudices of the scientific community in their times (a prejudice that remains with us today). Also in the case of the intuitions of cognitive psychology, testimony tells us often not what the witness saw, but what his society thinks it natural to see (Nisbett & Wilson, 1977).

Summarising some of the wisdom of historiography as it applies to our case of introspection for technological human-like AI:

1. There is no mechanical logic of critical examination of testimony. But in technology, we do not need a clear mechanical criterion for *truth* as such. We only need some social (perhaps economic) criteria for *utility*, and we have some – empirical testing and market economics – see Section 10.5.
2. About the temptation to throw away all of subjectivity as non-scientific, we can adopt Bloch's advice that "It is always disagreeable to say 'I do not know. I cannot know.' It must not be said except after an energetic, even a desperate search" (Bloch, 1953, pp. 59–60). But even when we despair of getting the correct and precise answer, we have a "get out of jail" card – since we are dealing in a technology that aims to approximate, we can interpolate the voids in our knowledge (see Section 10.3.5).

10.3.2 Looking/Listening For

In acting in different capacities, or in different roles, we also *look for or listen for* different things. An example of the different types of "looking for" could be looking at the floor for a dropped coin vs examining the floor for structural damage. The externally observable actions of surveying the surface can be identical, but the intent, the mental activity, and attention are entirely different. This is true also of our internal looking/listening in introspection. As Schwitzgebel (2012, sec. 1.2) notes, we can introspect either attitudes such as beliefs and desires or conscious experiences such as emotions and images. The selection of what we listen for is volitional, we can choose to listen, together with the classic-AI people (especially the knowledge engineers) for beliefs and the application of rules, like in the case of the General Problem Solver (GPS) (Newell & Simon, 1961b). We can also focus on lower mechanisms.

Any report (not only introspective reports) beyond describing the subject matter also addresses a specific **audience**. On a trivial level, a bilingual person will issue his reports in one language at a time, the language of his audience. But also, any report will be couched in terminology that is expected to make sense to the audience: Stream of consciousness, data and algorithms, or beliefs and doubts, whatever the reporter thinks the audience expects. Here is one of the places where Simon and Dreyfus completely talk past each other: Simon is an objective scientist in the tradition of Watson, while Dreyfus is a phenomenologist, committed to subjectivity. They both listen for different things in their research and address different communities.

So when we watch our own mental processes or listen to ourselves thinking, we are always looking for something, and we look to issue some report (if only for ourselves) – there is no neutral observation. What should we look for? In what terms should a report be made? We are looking for AI designs. A design (in this context) is a formalisation of a process of data processing, so we are looking for **information-processing processes** in our mind. *That* is what we are looking for. But there are many pitfalls in the way: Our favourite theory (e.g. that humans are rational) can interpose itself into our observations. It is important to "bracket", or suspend, our beliefs and try to see the mental processes as they are (Gallagher & Zahavi, 2012). One of the most important things is "keeping our eye on the ball" of human thought as we truly experience it (insofar as possible) rather than how our culture might think our thoughts *should be.* That is how this approach differs from classic AI. However, we also need to "keep another eye" on programmability – or we will fall into the same trap as Dreyfus and his phenomenology, producing wonderful reports of no technological application (Dreyfus, 1965).

A possible question arises of how can the encultured mind look for or at the un-encultured mind? There are two answers here:

1. The first answer is that there is a category error in this question, as if the "encultured" and the "un-encultured" minds are two different entities "inside our head", and there is a problem for one to access the other. The reality is that being encultured or not is a matter of degree or a matter of level. In a sense, all we have is the un-encultured level – and it goes to great lengths to "behave itself", that is, to produce behaviour that is socially acceptable, encultured. So it is one and the same mind, just two levels – there is no access problem.

2. The second answer is that we should observe the un-encultured mind "carefully". We should use all our skill, refinement, patience, openness, etc. (all encultured properties we hopefully have) in order to listen to the un-encultured mind as truthfully as possible and use our (hopefully) good command of language and writing to produce as accurate and honest a report as we can.

10.3.3 Pollution

As we saw above, our listening determines what *kind* of introspection we do (beliefs, processes, sensations). It also colours the content of what we detect in introspection. Listening while being committed to some prior theory or model can lead to pollution of our introspection by our prior commitments.

An extreme example of what I call "polluting" introspection with prior theoretical commitments (in the context of an experiment) is beautifully recorded by Newell and Simon (1961a). This paper presents an experiment where the authors asked a student to solve a formal problem (while "thinking aloud", see Section 7.3.1), given certain symbols and manipulation rules. They "asked the subject to talk aloud about what he was doing – 'what he was thinking about'", and they recorded the entire session. Only a few lines into the (quoted) session protocol the experimenters ask the subject "Applying what rule?", rather than a more neutral instruction such as "What are you thinking now?" The assumption that the subject is thinking in terms of *rules* is polluting the evidence, even when the explicit instructions were to report *all* their thinking.

However, the pollution can be more subtle and self-induced. I would suspect that anyone saying something like "For me mathematics has always been the language of thought. I don't know precisely what I mean by that... Mathematics – this sort of non-verbal thinking – is my language of discovery" (Simon, 1996a, p. 106), is not being honest with himself or with us as his audience. Was mathematics always his "language of thought"? Even when he was 5 years old? Again, in introspecting for anthropic AI we need to get behind our "western, modern, well-trained and adult" thinking and aim for the underlying mechanisms – these cannot be explicit mathematics.

How can we defend against such pollution? First, we can make an effort to not project our theories or other cultural artefacts onto our introspection. This can be done, *inter alia*, by noticing our theories "coming to mind" and either setting them aside calmly, as a quiet choice, or turning our attention to how our thought processes specifically *deviate* from what such a theory might expect.

Next we can critique our introspections after the fact: Would such a mechanism produce the results we observe? As an example, if "mathematics" as such were indeed someone's entire system of thought, it would not produce mistakes, but we all do make mistakes. Ultimately, we need no *steadfast guarantee* against such pollution. Different introspections, good and bad, pristine and polluted, will simply produce a larger variety of software designs. These designs make no truth claims but are only candidates for a technology. As mentioned above, let a thousand flowers bloom.

For anyone who still feels that the quality should be improved, there are detailed guides from the era before introspection fell out of favour (Schwitzgebel, 2004), and there is a whole field of modern research (Froese, 2011; Jack & Roepstorff, 2003). Again, these may be useful, but there is no necessity in taking them too seriously. Mistakes are acceptable – luckily for us, we are operating in the context of discovery, *for technology*.

For an explanation why introspection would be a good source of ideas for anthropic AI designs, see Chapter 9. *Pristine* (non-polluted) introspection is better because the pollutions come from cultural artefacts, and we are aiming specifically for anthropic AI.

Again, somewhat polluted evidence is not catastrophic, since we are exploring the space of possible AI designs. But in aiming for novel anthropic designs, we should at least try to avoid such unnecessary interference from over-optimistic rationalistic theories. A useful distinction in avoiding the tried, tested, and tired theories of yesteryear is the distinction between knowing how and knowing that (see Section 6.7). The very idea that "knowing that" is a fundamental part of thinking is a western, modern, adult notion.

10.3.4 Introspection: Is It Above or Below the Culture Line?

There is another problem or seeming contradiction: When we introspect, often we come up with cultural products, like "I use mathematics" (to paraphrase Simon and others). But aiming at building anthropic AI, we should look for the mechanisms that are *below* the "culture line" – for the basic *human* abilities and skills that *underpin* culture (but see Section 6.5.1, where I cast doubt on the very concept of "layers" or "levels" in the mind).

Introspection, as Nisbett and Wilson argued, shows us the *products* of some unconscious, innate processes, so in a sense we can see *what* we are thinking but not *how*. Here again I must protest that in terms of technology this is not a problem: In seeing "what" we think, with the ever-better resolution of practised introspection, aiming always to see more, we will have enough of a picture of *what* is going on to interpolate (below).

So are we introspecting at the cultural or subcultural level? Insofar as possible, we aim to introspect at that "boundary", but again insisting too much on exactness here is a fool's errand: It is not the distinctions we are ultimately after, it is the technologies.

10.3.5 Interpolation and Approximation

10.3.5.1 The Holes in Introspection

The consensus in cognitive science seems to be that introspection may tell us *what* is being thought about but not *how* this thinking is accomplished (Nisbett & Wilson, 1977).

This is seen as a problem for introspection, but that problem is in using introspection for the science of psychology, rather than for technology. If we know only the outline of *what* is accomplished without the *how*, we can substitute whatever technical trick we have (in our skills as programmers) to achieve the same in a computer. For example, we do not fully understand how long-term memory works in humans, and the introspection that "I just recalled my first day in school, the weather was dreadful!" – does not help us explain *how* the memories are stored in the brain. But in technology, we can be far more relaxed – if we need some long-term store of information, we can use an SQL database. Here we see the "cash value" of the insistence that technology and science have different criteria for truth. We need not obsess about the true mechanism of memory together with the cognitive psychologists – we can just go ahead and write code. The gaps between the different moments in introspection ("trying to recall… recalled!") are a problem for science and not for technology, for psychology and not for AI.

The proposal of using introspection in AI design is not a proposal for a new "do-all" technique like expert systems or "deep learning" with which often are deployed as an entire solution. My proposal is to use introspection to design systems that use and come on top of any and all previous technologies. This is very much like Minsky's "scruffy" AI (Minsky, 1991). So we should use introspection for the overall design and perhaps for some of the components – but as technologists we should not shy away from using existing techniques as part of the design.

Note that also when humans teach each other skills (like making a cappuccino with an espresso machine), the teacher does not teach how to move one's hand or how to lift the milk canister. The assumption is always that more basic skills that can be used *pre-exist*. In AI, some of the more basic skills may be implemented using an introspection-based algorithm, some can be implemented using some other AI, and some can just be hard-coded.

10.3.5.2 Opportunistic Approximation

When we need to implement some mechanism gleaned from introspection, we often do not have enough information on what the mechanism does *precisely*. For example, we humans may forget something or overlook the best option in some fraction of the times we try to achieve a task. We can use crude approximation, like "50%", and later tune that parameter if the result is not a good match of the observed introspection or behaviour. Moreover, we can sometimes match a phenomenal process that needs to happen "occasionally" with some computational process that would be expensive (say in CPU time). An example of that is given in Section 12.3.5. These are just conveniences, and as long as the AI works and produces credible behaviour, they are OK. Again, we are not doing science.

10.3.5.3 Analogue Cannot Arise Out of Digital

An objection may arise that the subtlety and fluidity of our subjective mind cannot be captured by the 0s and 1s of a computer (this is similar to Dreyfus's objections). Though it may be true that humans are essentially analogue and computers are essentially digital[2] and therefore cannot be the same, we still can approximate analogue phenomena to an arbitrary precision, especially with the current availability of virtually unlimited computation power "in the cloud". Just as we can implement floating-point numbers as substitutes to real numbers, and we can add precision by adding bits, and just like we can simulate the earth's atmosphere for weather forecasts by simulating the physical conditions in "air cells", so we can make an approximation of the fluidities of human subjective experience.

10.3.5.4 Being Analogue Does Not Mean It Is Not Digital

On the contrary, one could speculate that maybe humans' nonideal, **informal behaviour is nonetheless produced by an underlying ideal mechanism**, perhaps

---

[2] Brian Cantwell Smith would protest that computers are in the world, subject to the same physics, and are only "ideally" digital. Though interesting, this point does not affect the argument here.

in a similar way that deterministic behaviour by a computer can be used to simulate and predict seemingly chaotic systems, such as the weather. My response is as follows:

1. It is highly unlikely that there is such perfect order as Case-Based Reasoning (see Section 11.2) or Intel processors underneath our rather non-formal experience of ourselves dealing with the world. There seems to be nothing in the brain that operates digitally or at a sufficient frequency to "simulate" our informal experiences.
2. If there were even a likelihood of such an underlying order, then the onus to show that such an order exists would surely be of those who propose its existence and not on those who deny it (by Occam's razor or in analogy to Russell's teapot (Russell, 1952)).
3. Regardless of whether such an order ultimately exists underneath the seeming informality, such a mechanism for producing chaos out of order is not visible to us in any form that can be used to base technology on it.

10.3.6 *Multiple Iterations, Multiple Mechanisms*

In using introspection as a basis for AI, we may introspect even briefly, not too thoroughly, stop and implement the model we came up with, and then come back and refine our introspection and our model again, and then refine the code. There is no necessity to produce a complete tome of phenomenology before we start coding (unlike Dreyfus).

As we will see in the examples, (one could argue that) fuzzy logic was based on introspection, saying that the boundaries of concepts are not clear-cut but fuzzy. Zadeh did not deepen this introspection nor did he broaden it. Deepening it would mean further exploring the ways that concepts behave in our subjective experience and broadening it would have to do with adjacent mechanisms, say memory or action choice.

Zadeh used introspection for this one element and fell back on to logic, mathematics, and the pre-established tradition of expert systems. It seems likely that if we want to create anthropic AI, we will need to introspect multiple mechanisms and *not* include any artefacts of a specific culture, like mathematics or logic. We most probably need multiple novel elements, conjoined in a way that respects our introspective observations, not some "neat" architecture (Minsky, 1991). These elements can be added gradually, interspersed with experimentation for feedback on how each step of the development of the AI design works, and allowing further introspection at each stage, looking at how our own thought processes differ from the model.

10.3.7 *Personnel*

In a sense, this book flies in the face of the traditional division of skills and mindsets between the hard sciences (STEM) and the humanities and also is distinctly non-cooperative with psychology in its quest to become an exact science. But this is not just a theoretical point: In terms of personnel, if one wants to develop anthropic AI using introspection, perhaps STEM education and programming skills are not the principal skills that are needed. If indeed introspection is key, there is a need for people who are good at that. I would wager that people with a sense of poetry, drama, literature, etc. may be useful members of a team developing AI. Such a project needs people who are more at home with the soliloquy than with the compiler (Snow, 1964). We have done mathematics and cognitive theory-based AI for long enough. It is time to try something radically different, rather than "returning to cognitive science" (Langley, 2006).

That may have been a little overstated. In any team where software is developed, programmers are key. But the "architects" of the software must be informed by introspection rather than by the latest software development fad. It would of course be a good idea to have the entire team be composed of people who are good introspectors, knowledgeable about all exiting AI techniques, and also good programmers. It is unlikely that any team will manage to recruit more than one or two of these fully interdisciplinary workers, if that. Instead, it is enough that the introspectors have a vague idea of programming, so that they produce models that can be at least approximated into some software design. The software architects, doing the design, should at least have a healthy respect for the introspection process but need to have a fully professional grasp of programming, so that the programmers would fully understand what is required software-wise. Again, "doing subjectivity" or introspection is not one thing, a box to be ticked, but is an ongoing and iterative process. This should not be taken lightly.

Interdisciplinary thinking is not just desirable to "compete with the Russians" as Snow (1964) demanded. Interdisciplinary work is a positive requirement for developing anthropic AI. These different disciplines may be found in the same person or in a team that works well together.

10.4 ■ Project Expectations

Consider the (currently impractical) idea of building AI by simulating every cell and interconnection in an entire human brain (as in the blue-brain project (Markram, 2006)). Since the AI would be constructed according to some scientific model of the brain that would initially be quite inaccurate, we should not expect the mind emerging out of such a simulated "brain" to necessarily be sane, of sound intelligence, or interested in communicating with us humans. This arises from many possible causes: Many parameters will be inaccurate, the simulated brain would hardly undergo a normal social development, etc. (Idan Segev, personal communication, 2011). In such a set-up, we would be delighted if we get a mind capable of *any* learning in even very few of the cases.

Similarly, in an AI system that is sufficiently "low level" even if not as low as the cell level, we should expect a relatively *low success rate* in engaging with the environment in a way that would be meaningful *to us*. In aiming for anthropic, that is, subcultural AI, we are in the danger zone, courting those difficulties. Perhaps, we will need two distinct phases of development – the one where the anthropic model is being developed "for its own sake", brought to a functional level "in the laboratory", and a later "implementation" phase where only the better specimens of the original model are actually used in implementing practical technology. Only in this implementation phase would a normal technical evaluation make sense.

10.5 Testing and Evaluation

Recall that the purpose of using introspection is both to generate a more anthropic AI design and to broaden the bases for AI development. As a technology, anthropic AI must ultimately pass muster as being fit for purpose, workable, and marketable. However, in the development stage, if one is interested in how anthropic their technology is, the following points may be of use.

The purpose of anthropic, non-acculturated AI is to create human-like systems that can learn as flexibly as humans are flexible, without being pre-committed to a specific way of doing things. So we are interested in how human-like an AI system is, compared to other systems.

A conservative evaluation of any design should be empirical. As alluded to in Section 10.2, any evaluation can follow an objective or a subjective (quantitative) path. Further (and less conservatively), some qualitative feedback may be of use.

- In the objective path, both humans and introspective-based systems are put in similar circumstances, and measurements are taken of various parameters. The more **similar** the system is to the human, the better it models a human. This is similar to cognitive simulation in method though not in intent – again science vs technology.
- The subjective path for evaluating an introspective system would involve producing (say) a video of the performance of various algorithms (and perhaps also of humans tackling a task) and asking a sample of disinterested observers to give their impression of "how human or machine-like" each video seems. The data collected would be processed using standard interview-data methodologies, as in the social sciences.
- Qualitative feedback could also be of interest, collecting the comments of the observers as feedback for the developers.

The choice of evaluation methodology would be influenced by the aims and circumstances of the project.

It's high time for some full-cycle examples of AI based on introspection.

Chapter 11

Examples

We will start with examples from existing artificial intelligence (AI) and move on to novel algorithms. The first example, fuzzy logic, will demonstrate a minimal case of using introspection for AI. The second, Case-Based Reasoning (CBR), will show a more developed example of how this design could have evolved using introspection (though historically, it is not clear whether introspection was involved). The third example will be "AIF0", my first experiment in developing introspection-based AI, followed by AIF1 (a failed effort) and (in the next chapter) AIF2 – a successful and interesting design.

Throughout the presentation of these examples, one must recall that the concern being addressed is technological, not scientific, so the very question "is it correct?" is less to the point than "does it work?" This calls for a few clarifications:

1. The introspection data presented in the (later) examples is derived just from ***my* introspection**. I present it "as is" without any attempt to argue for it, amongst other reasons because it is not clear what sort of argument *can* be presented for introspective data. Regardless of the accuracy or veracity of the introspective reports below, what I am arguing for is the *methodology* that uses introspection as a basis for AI designs. Anyone can use this methodology to design AI based on their own introspections (see point 7 in Section 8.7).

2. Building on that point, since the examples presented are only *examples*, from one person's introspection, no claim is being made that the resulting designs are **good** in and of themselves, and therefore, I will not present comparative data trying to prove that any of these example designs are better than any existing design by some objective criteria. Any competitive evaluation would fall outside the scope of this volume. The claim is only that it is ***plausible*** that they would be more human-like, by using an anthropic (Chapter 6), introspection-based design process. The focus of this book is showing a new

methodology, a different way of *developing* anthropic AI based on the deliberate use of introspection. I am not arguing here that the example designs are fit for any specific purpose, only that they are *likely* to be more anthropic and demonstrate the fecundity of the approach.

3. The focus in AI design is **technological**, and the criteria of success for technology are lower than for scientific truth (see Section 5.1.3). However, once a design exists (regardless of its source), a model based on such a design could be proposed as a scientific model (theory) in psychology, similar to how some simple neural networks are proposed as theories in cognitive psychology (Altmann & Dienes, 1999). People who want to resurrect subjective psychology from Watson's blows may hold hope for such theories. This should be contrasted with Wheeler's (2005) approach, which sees AI as "the intellectual heart of cognitive science" – he is interested in the science primarily. Here it is technology first. That changes the level of truth we need to ascribe to our models and allows much more freedom. We are not doing science here, in any case not directly.

The first two examples, fuzzy logic and CBR, are given as a "warm up", to illustrate some points. The historical evidence as to the degree to which introspection was used to develop these designs is very partial and at times contradictory. Rather than worry about these historical points, I will present them *as if* there was indeed a deliberate use of introspection in both cases, as examples for: (1) how introspection could be used, in a minimal way, and (2) how we can step away from the boolean, overly rational AI. The algorithms are also worth mentioning as "neighbours" of the original designs to be presented later.

Environment

In all the following examples other than the first (fuzzy logic), the environment is a game-like situation, where the AI can take actions in the environment (from a predefined set) and gets feedback in the form of a score.

Actions come from the range of available actions that can be performed by the machine.

The outcomes of the machine's operation are given as **score** inputs. The scores allow measurement of progress towards one or more goals and/or adherence to one or more principles. Scores may be provided from the environment or from a subjective source such as a human observer.

11.1 Fuzzy Logic

Fuzzy logic shows, in one isolated and clear case, how introspective AI could work and how it did in a *minimal* way. The fuzzy notion arose from Lotfi Zadeh's (1965) self-observation that in human concepts, the boundary between membership and non-membership of a class (or set, or concept) is not a square wave or all-or-nothing affair.

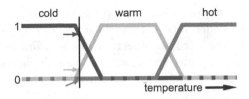

Illustration 11.1   Fuzzy logic. Source: Wikimedia.

The "fuzzy" notion is the idea that things need not be 100% members or non-members of a set, or category, or concept. The example in Illustration 11.1 shows that a specific temperature, say 10°C (shown here as the vertical line) can be seen as being 90% cold and 10% warm. So the temperature "10°C" is only a part-member in the concept or set "cold" and likewise for the concept or set "warm". One of the applications of fuzzy concepts is in formulating rules for expert systems, allowing words like "a little", "somewhat", "very", etc. to be given numerical meanings, and expert-system rules to say things like "when the boiler is somewhat warm, do X". This is a language closer to the (human) expert's language. The eventual decision processes (de-fuzzyfing) vary between implementations (McNeill & Freiberger, 1994). To clarify the terminology, fuzzy *sets* allow parsing of notions such as "somewhat warm", while fuzzy *logic* is a design for combing such notions, similar to standard logic's AND, OR, etc.

To see how fuzzy logic can be seen as a minimal case of "introspection-based AI", let's trace the process of turning an introspection into an AI design using the terminology of Section 10.2, explicitly referred to here in **bold type**. Zadeh (supposedly) aimed to represent the way he *actually* thinks (phenomenologically) rather than the way that a logical, mathematical, or scientific mindset would urge him to think (this is the intention to introspect). Out of his **introspective vision**, Zadeh chose to concentrate on (or **listen for**) the boundaries of concepts or "sets" as he called them in his paper (1965). Regardless of any complexities in his introspective vision, he chose to **articulate** his **model** of his observation as allowing each object to be a member of any concept or set to an *extent*. This extent is expressible as a percentage or as a real number between 0 (non-member) and 1 (full member).

Later (in the **software design** phase), Zadeh chose to approximate the boundaries of the concepts using simple mathematical curves, such as the straight linear function seen in Illustration 11.1. The compromise involved with this approximation for the sake of **programming** is clear – the diagonal lines in the diagram above are unabashedly mathematical (this is a case of opportunistic approximation, see Section 10.3.5.2) and therefore not precisely human or introspective but are still significantly more representative of the human situation than assuming an all-on-nothing (square wave) membership of a category.

Again, we should not err (with Dreyfus) into an excessive belief in phenomenology or the phenomenological literature: The idea is to introspect in order to create usable designs in a finite (development) time. It is fine to approximate. On the other hand, Zadeh is an excellent example of how one point of introspection is taken and then embedded in a mathematical framework (set theory, logic…). Zadeh is not doing full-blooded introspection – he is committing one little introspective sin, so to speak, and hurries back to the safe shores of mathematical orthodoxy. So yes, he used introspection as a basis for AI but did so sparingly and shyly (see Section 8.3).

Some may object to any discussion of fuzzy logic, in that it has been shown to be a specific case of statistical AI and therefore of no lasting contribution. That would be missing the point here – here, we are discussing the method of invention. The fuzzy notion, like most other notions, is limited, perhaps already obsolete. It is here to demonstrate a minimal usage of introspection, and how it was done shyly.

11.2 Case-Based Reasoning

CBR has its roots in scripts, dynamic memory, and other cognitive theories. One could tell a (perhaps reconstructed, perhaps speculative) story about how CBR was arrived at, in order to illustrate the point of introspection for AI. As we saw in Section 8.3.1 (in an interview with Turkle), Roger Schank explicitly admitted to using introspection – however, he expunged any mention of introspection from his published AI papers (Nilsson, 2010, pp. 400–402; Schank & Abelson, 1977; Schank, 1982).

CBR is of interest because it exemplifies how some of AI *was* based (rather poorly) on introspection, and because it is a stepping stone towards presenting the next, more interesting (and original) examples.

CBR[1] attempts to solve every problem (or situation) the agent may encounter by looking into a database of previously encountered problems and solutions and selecting the best solution available. In some cases, the solution is adapted for the current case, before it is executed. The slogan for CBR is the four "Re"s: "retrieve, reuse, revise, retain". This design has had some success and has many variants.

A reconstructed/speculative story on the origin of CBR could go like this: While playing the **role** of competent administrators (see Section 9.3.1), the inventors asked themselves "what would *I* do?", "How do *I* solve problems?" They came up with the answer of reusing solutions that have been accumulated

---

[1] Some argue that CBR is a methodology rather than an algorithm, since in its purest form it advocated only the 4 "Re"s, retrieve, reuse, revise, retain. The details on how to do each of these steps remained unspecified. However, if one wanted to be pedantic, any algorithm that includes even something as simple as "add 1 to a" is underspecified, in that the exact behaviour of a in terms of overflow is left unspecified. In our case here this point is not so important. The term "methodology" is used in this book for an approach for developing *new* AI designs, and the term "design" for algorithms and families thereof (I. Watson, 1999).

in their own memory from previous encounters. The design does not specify where the original database comes from or how new solutions are generated for problems never encountered before – again like a competent administrator, the assumption is that the computer has already seen all the relevant cases and can make minor adaptations. Hence, at its most primitive, CBR is little more than a directory of solutions.

Note this latest term, "**solutions**", which suggests that the following assumptions are being made:

1. That the world in which the agent is operating is made of distinct "problems", presented one by one.
2. These problems admit of solutions, that these solutions are clearly and obviously distinct from non-solutions, which would be labelled *wrong* and as useless behaviour.
3. That the database already has such a solution in store for each problem to be encountered or a solution that can be readily adapted for any presented problem (the "revise" stage).

So we see that CBR is made in the image of an idealised, rational administrator. Solutions are distinct from non-solutions, there is no matter of degree of "goodness"; where all the assumptions of this design are correct in the world in which the AI operates, then the design would produce ideal behaviour based on the available information – bounded rationality (Simon, 1955). There is nothing wrong with all that, except it does not meet *our* agenda of producing anthropic AI.

The assumption that solutions are clearly and immediately separable from non-solutions is unrealistic and will fade away as we progress to a more introspective designs, such as the following.

11.3 AIF0[2]

This example demonstrates moving away from the mathematical towards the more introspective. It is a first step of technical novelty, with two more to come. As a point of nomenclature, I will use "select" for picking a *subset* out of a bigger set (a bit like SQL uses that word) and will use "choose" for the *one* final decision of an algorithm in a specific round.

I will describe the process of introspection (the contents of introspections are underlined), and the processes of software design, running and results, and will later discuss the implications of this example.

---

[2] Artificial Intelligence Framework.

11.3.1 Introspection

One could **observe** that in everyday life, <u>I often use suboptimal solutions for problems</u>, not because I have not encountered a better solution and not because it is "good enough" (Simon's satisficing) but just because it is not in my nature to always do the perfectly correct thing – either <u>through ignorance, confusion (mis-execution),</u> <u>or through playfulness or exploration</u> (remember we are *not* aiming for emulating the well-trained scientist or soldier). So in terms of introspection, <u>I do things that I</u> <u>know (or hope, or believe) will work best, but I do not necessarily choose the best of</u> <u>the options I know of. Sometimes I just guess, or do something new, even if I know</u> <u>a good response to a situation. I also sometimes mis-execute my intentions.</u>

Here is an **articulation** of the following innovations over CBR, a **model**:

1. Not one "solution" is chosen, but several are selected
2. One of these is chosen with some random element.
3. The very notion of "solution" (as in a 1-0 solution-or-not sense) is gone and is replaced by the notion of "the best few we know". Therefore, the assumption that we have a correct solution for every prospective problem or even one "good-enough" solution is relaxed and replaced with "the best few we have".
4. Unlike CBR, where "the" solution (or "the best" solution) is chosen and used, in AIF0, there are the following steps. First, multiple similar cases are selected (perhaps up to some threshold of similarity), and next, these similar cases are sorted by expected outcome, derived from the episodes' score as found in the memory bank. In a relatively rare case, a random action is performed.
5. A score, or feedback, is collected from the environment.

11.3.2 Implementation

In the process of **software design,** we must approximate the introspective model using a software mechanism, so in this case we can use the following approximation for fallibility and playfulness of the human: Use the best "case" solution only half of the time, and the second best "case" in another 1/4 of the cases, and so on for the next 1/8 and 1/16 of the cases. In the last 1/16 of the cases, we can have the software choose an output at random from the repertoire of possible responses (this is an example of "interpolating" a mechanism, see Sections 10.3.5.1 and 10.3.5.2). This mechanism facilitates learning, so this design can bootstrap its own knowledge bank, without any prior knowledge.

Pseudocode:

■ For every situation:
 – Select all similar situations from the past (similarity can be crudely defined as equality for the time being)
 – Of these similar solutions, select the top best (outcome) four cases that were used and sort them by score

- — *i* ← first case
- — While *i* is a valid case
  - • Flip a coin (50% chance)
  - • If heads
    - ■ Choose the *i*'th case (go to label "DONE")
  - • else
    - ■ *i* ← next case
- — When the "while loop" ends, choose a random action
- — DONE:
- — Perform the chosen action in the "world" (which is probably a micro-world, simulated), collect a score, store the case, and repeat from the start for next input.

All that is left of the original introspection (that was not in CBR) is

1. That we select *multiple* cases
2. Choose from these *non-deterministically*
3. On an ongoing basis, allow completely random choices in a fraction of cases.

This is a stepping stone, and this is a technological project, so adding three features at a time is a reasonable step.

Note also that the whole issue of "**similarity**" is being brushed neatly into a subroutine (as it is in CBR). The following example will use identity as a crude form of similarity.

11.3.3 *Example Run, Statistics*

This algorithm was run in a world consisting of a game where each input, *A*, *B*, *C*, or *D* should be matched with 1, 2, 3, or 4 as output, respectively. A successful match scored 1, an unsuccessful match scored 0.

Each "case" starts with the algorithm getting an input of either *A*, *B*, *C*, or *D*. The algorithm produces an answer, 1, 2, 3, or 4. Below is a trace from an example run.

Explanation of the trace: Please follow as an example the highlighted line number 45. Every iteration number is followed by the input ('*A*'–'*D*'), then the four "best matches" (selected options) are presented (represented by their iteration number) from which the algorithm will later choose. These four "best matches" are represented by the "iteration number", so in our (highlighted) example, the input "*C*" is similar to all previous instances of a "*C*" input, and these are sorted by score, and the best case is 18, followed by 19, 36, and 39 (in all of which the program scored 1). Note that in the first few lines of the trace, where there are no precedents to follow, an index of "−1" is shown. Next in the output line is the index of the chosen option, 0–3 (for the four possibilities) or *R*, if a random action was selected. Note that when there are few options available (near the top), then the random option is common. Next the output is shown and the score.

```
ITER  Inp.  Options to consider (4), selected      Score
   0, in B: ops(   -1,    -1,    -1,    -1)-> R out 4, S= 0
   1, in C: ops(   -1,    -1,    -1,    -1)-> R out 1, S= 0
   2, in B: ops(    0,    -1,    -1,    -1)-> R out 3, S= 0
   3, in A: ops(   -1,    -1,    -1,    -1)-> R out 2, S= 0
   4, in D: ops(   -1,    -1,    -1,    -1)-> R out 3, S= 0
   5, in A: ops(    3,    -1,    -1,    -1)-> R out 2, S= 0
   6, in C: ops(    1,    -1,    -1,    -1)-> R out 4, S= 0
   7, in B: ops(    0,     2,    -1,    -1)-> 1 out 3, S= 0
   8, in C: ops(    1,     6,    -1,    -1)-> 1 out 4, S= 0
   9, in D: ops(    4,    -1,    -1,    -1)-> R out 2, S= 0
  10, in A: ops(    3,     5,    -1,    -1)-> 0 out 2, S= 0
  11, in D: ops(    4,     9,    -1,    -1)-> R out 1, S= 0
  12, in A: ops(    3,     5,    10,    -1)-> R out 2, S= 0
  13, in B: ops(    0,     2,     7,    -1)-> 0 out 4, S= 0
  14, in B: ops(    0,     2,     7,    13)-> 0 out 4, S= 0
  15, in A: ops(    3,     5,    10,    12)-> 0 out 2, S= 0
  16, in B: ops(    0,     2,     7,    13)-> 1 out 3, S= 0
  17, in B: ops(    0,     2,     7,    13)-> 2 out 3, S= 0
  18, in C: ops(    1,     6,     8,    -1)-> R out 3, S= 1
  19, in C: ops(   18,     1,     6,     8)-> 0 out 3, S= 1
  20, in D: ops(    4,     9,    11,    -1)-> 2 out 1, S= 0
...
  35, in B: ops(    0,     2,     7,    13)-> 0 out 4, S= 0
  36, in C: ops(   18,    19,     1,     6)-> 0 out 3, S= 1
  37, in B: ops(    0,     2,     7,    13)-> 1 out 3, S= 0
  38, in A: ops(    3,     5,    10,    12)-> 1 out 2, S= 0
  39, in C: ops(   18,    19,    36,     1)-> 0 out 3, S= 1
  40, in D: ops(    4,     9,    11,    20)-> 1 out 2, S= 0
  41, in A: ops(    3,     5,    10,    12)-> 0 out 2, S= 0
  42, in C: ops(   18,    19,    36,    39)-> 1 out 3, S= 1
  43, in B: ops(    0,     2,     7,    13)-> 0 out 4, S= 0
  44, in C: ops(   18,    19,    36,    39)-> 0 out 3, S= 1
  45, in C: ops(   18,    19,    36,    39)-> 3 out 3, S= 1
  46, in A: ops(    3,     5,    10,    12)-> 0 out 2, S= 0
  47, in D: ops(    4,     9,    11,    20)-> 0 out 3, S= 0
  48, in C: ops(   18,    19,    36,    39)-> 0 out 3, S= 1
  49, in D: ops(    4,     9,    11,    20)-> 2 out 1, S= 0
  50, in A: ops(    3,     5,    10,    12)-> 0 out 2, S= 0
  51, in C: ops(   18,    19,    36,    39)-> 1 out 3, S= 1
  52, in A: ops(    3,     5,    10,    12)-> 0 out 2, S= 0
  53, in C: ops(   18,    19,    36,    39)-> 0 out 3, S= 1
  54, in A: ops(    3,     5,    10,    12)-> 0 out 2, S= 0
  55, in C: ops(   18,    19,    36,    39)-> R out 4, S= 0
  56, in B: ops(    0,     2,     7,    13)-> 3 out 4, S= 0
```

```
57, in C: ops(  18,    19,    36,    39)-> 0 out 3,  S= 1
58, in A: ops(   3,     5,    10,    12)-> 0 out 2,  S= 0
59, in C: ops(  18,    19,    36,    39)-> 1 out 3,  S= 1
60, in C: ops(  18,    19,    36,    39)-> 0 out 3,  S= 1
61, in A: ops(   3,     5,    10,    12)-> 2 out 2,  S= 0
62, in A: ops(   3,     5,    10,    12)-> 0 out 2,  S= 0
63, in C: ops(  18,    19,    36,    39)-> 2 out 3,  S= 1
64, in B: ops(   0,     2,     7,    13)-> R out 2,  S= 1
65, in A: ops(   3,     5,    10,    12)-> 2 out 2,  S= 0
66, in A: ops(   3,     5,    10,    12)-> 2 out 2,  S= 0
67, in A: ops(   3,     5,    10,    12)-> 2 out 2,  S= 0
68, in C: ops(  18,    19,    36,    39)-> 1 out 3,  S= 1
69, in D: ops(   4,     9,    11,    20)-> 0 out 3,  S= 0
70, in C: ops(  18,    19,    36,    39)-> 0 out 3,  S= 1
71, in D: ops(   4,     9,    11,    20)-> 0 out 3,  S= 0
72, in D: ops(   4,     9,    11,    20)-> 1 out 2,  S= 0
73, in C: ops(  18,    19,    36,    39)-> 0 out 3,  S= 1
74, in C: ops(  18,    19,    36,    39)-> 1 out 3,  S= 1
75, in C: ops(  18,    19,    36,    39)-> 2 out 3,  S= 1
76, in B: ops(  64,     0,     2,     7)-> 0 out 2,  S= 1
77, in C: ops(  18,    19,    36,    39)-> 0 out 3,  S= 1
78, in B: ops(  64,    76,     0,     2)-> 1 out 2,  S= 1
79, in A: ops(   3,     5,    10,    12)-> 0 out 2,  S= 0
```

Note that by the end of this trace (80 rounds) the machine has learnt about the mappings for B and C but not for A or D. This will likely happen later in the run and the entire mapping will be learnt. Illustration 11.2 shows an average of the scores of 10,000 runs of a 2,000-round game.

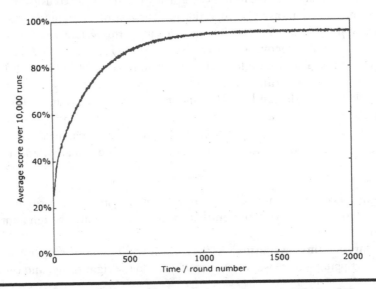

Illustration 11.2 Statistics on the Learning of AIF0 on the *ABCD* -> 1234 problem.

Note that the theoretical maximum that this graph should approach can be calculated as follows:

Once the program has run for long enough to have four samples of a correct response for each possible input, it will usually choose the correct answer based on this accumulated experience. The chances of it choosing a random choice are $0.5^4 = 0.0625 = 6.25\%$. If the software chooses a random action, it still has a 25% chance of choosing the correct answer randomly, so the ultimate error rate should be 4.68%, and the success rate should be 95.32%, as we indeed see in the graph above.

Consider the following modifications:

- If the rules of the game (the correct mappings between *ABCD* and 1234) change midway through the game, this would lead to much confusion. A slight variation, making the "case number" part of the input that is compared by the similarity function, would allow the algorithm to recover from a change in the rules as it would prefer more recent "cases" since they would be more similar to the current case.
- Adding a random small "noise" to the score does not change the results noticeably, though it makes the "similarity" more like a real-world scenario.

Recall, the purpose of this algorithm is only as a simple example to illustrate the wider point about the methodology. In subsequent section, this will be built upon.

11.3.4 Discussion

Some of the observations in the introspection above could be reached using other, more objective, means. As long as an introspection gives us *some* new insight for a design, that insight is worthy of our consideration. In following introspection rather than mathematical correctness, we move away from rational AI towards anthropic AI, away from classic AI towards subjectively informed AI, away from classic AI and towards Dreyfus.

In this specific algorithm, we introduce *mistakes* (not choosing the best option, the 1/16 chance that the result will be random), but we gain the algorithm's ability to bootstrap its own knowledge, that is, to learn, starting from an empty database. Moreover, we gain the ability to recover from a midway rule-change. Also, through introspection we uncover three distinct sources of sub-optimality, and these are reflected in the software design:

- **Ignorance** – we simply do not know a better response to a situation. This is reflected in the AI design in that the software can also be ignorant of the "better solution".
- Confusion (**mis-execution**) – "the spirit is willing, but the flesh is weak"[3] – like tripping – there was a full intention to do the right thing, and the execu-

---
[3] Matthew 26:41.

tion failed. This is mainly reflected in the possibility that only the second to fourth options will be chosen. It is also reflected by the "random answer", the fifth option in each decision.

■ **Playfulness** – Humans (not well-trained soldiers) often do not go for 100% accurate performance, since they find it boring. Humans like experimenting – we could call it playfulness. Contrast a 2 years old with undergraduate students and with elderly people: the older a person gets, the more they tend to refrain from experimentation and play behaviour, and the more you can expect them to "behave reasonably". This tendency to reduce exploratory moves (playfulness) with time can be reflected in the algorithm by gradually, during the runtime of the above design, moving the chance of using each selected case up from 50% to say 70%. The result would be that, gradually during the game, the chance of a random choice moved from 0.5^4 (6.25%) to 0.3^4 (=0.81%). This will allow for sufficient experimentation in the early stages but will allow a better result later on – at a cost to the learning ability later on. This modification of this "decisiveness" parameter during the run is one of the variations possible with this design (see Section 13.2). Playfulness is reflected mainly in the random action and also somewhat in the possibility of choosing the second to fourth options.

11.3.4.1 Details and Parameters

Not every aspect of the code reflects introspection directly, for example the notion of "flipping a coin" in this particular way is just an attempt to approximate the apparent randomness in the introspected process. Note also that the parameters "50%" (coin flip) for decisiveness or "4" (number of attempts) are **arbitrary**, and may be tuned to get different behaviours. Note also that these details are crude and mathematical and have no basis in introspection whatsoever. This is part of the compromise between classic AI and subjectivity and is in line with the precedent of fuzzy logic, where the fuzzy edges of the concepts are assumed to be linear or described by some other simple function.

A question might arise here as to what degree can these arbitrary **parameters** be tuned away from the initial values (50% and 4 here) before the AI method can no longer be considered "based on introspection". Being interested in technology, I view this question as scholastic (in the derogatory medieval sense) – as long as an activity (introspection) generates worthwhile ideas for designs it is worth pursuing, but the purpose is *not* "good" or "pristine" introspection but rather forwarding our human-like AI technology. So we may use introspective ideas to create designs, and later we may, if it behoves our purpose, abuse the introspection by using some introspectively implausible parameters. Let a thousand flowers bloom.

11.3.4.2 Why This Is More Anthropic

AIF0 is more "human-like" or "anthropic", since humans do not have a pre-existing database of cases telling them that solution Y for situation X is correct, optimal, or "a solution" in some predetermined sense. Humans struggle along in situations as they can with the information they have (not "as best"!).

The best response available to a human may be (objectively) quite bad, and moreover, once a **"bad habit"** of using a bad response has established itself in a human mind, it may be seen (subjectively) as "the best I have", even if an external observer can rightly judge the habit to be bad. A brief exposure to a better response to a situation may not cause an immediate overall switchover to the better response, like any rational system would. By sheer "bad luck" or "pig headedness", the better response may be neglected (examples of this below).

Mistakes are made. This is a hallmark of non-rational, nonideal AI.

11.3.4.3 Similarity

An important issue in many AI algorithms is the notion of **similarity**, often hidden inside a similarity function. The issue of how to judge the similarity of two inputs is easy only insofar as the input is *very* primitive, ideally discrete digital data. When the inputs are images with millions of multiband pixels, or worse, videos, or "situations" (in the phenomenological sense) – then the issue of what is similar explodes into an impossible imbroglio. Considering our commitment to producing actual AI designs, we cannot just throw our hands up in despair à la Dreyfus, but we have to, in each implementation, come up with some similarity function, just as CBR does. This gets more complex with the complexity of the examples and always involves a wrenching sense of not doing justice to the real notion of similarity – but software *must* be written. The similarity function, in principle, can involve another, entirely different AI algorithm from the main one, such as one of the many derivatives of the neural net concept, "nearest neighbour" by Pythagorean distances in some vector space, a genetically evolved similarity function, etc. We can also experiment with different approaches, as with any technology.

One must recall that AIF0 is a simple example of the concept of AI based on introspection, and the resultant design is no more than a preliminary caricature of anthropic thought, a beginning of our project. We aim for phenomenologically more correct stuff, see below.

11.4 AIF1

The purpose of this example is to show how introspection can be deepened, and more introspected mechanisms can be brought into software.

Introspection: I observe that all thoughts (including those about possible actions) have a time dimension, they do not appear as closed "cases" but as "episodes" over time. Once I commit in my mind that currently unfolding events are similar to some episode or sequence of events in the past, I treat the whole sequence form the past as the "case" I am following, perhaps in a similar manner to AIF0.

Attempted approximation: I tried using an instance of the precious algorithm (AIF0) to determine the beginnings and ends of sequences and use another instance (of AIF0) to select sequences and produce behaviour.

Having coded a version of this algorithm, it failed to produce behaviour better than noise (no useful learning). The algorithm that was supposed to find meaningful beginnings and ends to sequences of events did not train meaningfully, probably (analysing retrospectively) because the idea that there are clearly defined beginnings and ends was wrong. Perhaps, the success of AIF0 led me down the dangerous path of wanting my new "pet technique" to be *the* building block of future AI. This temptation to want all of intelligence to come out of a single idea is tempting, and several AI approaches have this "imperialist" view of the scope of use for their favoured idea: Logical AI and neural nets spring to mind, as does the critique of this over-optimism verging on hubris (Dreyfus, 2012).

On the positive side, this is an example of iterative introspection. Having achieved a first success with AIF0, I went back and refined the introspection, adding a time dimension.

Chapter 12

A More Sophisticated Example

The purposes of this example are

- To further deepen the introspection.
- To demonstrate how complex introspections can be approximated by code, sometimes in an opportunistic way.
- To show how a failure (AIF1) need not imply a retreat and that the solution could be in even more ambitious introspection (reminiscent of Dreyfus's demand for an even "*more* Heideggerian" artificial intelligence (AI) (Dreyfus, 2007)).

Furthermore, this example demonstrates

- Smooth acquisition of skills by interleaving multiple "cases", recalling Dreyfus and Dreyfus's work on skills (1986).
- A possible concrete manifestation of Gadamerian AI as recommended by Winograd and Flores.

12.1 Introspection

The **introspective vision** became clear gradually — first I was displeased with the idea of discreet "sequences" — it seemed too constrained, too on or off. Then (while driving), I noticed how I was following *multiple sequences*, simultaneously — but could not quite put it into words. These sequences seemed to have to do with different aspects and eventualities of the driving and of whatever else was on my mind. However, this vision came initially with none of the below orderliness – all I could do to hold on to the vision was to point to the Beatles' song "Across the universe":

> Words are flowing out
> Like endless rain into a paper cup
> They slither wildly as they slip away
> Across the universe

Needless to say, this is technologically useless. A more comprehensible **articulation** of this image emerged over the following few days, making the notions of "flowing" and "slipping" more concrete:

- The sequences (of AIF1) also known as "lines of thought" are not as on or off as in AIF1 but fade in and out without clear beginnings and ends.
- There are multiple such lines "being followed" simultaneously, to varying degrees.
- Actions are usually selected out of one of these sequences, again, aiming for the best future outcome but often missing.

Over time and in different contexts, the terms "episode", "sequence", "line/thread/ train of thought", and just "line" were used, are equivalent, and represent a sequence of events in the past, being "followed" in the present, since it is similar to current events. Note that the sequences that are present but less dominant play the role of the "recesses of the mind".

12.2 Introspective Model

At any point, there are multiple different things "on one's mind". These "things" (hereinafter "lines of thought" or just "lines", sequences, etc.) are not static but take the form of a sequence of events from memory, that are similar (or relevant, see below) to current unfolding events. Such "lines" are followed in the sense that the "current" part of the sequence advances in time as reality advances in time, like (when singing) we do not need to consciously "advance" in the lyrics and in the music when singing, but we just go with the flow of the memories of having heard or sung the song before. A 15 s phrase in the remembered song will be reproduced in a time not too unlike 15 s.

An action is selected out of the options presented by these lines of thought, as follows: If in line "*a*" one did A, and in line "*b*" one did B (and these are all the "lines" "on one's mind" simultaneously), it is probably correct to assume one will do either A or B.

There is a preference to selecting an action that would be beneficial, so each line is given priority based on the anticipated reward occurring in the proximate time (the anticipated future or the yet to be replayed part of these remembered lines in the past).[1]

Of course this is still only a model, and many details are missing to recreate the original introspection. This is left to future work. It is doubtful if we can ever fully model our introspections. But we also can't fully model real numbers in a computer – approximations are good enough for technology.

The next step should be to find a formalization in software and data that will create an approximation of simultaneous "lines" or "trains of thought", drifting in and out of some group of thoughts, perhaps called "consciousness".

12.3 Software Design

The details of the design will be presented in an order that moves from some preliminary remarks, to the functionality visible in the introspective model, and then to the technicalities inherent in any design. These later technicalities are details of implementation that need to be addressed, like an integer's number of bits must be determined and whether it is signed or unsigned; in this design, there are many such details.

12.3.1 Preliminary: Sequences in Software

Recall that the introspections called for "lines of thought" which "fade in in and out without clear beginnings and ends". This is not the common way of doing anything in computing. Usually we need a beginning in order to (1) find the data, (2) not start before the data, over-running something else, and (3) have a starting point for some loop or process. We need an end for similar reasons: (1) not to overrun some other data and (2) provide an end point where we can say our work is done. If we can achieve similar functions in AIF2 using different means, then we will have a reasonable design "without clear beginnings and ends".

Traditionally in programming, one would assume that a sequence would be represented by a formal array, a consecutive group of memory locations or by a linked list. That means that a sequence has a clear beginning and end, and there is some pointer or index pointing to the "current" position. Consider printing out a string 40 characters long:

Assuming "a" is a character array representing a string and "i" is an integer:

■ for $i = 0$ to 40
  – putchar ($a[i]$)

---

[1] This is reminiscent of Husserl's "protension" (Beyer, 2015).

Or consider printing a string which is a null-terminated sequence of bytes in memory, pointed to by "p", "q" being another pointer:

- $q = p$;
- while (*q is not null)
    - print *q
    - q++

Consider further a linked list of characters:

- z = head_of_list
- while z is not null
    - print z.data
    - $z = z$.next

In all cases, there are

1. A data point marking the beginning: "a", "p", "head of list"
2. An index, traversing the data, "i", "q", "z"
3. An indicator of the end, "40", the null character at the end of the string or the null pointer at the end of the linked list.

In AIF2, as we will see below, the beginning and end are abstracted away. There are separate mechanisms for "starting" or "ending" sequences. The only mechanism we need most of the time is just a pointer into the "current" moment in a sequence. This is a step away from the rationalistic view that we need strict control over beginnings and ends, and towards the subjective experience that all we have at any point is the now, with the various memories, thoughts, and tunes going through our mind.

It so happens in AIF2 that the sequences are advanced by one time unit, represented by a "1" in the indexing of any area of the memory bank, but at the same moment the memory bank is growing by one unit every iteration, so there is no danger that the sequence data type will "overflow" its end. We are now ready for the main design.

12.3.2 A Novel Data Type

Here I introduce two closely related novel data types: a "sequence" and a "table" of sequences. Sequences will usually be used in groups of a few at a time, such a group being called a "table". The sequences are based on (and refer back to) a history database of all the history of the program's current run. The history database is not novel and can be stored as an array.

All the "personal history" of the AI system is saved, including inputs, outputs, and scores (from the outside world or microworld). This array starting at 0 and ending "now" is represented as the "history database" in Illustration 12.1.

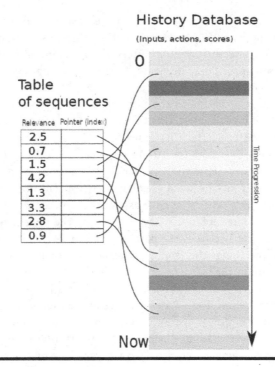

Illustration 12.1   AIF2 data types.

The "sequence" data type is designed to represent a single train of thought, or line of thought, or a scenario that occurred in the past. Every "sequence" is comprised of two scalar values: One is an **index** or pointer into the history database. This index points to a moment in time in the past that is analogous to the present moment in time. The **relevance score**, which is a (discounted) accumulating score of the similarity between the events in the sequence and the events as they are actually occurring in the situation facing the system. Every instance of a sequence represents a sequence of events (a scenario from the past) that is considered to be similar to the present and therefore describes *a possible outcome* in the future, as seen from the current time. In Illustration 12.1, the similarity is illustrated using colours, representing the observed characteristics of individual events. Note that the last two colour blocks are purple and green, incidentally very similar to the two blocks just prior, and hence, the sequence following only two steps behind the present has a high relevance, "4.3". The second most relevant sequence is in the very beginning of the history database, but the blue is not quite the same as the purple, hence, the lower relevance of "3.3", still high.

As these scenarios are inside a history database, populated by the past experiences of a specific run of the AI implementation, this represents the AI system's own "personal" experience. Each sequence represents an option for action (the one taken at that point, or shortly thereafter, in the past) and also represents a possible outcome arising from the combination of the current situation and the action. Assuming that events occur in regular intervals, say of one second, then for every second that elapses in the "outside world", the index component of all sequences must be incremented, and the relevance scores should also be updated based on the similarity of current events to the next event in the history database at each sequence's new "present". Hence, this is not a static data structure but requires ongoing maintenance, to keep it "in the now".

Typically, a "table" would have 20–40 sequences in it. This data type is novel in that it is designed to imitate the way that multiple thoughts drift in and out of consciousness – therefore, the sequences have no clear (abrupt) beginning or end (see Section 12.3.1). In a sense, the table as a whole represents the "consciousness", and the relevance scores represent "how conscious" the system is of a particular train of thought or scenario from the past.

So to sum up the above, the sequences in the table each consists of a relevance score and an index pointing into a specific time in the past, that is part of a sequence of events that resembles current events. These pointers move forward in time in sync with the present time. The relative salience of each sequence to current events is measured by the "relevance" score (maintained next to the pointer in the table). This relevance is adjusted gradually, according to the similarity of current events to the events in the past sequence, so these sequences fade in and out in terms of their applicability to the current situation.

Occasionally, the least relevant sequences are discarded from the table, as their relevance score drops below a certain threshold. Once the table is depopulated (say below 10 sequences), it is replenished (this is a computationally expensive operation, see Section 12.3.5).

Returning to Illustration 12.1, we can see eight sequences in a table (on the left), each with a relevance score and a pointer or index into a (greatly truncated) history database of all events (represented as coloured blocks) from the beginning of the run until the present moment. Assuming that the relevance score is overwhelmingly influenced by the last two events, you can see that the scores reflect how similar (or not) the last two blocks in a sequence are to the most recent two events in the chart, at the bottom of the coloured history database.

12.3.3 Decision Process

A word is due about **relevance** (mentioned above) and **desirability**, which is the expected score over time in the future, for a specific sequence of events in the table.

These two key notions are similar, yet in a sense mirror images of each other:

The "relevance" of a line is determined by how similar events *in the past* have been to *current events*. In a sense, it is simply the (discounted) extension of the notion of "similarity" over time. Similarity is always already determined in the past – since we do not know the future, we cannot compare future events (in reality) to the "future" of a line of thought. So relevance is in the past and plays a corresponding role to similarity and is constituted from similarity. The difference is that relevance is stretched over time.

On the other hand, "desirability" is the expected value "promised" by each of the "lines" in the future. It is calculated from the "score" events in the "future" of each line and is recalculated for the most relevant lines at each iteration. Desirability represents what the (naïvely) expected reward is in the case in which we end up repeating the same scenario. The AI system can "push" the present situation towards a repetition of a specific scenario by choosing the same actions that it took in that past relevant scenario. In a sense, this is the whole point of the "intelligence" of this design: Try to repeat successful scenarios from the past. For all the changes, this is still quite similar to CBR.

The decision process is as follows. For each action/output required:

- The top (say 10) most relevant lines are selected from the table.
- These lines are sorted by desirability, and the top (say 4) most desirable lines are further selected and sorted by desirability.
- A specific sequence (or random action) is chosen in a repeated round of coin-throwing, similar to AIF0 (see Section 11.3.2). At a low probability, a random action is chosen.
- The action taken in the chosen past sequence is duplicated (or a random action).

The random element (like in AIF0) allows novel actions to be tried out within the normal process of responding to the environment, in contrast to many learning systems that have a distinct "learning" and "doing" phase.

Several possible future variants will be discussed in Section 13.2.

12.3.4 More Details of AIF2's Implementation

As we see from the above discussion, there are many details missing from the picture. For now, let's assume that we have a sequence (or a table of them) already set up, and all we need to do is maintain these and take decisions. Illustration 12.1 assumed that only about two events (the current and previous ones) make the lion's share of the "relevance" of a sequence.

Every instant in time (the coloured blocks in Illustration 12.1) is an **event**. An event can either be an input from sensors, or an action that the AI algorithm outputted, or a score event.

There is a **similarity function**, taking two events as arguments, and returning a value between 0 and 1 that represents how similar they are, 1 for identical and 0 for completely dissimilar. The similarity function's exact implementation is not part of the specification of AIF2. This function can be hand-tailored or evolved using some learning algorithm.

Relevance is calculated as the previous relevance times some discounting factor, plus the current similarity minus 0.5. Note that relevance is not bounded in any range. If relevance drops below some threshold (another parameter of the design), then the sequence is dropped from the table. If a table is no longer sufficiently populated (drops below a certain amount of sequences) then it is repopulated, see below.

12.3.5 Dynamics of the Sequences Table

To populate a table of sequences (either initially or when the number of sequences drops below the repopulation threshold), a scan is performed of the entire history database to find any consecutive events that would have high relevance, based on the currently recent N events, this N being the "look_back" parameter. In principle, if computational time were not an issue, such a scan should be done frequently, maybe with every input, so that any sequence that is relevant enough goes into the table, however, considering that sequences stay in the table for a while, it may be enough to scan for new pertinent sequences only occasionally. This also reflects the introspective observation that not all relevant scenarios from out past are always considered, we often forget things, in ways we do not understand. Matching this forgetfulness to the computational high price of repopulating the table is an opportunistic approximation – there is no good reason to think that these would match up, but we need to approximate in order to code (see Section 10.3.5.2).

Because of the computational cost of scanning all the memory for populating the table, we can maintain a bigger table of scenarios than would be warranted by the introspection (say 20–40) and select only the top (say 10) "most relevant" scenarios every time we need to make a choice about an action. To choose an action from one of these 10 most relevant scenarios, we sort them by expected score ("desirability") and like AIF0 select the best in 50% of the cases and so on for four scenarios, with a possibility of a random action (see AIF0 in Section 11.3).

Note that the active "scenarios" drift in and out of this "top 10" category, as they are selected from a bigger table. Also "scenarios" do not have predetermined beginnings or ends – when a situation (in the present) is similar enough to a situation from the past in the table, it drifts into the high relevance end of the table, and when a scenario drifts so low in relevance, it is silently dropped but only a few iterations after it is no longer considered a "top 10" scenario. This gives this design some "softness" – mental events are rarely abrupt.[2] A sudden change in the environment would cause most if not all sequences to drop out of the table rapidly, leading to a repopulation of the table that fits the new circumstances. The moments of "mismatch" between the table and the reality

---

[2] Husserl's "extension" comes to mind.

around the robot bear resemblance to similar confusion in humans, when the scene changes abruptly.

12.3.6 *Initial Conditions and Decisions*

Similar to AIF0, it is not a problem for a new instance of the system to act pretty much at random until it accumulates enough experience to draw from, so the initial conditions of the design are of secondary importance; we can assume that we have at least a minimal database of past events, including a record of inputs, actions, and score events. This initial experience can be accumulated by simply letting the design flail around, randomly, for a while. We can also assume the table has been populated as per Section 12.3.5. We must recall here that a complex system such as AIF2 may, like the "blue brain" project, often produce a non-functioning intelligence or an intelligence uninterested in learning to deal with the problems we present to it (see Section 10.4 and the examples below).

12.3.7 *Further Parameters*

Many parameters are involved in this AI algorithm. Here is a partial list of issues and parameters that need to be tweaked is provided in order to demonstrate the complexity. In the experiments run so far, many of these were assigned arbitrary numbers, and many (including the weights of the similarity function) were tuned using a genetic algorithm.

In terms of calculating "desirability" (see Section 12.3.3):

■ **look_ahead** – determines how many events in the "future" to consider when calculating desirability

In the context of choosing the sequence to use to guide current action, I have so far spoken of four iterations of coin tossing at a 50% chance each. These numbers can vary from one run to another:

■ **decisiveness** – the factor in the random decision, typically 0.5
■ **max_cases** – how many times to try the coin tossing (and thus the chance of exploratory moves), typically four.

The "decisiveness" parameter may change over time *during* runtime, following some function – for example, it could become linearly higher.

■ **var_decisiveness** – (boolean) use variable decisiveness
■ **algebraic_form** – the equation for variable decisiveness, typically linear
■ **vd_parameter_a** – the first parameter for calculating variable decisiveness
■ **vd_parameter_b** – the second parameter for calculating variable decisiveness.

In terms of table management, we also have

- **table_length** – the maximum size of the table
- **think_about** – the maximum number of events to enter a non-empty (and non-full) table
- **init_relevance** – initial relevance of events that enter the table
- **max_relevance** – max relevance of events in the table
- **recent_prior** – (boolean) do recent events have priority (in the similarity function).

There are several more parameters. The point here is that the complexity of introspective algorithms is larger than those produced by mathematical models, but it is still manageable. The fact that human-like AI is difficult should not stop our exploration.

12.4 AIF2 Example Runs

Some example runs are documented in three videos found in http://tinyurl.com/hycenh9.

The three videos show the performance of AIF2 in a car-driving game, approximated from the work of Togelius et al. (2007). The purpose of these examples is to give *a taste* of what is achievable with AIF2 and more generally with introspection-based AI. Proper controlled evaluation and discussion of these results lies outside the scope of the current project. Note that, as was expected and as explained in Section 10.4, relatively few runs learnt at all. The examples below were selected for emphasising specific points, rather than for being typical. They are quite dissimilar.

The game in these examples consists of a "car" on a "track" that needs to race and accumulate as much distance in a given time. In the usual case (presented here), the car's driving software is entirely naïve at the beginning and learns solely by getting a +1 score on moving in the right direction, +10 for passing a waypoint at a predetermined proximity, while moving forwards (there are eight of them, marked in blue, except the next one which is brown). The agent gets −10 points for colliding with a wall.

The car has six directional sensors (no diagonal sensors in the back) that feed in the distance to the nearest obstacle and a directional (polar) feed pointing at the next waypoint.

12.4.1 Learn 1

Discussing the experiment recorded in the video "learn1.avi" (see link on the top of Section 12.4): In this simulation, there was a bug in the physics engine (leading to an undefined state), so occasionally the car-racing game is reset to its initial state, without resetting the AI software. The question of how skills are learnt best, in an ongoing engagement with the problem or with repetitive restarts, remains open.

Note that the car initially flails about, starts improving slowly, and by 1:35 manages to get beyond the "choking point" above the top-right corner. By 2:30, some skill in not crashing begins to emerge, but mostly the car still crashes a lot. Around 3:30, it is completely lost. Around 4:30, it develops a (bad) habit of crashing into the wall repeatedly, but by 5:00, it rather suddenly starts to drive skilfully with no crashes for 65% of the round, recovers from a bad spell after a crash, and completes several full rounds, with few crashes. The rounds complete at 5:26, 5:37, 5:48, and 5:58.

The learning process is reasonable, in terms of our expectations: It is cautious and experimental. The system has initial difficulties and finds the top-right corner, which is tight, more difficult than the others. Once a full round is completed, the skills accumulated in traversing the beginning seem to kick in and serve to support the future circumnavigation of the track. The algorithm is behaving as expected.

12.4.2 Learn 2

Discussing the experiment recorded in the video "learn2.avi": The physics engine was fixed, so there are no "resets". Note that the track is a bit more difficult, with some more obstacles on the outer side of the track. After initially flailing about, going mainly backwards, at 0:14 the player gets into a strange mode of banging itself against a wall (in reverse). At about 1:00, it discovers that staying still is better than getting repeatedly penalized, and at about 1:05, it starts racing (quite wildly) towards the waypoints. Other than another spate of banging against the wall at around 1:45, it learns to run around the track with less accidents, until the end of the video clip. It is interesting that "learn1" learnt step by step with great caution, while "learn2" spent much time being unproductive but was significantly more reckless and "enthusiastic" in learning for the rest of the time.

The repetitive behaviour is interesting, not in being repetitive (that is something that most software does) but in being able to break away from the repetitive behaviour without any explicit intervention. Even after a pattern of behaviour establishes itself, the algorithm can break away from it. Here we see the benefit of the "random action". Once the program gets out of this repetitive phase, its learning seems to display far less caution than "learn1".

12.4.3 Learn 3

Discussing the experiment recorded in the video "learn3.avi": It is a different track, and as usual, the player flails about. However, in this case, it develops a strange waltz-like strategy, of going around in arcs backwards and only occasionally going forward just to collect the score at the waypoint. It also (like "learn2" at 1:00) discovers at 1:35 that staying still is an option that is better than bumping into walls but not as satisfying as getting more waypoints. This "waltz" strategy works but is suboptimal. In this, it is like many habits of intelligent creatures.

12.5 Discussion of AIF2

Each of these runs develops **its own way** of doing things, like a "personality".[3] These idiosyncratic development patterns are very encouraging in terms of producing anthropic AI, since humans are also diverse, non-optimal creatures. Another point of similarity with the human condition is that there is no pre-knowledge of the range of scores – AIF2 learns by preferring the better, not by aiming for the best.

One may raise the classical problem of "credit assignment" in AI – how does this design attribute the good or bad scores it may get from the environment to particular causes? This does not arise, since there are no cause–effect pairs, even statistically, like in a Markov chain data type (see Section 12.6.1). The score events are simply registered as part of the history and will sit there until that part of the history database becomes part of a relevant sequence, in which case the scores will be part of a desirability calculation, and hence will "motivate" the action taken at the time either positively or negatively.

AIF2 demonstrated a complex design that deepened the introspection in the face of the failure of the previous design (AIF1). Using introspection as a basis for AI is not guaranteed to work, but in this case, it did. This design is introspectively much richer than any other design encountered in the literature. Moreover, the introspected mechanisms as implemented in software present some surprisingly realistic behaviour, delivering some evidence for the anthropic approach. Anthropic AI was defined as pre-programming only the basic intelligence, without any cultural commitments, and letting each instance of the program learn, or develop, its own "culture". The above runs demonstrated that a game can be learnt from scratch, displaying a diverse range of responses to a similar environment. This diversity also speaks to the human-like character of this model.

Even though AIF2 is the last algorithm in this volume, it is not the end of the exploration. It should be seen as a basis for further development, see Section 13.2.

12.6 Consequences of the Examples

12.6.1 AIF Is More Like CBR Than Like Reinforcement Learning

The AIF2 design can be seen as similar to reinforcement learning (RL), in that it navigates a situation using a closed list of actions and takes feedback from the environment. It can also be seen as similar to Case-Based Reasoning (CBR) since it uses stored episodes as "solutions" for future situations. The RL paradigm includes the notion of a Markov chain and of a closed universe of states that can (at least

---

[3] A highly qualitative observation is that the player or "car" in these videos seems (to several observers) to be rather "cute" – whatever that means. Exploring this question is outside the scope of this project.

in principle) be explored exhaustively. CBR on the other hand is more open ended and more modest, in that it does not aim at an overall solution (a fully understood Markov chain) but at "the best we have". In this sense, it is closer to the AIF family, which being introspective does not aim (even theoretically) at infallibility. Moreover, the AIF family of designs has as its main data store a historical database, more like CBR's store of "cases", and not some statistical summary of weights or probabilities like RL. AIF0 even retains the separation into discreet "cases".

12.6.2 The "Sequence" Data Type

Probably the most interesting technical contribution that AIF2 makes is the introduction of the "sequence" data type as a building block for AI systems (in Section 12.3). This allows the representation of multiple fading trains of thought that originate from the memory of past experiences.

Even if AI practitioners were to ignore all the arguments presented in this book and will not consciously seek to use introspection, the mere introduction of such subjectively informed designs into the discourse will broaden the field of "allowed" or "respectable" discussion. Considering how infrequently non-philosophers read philosophy, perhaps that is the most that can be hoped for in terms of any impact of this work on the technology debates and marketplace, at least in the short term.

12.6.3 Dynamic Symbols

Consider AIF2 as a model of the working of the mind. It can be viewed as matching events from the past to the present, if you so will, "interpreting" the present using the past as the source of possible scenarios with which to understand the current situation. Each AIF2 run creates its own history database which it uses to interpret future events.

In classic AI designs, the symbol system in terms of which the world is construed is predetermined by the programmer or knowledge engineer using a fixed vocabulary. The classic AI system does not "grope around" looking for a vocabulary through which to construe a situation. Neural nets (in the learning phase) do "grope around" and are adaptable in unpredictable ways, but we cannot see (at least usually) a signifier-signified relationship at all. In AIF2, conversely, the very *terms* of understanding are a product of the lifetime of the system itself. AIF2 understands the current situation in terms of its previous memories. A past memory that is used often can be construed (by us, as observers) as serving as a symbol or a concept "describing" or "interpreting" the present.

It is as if classic AI's version of the human has been given a language by some supernatural being, and the designed "mind" is confined to use only that language while AIF2's "mind" evolves its own concepts to deal with any situations that it encounters with any regularity. This development of the mind may even occur socially, in future settings. That would be a rudimentary culture.

These dynamic symbols have technical and philosophical consequences:
Technically:

- Since there is a symbolic relationship, there is an "understanding X in terms of Y", one can debug such a system more intuitively than a neural net, without committing to the rigidity of a predetermined set of symbols.
- A system that has both plasticity and sentence-like structures can adapt to cultural factors that are particular to the environment of every particular run, even in a temporary manner. Classic systems have little plasticity, and neural nets have nothing that resembles sentences or structures that could accommodate the cultural transmission of habits.
- A future, more sophisticated system based on this approach also would allow for reflection on its own practices: Introspection by the AI rather than by the developer (contrast with Section 5.3.2).

Philosophically, this notion of viewing past sequences as representations of sorts can be an interesting input to the debate on representations (Shanon, 2008): In a new sense, AIF2 harvests its own symbols, turning past events into symbols and past sequences of events into representations for understanding the future and speculating about it (see also Section 13.4.4).

12.6.4 How AIF2 Is Gadamerian

AIF2 (as presented above) reflects many of the characteristics that Winograd and Flores (1986) view as interesting in Gadamer's hermeneutics (see Sections 2.4.2 and 2.5). This avenue of research seems to have been so far neglected in the AI literature.

AIF2 does little but match previous episodes from memory to the current evolving situation. Even doing just that can be seen as interpretation of a crude type, a bit like CBR interprets the situation as being similar-enough to a past "case". But AIF2 goes further and allows the current situation to be matched with more than one sequence and thus be interpreted and reacted to using a *blend* of previously experienced scenarios.

Recall the name of Gadamer's main work – "Truth and Method". Truth stands for the brute facts of the text (or the "sense data"), and method is all the wisdom, methodology, and experience the reader brings to bear. Every person's "method" is a result of their own life experience, education, and other memories – ultimately these are all stored in the individual's memory (discounting any Jungian-type "collective unconscious"). So according to Gadamer, all interpretation is done using the past memories of the individual – and the AIF family of designs provide a mechanism for implementing such a system. Recall also that Gadamer viewed the act or interpretation as a "merger of horizons" – the outer horizon of "truth" – sense data, and the internal horizon(s) – of "method" or memory. Gadamer also stressed the unavoidable existence of "prejudices" – and we can see even in AIF0 that once a "habit of thought" is established it is difficult to dislodge.

Chapter 13

Summary, Consequences, Conclusion

This last chapter gives a summary and discusses the possible consequences of this work:

- For artificial intelligence (AI) practitioners, future possible extensions of the AIF family of algorithms
- For cognitive scientists, the possible impact of this research
- For philosophers, the manner that introspective ideas developed here may serve to "underpin" some ideas
- Some more outstanding questions.

13.1 Summary

This book argued, in the field of *technological* AI that **introspection is recommended for developers of anthropic AI**. It explored the conceptual space between phenomenology and AI, mainly classic AI.

A double crisis exists in AI: There is a dearth of new conceptual frameworks, and there is a neglect of the actual complexities and paradoxes of human thought (as revealed subjectively) in favour of a rationalistic viewpoint.

The **frailty** of human intelligence was surveyed on the individual, political, and scientific levels. Several unwarranted **assumptions** that have embedded themselves in our culture have had an adverse effect on our ability to think about AI. Some of these were enumerated, and their history briefly mentioned.

The project of this volume was to mitigate the faults of excessive **rationalism** using the subjective (standing with Dreyfus, and Winograd and Flores, against

Watson, Simon, and their followers). This turn to subjectivity is done while still being committed to producing concrete working software (standing with the mainstream AI community, against Dreyfus et al.).

Human-like AI was discussed as distinct from the ideal/rational type following Russell and Norvig (2013). Human-like AI is required for applications where smooth interaction between unskilled people and robots is key. Human-like AI has so far received far less attention than ideal/rational AI, both in research and in education. Technological AI was distinguished from scientific AI – this book focussed on human-like AI as a technology.

Within the context of the search for human-like AI, **anthropic AI** was defined as emulating the fundamental intelligence inherent in humans that makes learning and acquisition of culture possible. This was contrasted with the "western, modern, well-trained, and adult" intelligence that is so often sought after in AI but is a contingent fact which is only true of our particular current culture. COG and CYC were recognised as earlier efforts that initially constructed a fundamental intelligence and then aimed to acquire the necessary skills and/or knowledge by a learning process. Scientific models of the human mind (available for technological implementation) provide only models that are "too high" (like logic and cognitive simulation) or "too low" (like neural nets) for the purposes of anthropic AI.

Starting the work of rehabilitating introspection for the purposes of AI, **subjectivity** was shown to be a valid angle of research for AI, and some examples of cognitive science touching on subjectivity were presented. Within the subjective realm, the phenomenological critique led by Dreyfus was surveyed and critiqued for being only negative, not producing any concrete software designs.

Perhaps the most subjective approach of all, **introspection** was discussed and shown to be suspect not only for reasons given by Watson but also in principle: It is impossible to make neutral, interpretation-free observations even in the natural sciences, so we have no reason to expect the situation to be any better in the subjective realm.

Regardless of the above, cognitive science treats introspection as being an **illegitimate** method. Bringing in the distinction between the context of discovery and the context of justification, *any source of ideas* in science is legitimate, so introspection is rehabilitated as a legitimate source of discovery, of ideas, for science. Moreover, the level of truth required for *technology* is significantly lower than for science, so introspection (for AI as technology) has been fully rehabilitated from the traditional 20th-century view that it is "wrong", "disallowed", or illegitimate for some other reason. Somewhat strangely, AI researchers *have* used introspection, not least Simon. However, they have not used introspection full-bloodedly – they most often tend to expunge any reference to introspection from peer-reviewed publications and deal with it sparingly and shyly. Sherry Turkle's description of how the field of AI relates to introspection came nearest to this analysis, but it remains sociological and factual rather than analytical. Phil Agre also gave an outline quite close to the one presented here but shied away from introspection as such, eventually trying to create Heideggerian AI, but "by his deictic representations, Agre objectified" the ready-to-hand, thereby missing the phenomenological point (Dreyfus, 2007). No researcher did introspection for AI as it is proposed here.

Introspection was shown to be a positively **plausible** basis for AI, since it is used reliably in education: In teaching skills, in order to generate their narrative, instructors either recall the narrative used to instruct themselves years before (unlikely) or generate a narrative by self-observation. When the skill being taught is a mental skill, this involves *mental* self-observation – introspection. The success civilisations have in transmitting mental skills from one generation to another serves as testimony that this kind of introspection works, that is, introspection *is efficacious* in transmitting skills from one human to another, and therefore, introspective reports contain some sort of information *that may well be efficacious* in replicating human mental skills in software.

Examples were given for the use of introspection as a basis for designing AI software, and the new possibilities allowed by the rehabilitation of introspection for the development of AI designs were shown. Previously, insofar as introspection was used at all in AI designs, it was used as a basis for a single mechanism, which was later integrated into the mainstream mathematical framework of the discipline. The examples showed how *multiple* mechanisms can usefully be adapted from human introspective reports into an AI system. Sometimes where one or two mechanisms fail to produce a useful result, going for *more* introspection rather than less allows for the creation of a working system. This was impossible while introspection was minimised, treated as somehow illegitimate in AI research contexts.

An advanced example was described that brings forth a novel data type that not only represents past episodes, but in a sense, allows them to be re-enacted in the mind, in sync with current experience. Multiple such trains of thought fade in and out of significance. This was analysed in terms of representations, a central area of debate in cognitive science, and the notion of "dynamic symbols" was observed. These symbols are used in systems that understand the world through a vocabulary that is *not predefined*. This was shown to fit with the Gadamerian world view, thereby providing a concrete manifestation of one of Winograd and Flores's desiderata. This can be seen as a step towards Heideggerian AI, since Heidegger viewed Gadamer's work as a detailing out of his own work in hermeneutics.

13.2 Future Technical Work

Beyond AIF2, as presented in Chapter 12, the following variants could be of future interest:

1. The internal parameters of the algorithm may vary over time. For example, this has already been implemented regarding the weights of the randomised selection. This can make the algorithm more "decisive" or "conservative"

(more likely to select the better episodes) over time. This is based on the introspective observation that with skill less experimentation is done and the external observation that people (and other mammals) become more conservative as they age.

2. The set of **actions** (available in the environment) may vary over time or as a result of developments within the game/environment. This is planned to accommodate the discovery over time that some actions are not available or the stumbling on to new options. This further moves away from classic AI's Markovian assumption that the group of possible actions is an (often small) finite set.

3. The **score** (given by the environment) is currently a simple number indicating an overall assessment of the outcome but could be comprised of a few separate components, for example, indicative of progress towards low-level and high-level goals or short-term and long-term goals. This is an attempt to deal with the existence of several goals, perhaps on different scales, simultaneously.

4. Even in the case of a random action, various actions correlated to particularly undesirable outcomes may be excluded from the range of options (a "**Panic** mode"). This is based on the observation that we may be adventurous only within certain bounds and not only reward-seeking but also catastrophe-averse.

5. The **history database** may be entirely "real" (derived from the current run) or may be a "manufactured history" including "transplanted experience" from another run and/or a manually encoded history to provide the algorithm with a starting baseline of experience. This is to allow for pre-taught robots or for Chomskyan (or Plato's Menon) pre-known skills.[1] The transplanted history could also be derived from some process, such as crossing between two "parents", providing a new medium for genetic ideas.

   The idea of starting afresh while being "convinced" that there is a lot of history is reminiscent of how computer systems resume after being "hibernated" (as opposed to "suspended").

6. **Pruning** of the historical database can be performed on the basis of discarding the oldest data (suitable for rapidly changing environments) or on the basis of other criteria such as discarding historical episodes which resulted in mediocre desirability of the outcomes. These (mediocre) memories would not be particularly useful either for reuse or for avoiding past mistakes. This is based on the introspection or observation that we forget mainly the mundane.

7. **Federating** – This algorithm may be used in multiple instances, sharing the same timeline and history database. This could be useful, for example, to control different time resolutions or to have some "controller" select which of several machines implementing different skills/strategies should be used

---

[1] This is a bit reminiscent of the "young earth" argument trying to reconcile the geological record of life existing for millions of years with the biblical story that makes the earth under 6,000 years old.

at any time. This is also an attempt to deal with the existence of several-scale goals simultaneously and other possible complexities.

8. The parameters of the **similarity** function may be tuned by a genetic algorithm. This is to address the fact that we have no special insight (introspective or otherwise) into the well-known problem of defining similarity.

9. The other ("**technical**") parameters of the algorithm may also be tuned genetically. Examples of such parameters are table size, thresholds, and the parameters for randomised selection. This is not introspectively motivated but aims to tune the many arbitrary decisions made during the process of approximating from the introspection towards a formal algorithm.

10. The time parameters could be made more continuous, in a sense using real numbers as time indexes. This would move further away from Case-Based Reasoning (CBR), in that time becomes less atomic. It would also require the similarity function to compare not atomic events but "moments" that would perhaps have some duration.[2]

11. So far, sequences are recalled in "real time", the sequences being advanced by one-time unit for every time unit elapsing in the external world. Allowing some flexibility will allow for slowing down or speeding up the memories. This will allow the AI to experiment with applying skills at varying rates.

12. In a sense, in AIF2, the sequences of memory are themselves being experienced, in that they "play out" in sync with the unfolding (real) events and move in time. But in a stricter sense, this mere following-along is part of the interpretation but not part of the experience being interpreted, in that the recalled sequences never move into the "current sense data" that is compared backwards to previous sequences in memory. One could envisage a system, where we explicitly make the contents of past sequences being recalled part of the "present sense data". This would be a most interesting area of research, since this opens up the possibility of an AI system recalling "that it had such a combination of thoughts before" and suchlike. This may also be the beginnings of self-reflection, perhaps machine consciousness (Gamez, 2008) and perhaps even introspection by the AI, see Section 5.3.2.

13.3 Possible Consequences for Cognitive Science

13.3.1 Models for Scientific Psychology

An important distinction used to construct the argument can now be relaxed a bit, in order to show some further potential utility. Parts of the introduction were spent making a clear distinction between technology and science, and some of

---

[2] This again is reminiscent of Husserl's extension and protension.

Chapter 8 (especially Section 8.2.4) presented the distinction between the context of discovery and the context of justification in science. The argument claimed that introspection was a legitimate source of ideas because it was only used in the context of discovery, and moreover, it was only being used for technology. We can now relax this a bit and discuss the interaction between these. In a sense, we "must throw away the ladder" after we have climbed it (Wittgenstein, 2001b, sec. 6.54).

Recall that:

1. All ideas are allowed in the context of discovery *even* in science—that is where this distinction originated.
2. Psychology already uses some AI programs as models or sketch theories about how cognition works, as Simon predicted that "…theories in psychology will take the form of computer programs" (Simon & Newell, 1958; Sun, 2008).

Introspection-based AI designs may be used as theoretical tools in psychology. In being introspective, these theories perhaps would have a better chance (than, for example, neural nets) to bridge the cognitive and personal-analytical branches of psychology.

13.3.2 A Response to Dreyfus's Critique of AI

AIF2 uses dynamic symbols "mined" so to speak, out of the input stream, to signify/interpret other events in the input stream. Unlike Simon's classic AI, there are no pre-fixed symbols, but nonetheless, there is a certain notion of representation.

Classic AI, insofar as it used introspection, used it both sparingly (simulating one mental mechanism at a time) and in an idealised manner. However, they did produce concrete working systems.

Dreyfus seems to get carried away with his title of "what computers can't do" (1979). His argument would have been better served by being called "What can't be formalised". But heavily informal systems, such as global weather, *can* be simulated by computer to any precision we choose. His argument that a 100% emulation of a human mind in a computer is impossible should not stop us approximating. I agree with Dreyfus that if one is looking to get to the moon, one should stop climbing the nearest tree and get into a warm room for some deeper planning. However, Dreyfus's discussion doesn't elevate us towards the moon even the few metres that classic AI's tree would, since no working software is produced by his approach at all. All Dreyfus does is show why Platonism/intellectualism will not get us there. He stops there, without proposing any concrete alternative that is better than that first tree.

This is why working examples are attached here. Dreyfus's founding contribution to philosophy of AI is not being belittled, but it is time to move forward to a more positive contribution and show what *can* be done, not just what *can't* be done.

13.3.3 Natural Language Processing

An application of the AIF family for natural language processing is worth exploring.

A more advanced version of AIF, where there would be (at least) two AIF2-type mechanisms cooperating, could be used to produce **language** – with one engine following structure (including syntax), producing (more or less) grammatical sentences, while another instance deals with the content, bringing up the relevant semantic fields – and somehow cooperating in producing the eventual sentence. Such sentences would hopefully be *mostly* but not completely grammatical, mostly but not completely on-topic – quite like human speech.

Conversely, in terms of understanding natural language, a more advanced edition of the AIF designs could also be used to understand different aspects concurrently – for example following the various grammatical rules and customs on the one hand and helping build a mental "picture" using the meaning of words by placing the various recalled meanings in the correct relations to each other (as the previously learnt grammar dictates). This would require having some "Cartesian theatre" or "imagination" able to draw mental pictures and the ability to react to these pictures in relation to the external reality.

13.3.4 Cognitive Models

AIF2 is entirely consistent, as an example for introspection-based AI, with some of the most popular views in cognitive science. The "predictive brain" concept (Clark, 2013) argues that the main (if not only) function of the brain is to predict the environment and to manoeuvre the person's body in such a way as to both minimise prediction error and produce the best possible results.

13.4 "Underpinning" Models in Philosophy

In this section, I will show how AIF2's "dynamic symbols" (Section 12.6.3) can also be seen as underpinning various ideas in cognition and philosophy. I use the term "underpinning" specifically to make a different point than "support". One supports a world view with arguments, showing why one should accept or believe in some position. When I say "underpinning", I mean that one could construct a software model that would operate in a way similar to the intellectual idea being examined. In a sense, this allows a philosophical model to "come to life" *in silico*. In another sense, "underpinning" is a software-based experiment, somewhat similar to a thought experiment. Like the thought experiment device, it *may* lend support to a model, but that would require clear argumentation. I will here argue that AIF2 or subsequent members of this family of designs can be used to underpin several philosophical concepts:

- Wittgenstein's "aspects"
- Gadamer's "prejudices" or "method"

- Dreyfus's demands from AI
- Wheeler's "action-oriented representations"
- Indian philosophy's *adhyasa*

The sections below show how, perhaps with some imaginative licence allowing for future research, the above philosophical concepts may be underpinned by an AIF2-like mind. Again, none of this is to claim that AIF2 or its derivatives are true, correct, or even superior to any other designs, past or future. The sole goal is to show how in a wide range of senses introspection-based designs can be useful.

13.4.1 Wittgenstein's "Seeing As"

Wittgenstein (2001a, p. 166) introduced the duck–rabbit drawing. When presented with this picture, people usually either persistently say that it is a rabbit or a duck, or that they see that both can be seen in the same picture. Most people after discussing the dual nature of the picture can see the duality.

Many AI programs that are logic or statistics based (say an expert system) would assign a higher probability to one or the other interpretations, by some function. Perhaps, the picture is indeed by some objective measure more a duck than a rabbit, but that is not how it is *for us* humans. AIF2, on the other hand, would either have past experiences of seeing the picture as a rabbit or as a duck and would repeat that habit, probably (just as a human) until shown the other option and would then alternate between the two. The very structure of AIF2 is similar to Wittgenstein's "seeing as" – it acts in any specific situation X based on one of a number of similar situations in the past. In that sense, AIF2 sees the current situation as equivalent to that past scenario.

13.4.2 Gadamer

Gadamer's view of hermeneutics is that we use our memories of the past (which form our "prejudices" or "inner horizon" or "method") to interpret the present (termed "truth" or "outer horizon"). We do not interpret the present using only one memory at a time as in CBR but use a blend of the memories available to us. AIF2 is to the best of my knowledge the first attempt to bring to bear on AI decisions such a time-based blend. For more details of how AIF2 is Gadamerian, see Section 12.6.4.

13.4.3 Dreyfus's Demands from AI

As we saw, Dreyfus's critique of AI was broad and unrelenting. Dreyfus also taught us the dangers of "first-step" fallacies (2012), so I cannot even claim that AIF2 or the whole introspective approach is a good "first step" towards appeasing his demands. What I can claim, that it is *a* step, perhaps "up a tree", but at least up a taller tree than existing AI, at least in the following sense.

Dreyfus outlines one specific element of what a more human way of doing things might be, in one type of skill acquisition:

> Now suppose that, in this random thrashing about, I happen to touch something, and that satisfies a need to cope with things…. I can *repeat whatever I did*, this time *in order to* touch something…. This is presumably the way skills are built up.

(Dreyfus, 1979, p. 253, stress in the original)

AIF2 does nothing if not "thrashing about" and later, in encountering similar circumstances, recalling the better and worse outcomes that were obtained in the past and giving a higher chance to "repeating" the beneficial action in the future. Like Dreyfus's description, there is no sharp distinction between a "learning phase" and a using of some formal stored knowledge. AIF2 therefore implements discovering skills and learning to use them in a more Dreyfus-like way than anything done before in AI (as far as I could discover).

If that were the entirety of Dreyfus's world view, one might be tempted to say that it is similar to reinforcement learning, but in Dreyfus's critique, it is part of a broad Heideggerian world view. The view presented in this volume is quite Gadamerian, and again, Gadamer's hermeneutics is only one element of the Heideggerian world view. So yes, perhaps even every *element* in our AI could be compared to existing systems, but the power of AIF2 is specifically in the blending, and the power of this volume's overall proposal is in showing how we can use introspection to generate *many* human-like AI designs.

13.4.4 *Wheeler's Action-Oriented Representations*

Wheeler (2005, pp. 195–196) recalls that orthodox representation theory (such as in classic AI) calls for representations that are "essentially objective, context independent, action-neutral, stored descriptions of the environment". He contrasts that with Brooks's "situated robots" that have no representations as such (recall Brooks's paper was entitled "Intelligence *without representation*" (1991)).

Wheeler mentions Clark's (1998, pp. 47–51) action-oriented representations as being halfway between mirroring the world and prescribing action. However, Wheeler critiques this "halfway" approach: The living organism has no interest in representing the world objectively as it is but only in terms of (ego-centric) actions. The representations of actions and outcomes do indeed reflect something of the world, but that "purely academic" part is of no interest to the living creature – "it is by adaptively mediating between sensing and movement that such inner structures earn their keep" (Wheeler, 2005, p. 197). Wheeler also points out that these structures represent knowledge-how, not knowledge-that. Note also that such a direct association between sensing and moving, without much if any intellectual content, is also fundamental to O'Regan's (2011) sensory-motor theories.

AIF2's "sequences" and "dynamic symbols" (Section 12.6.3) are good candidates for the role of Wheeler's action-oriented representations, at least as far as technological AI is concerned. They are used to predict possible consequences if certain actions are taken, based on the system's own past experiences. Arguably, that can be found even in CBR, not only in the AIF family. Unlike CBR, in AIF2, the representations/sequences can fade in and out and "cooperate" or "blend" – they are "softer" and allow for more subtle skills and skill combinations.

13.4.5 Adhyasa/Superimposition

Adhyasa is the Sanskrit[3] term for "superimposition" – it refers to people seeing in a situation some thing, distinction or circumstance that is not in the actual input. An example could be meeting a young person on campus, without conversation or prior acquaintance, and seeing them from a distance, perhaps carrying a computer, as an undergraduate. This idea of the bureaucratic definition "undergraduate" is added by the observer. Moreover, if you have just imagined the described situation vividly, you most probably imagined either a young woman or a young man, and they had some other specific features, like hair, clothing, etc. Not one of these details were in my description. All these details are added by the listener, "superimposed" on the basic situation, not really there. Similarly, all social constructs such as belonging to a nationality, etc. are not part of any objective reality but are superimposed by our understanding.

Again, like in the case of Wittgenstein's seeing-as, the case of adhyasa is similar to AIF2. The AIF2 agent is reacting according to the *predicted* consequences of its actions, predicated by past experience. It "sees" probable consequences before they arise. These consequences may well never arise, since the situation at hand may be entirely different from the memories of the AIF system. Again, no claim is being made that AIF is the only AI concept that could produce such behaviour. In the case of adhyasa, the phenomenon of "over-fitting" in machine learning also comes to mind.

13.5 Open Questions

This book has been an exercise in interdisciplinary work. I have already mentioned several areas for further research, much of which could be done by experts in the relevant specific fields. I am left with some observations and worries that do not fit neatly in any one discipline:

13.5.1 Dilthey vs Gadamer

Section 12.6.4 argued that AIF2 can be seen as a start in the pursuit of the long-awaited Gadamerian AI. However, this book did not advocate for taking

---

[3] Sanskrit is to India what Latin and Greek are to Europe.

phenomenological or hermeneutic texts as "gospel truth". It argued for personal introspection by the AI developer as a way to get at some mechanisms of the human mind in order to emulate them in software. In a sense, this volume promotes a Gadamerian approach for the content of the AI software, (following Winograd and Flores) but promotes a Dilthey-like approach to obtaining the ideas for building the software. Recall (from Section 2.5) that Dilthey called for a balance (in the person trying to understand some historical text) between "living experience" and critical thinking. For Dilthey, "living experience" meant that one should allow oneself to imagine what it would be like to be, say, Caligula in a certain situation, and try to use one's own reconstruction, like an actor's, to understand the dynamics of the situation. He then called for critical thinking to restrict those flights of fancy and make sure that they make sense in the historical context and in whatever other constraints are known to apply in the historical situation (Ramberg & Gjesdal, 2014).

This book suggests that one should use introspection in order to create in software models of how we humans may think. This is not restricted to "correct" introspection – the arguments above explicitly allow "bad", speculative introspection (see Section 7.3.5). This can be seen as the equivalent of Dilthey's "living experience". Our version of the restraining critical historical thinking is the demand that specific operational systems must be produced, run, and evaluated as a technology.

13.5.2 Further Unexplored Terrain

Two unexplored areas in cognitive science have been mentioned, that cry out for exploration – perhaps even more urgently for anthropic technological AI.

1. First, anthropology has been pointed out by Boden (2008, Chapter 8) as "the missing discipline" in cognitive science. My term "anthropic AI" only scratches the surface, in that I am interested in humans as such rather than in "western, modern, well-trained adults". However, there may well be some anthropological literature about cognition that has not been explored. A non-European phenomenology would be fascinating, which brings up the next point.

2. The literature on the structure of the mind in Sanskrit (and related languages) is vast. This is difficult to explore since beyond being mostly untranslated, these Indian traditions do not separate psychology, metaphysics, and religion to any degree that even begins to satisfy our western, modern expectations. Again, something being difficult is no argument for expecting it a priori to be wrong. Specifically for our interest in AI particularly and cognitive science in general, the Buddhist tradition has an obsession with enumerating lists of mental components of various mental mechanisms, if "mechanisms" is indeed the correct term.

13.6 Conclusion

This book argued that "introspection is recommended for development of anthropic AI". This should perhaps be the beginning of a retreat from science's domination over other areas of thought, specifically our thinking about human nature but also our thinking about technology.

In cognitive science, as Searle (1992, p. 115) puts it, we should (supposedly) "carve off and eliminate the subjective experience". I call for a moderation of that programme. Little be it for me to make direct recommendations about cognitive *science* in general – but in the field of human-like AI as a technology, this attitude has surely outlived its usefulness. Instead, we should return to an age-old piece of wisdom: "It is the mark of an educated man to look for precision in each class of things just so far as the nature of the subject admits" (Aristotle, 2009). By all means, we should render unto science that which belongs to science (see Matthew 22:21), but let's move on with the technology. We needn't wait for scientific precision.

If the full glory of human intelligence successfully emerges from the muck of human emotions and fragmented sentences, there is no reason to think that a human-like AI should emerge out of anything else.

Two final points:
1. If you want to comment on this book, please send me an email on book1@ freed.net.
2. Now that you have finished this book, go listen to "The Logical Song", by Roger Hodgson (Supertramp, 2009).

Bibliography

Agre, P. E. (1997). Toward a critical technical practice: Lessons learned in trying to reform AI. In G. Bowker, S. L. Star, L. Gasser, & W. Turner (Eds.), *Social Science, Technical Systems, and Cooperative Work: Beyond the Great Divide* (pp. 131–157). New York: Psychology Press.

Altmann, G. T. M., & Dienes, Z. (1999). Rule learning by seven-month-old infants and neural networks. *Science, 284*(5416), 875–875. doi:10.1126/science.284.5416.875a.

Amazon Prime Air. (2016). Retrieved September 24, 2015, from www.amazon.com/b?node=8037720011.

Ariely, D. (2009). *Predictably Irrational: The Hidden Forces That Shape Our Decisions.* London: Harper.

Aristotle. (2009). In W. D. Ross (Trans.), *Nicomachean Ethics.* Retrieved from http://classics.mit.edu/Aristotle/nicomachaen.1.i.html.

Augier, M., & March, J. G. (2001). Remembering Herbert A. Simon (1916–2001). *Public Administration Review, 61*(4), 396–402.

Austin, J. L., & Warnock, G. J. (1964). *Sense and Sensibilia.* Oxford, UK: Oxford University Press.

Baddeley, B., Graham, P., Husbands, P., & Philippides, A. (2012). A model of ant route navigation driven by scene familiarity. *PLoS Comput Biol, 8*(1), e1002336. doi:10.1371/journal.pcbi.1002336.

Bannister, R. C. (1991). *Sociology and Scientism: The American Quest for Objectivity, 1880–1940.* Chapel Hill: The University of North Carolina Press.

Bar-Hillel, Y. (2003). The present status of automatic translation of languages. In S. Nirenburg & H. L. Somers (Eds.), *Readings in Machine Translation* (pp. 45–77). Cambridge, MA: MIT Press.

Beyer, C. (2015). Edmund husserl. In E. N. Zalta (Ed.), *The Stanford Encyclopedia of Philosophy* (Summer 2015). Retrieved from http://plato.stanford.edu/archives/sum2015/entries/husserl/.

Bird, A., & Tobin, E. (2017). Natural kinds. In E. N. Zalta (Ed.), *The Stanford Encyclopedia of Philosophy* (Spring 2017). Stanford University: Metaphysics Research Lab. Retrieved from https://plato.stanford.edu/archives/spr2017/entries/natural-kinds/.

Bloch, M. L. B. (1953). *The Historian's Craft.* New York: Vintage Books. Retrieved from http://capitadiscovery.co.uk/sussex-ac/items/1081954.

Boden, M. A. (2008). *Mind as Machine: A History of Cognitive Science.* Oxford, UK: Oxford University Press.

Boden, M. A. (2016). *AI: Its Nature and Future.* Oxford, UK: Oxford University Press.

Bogen, J. (2014). Theory and observation in science. In E. N. Zalta (Ed.), *The Stanford Encyclopedia of Philosophy* (Summer 2014). Retrieved from http://plato.stanford.edu/archives/sum2014/entries/science-theory-observation/.

Bolter, J. D. (1984). *Turing's Man: Western Culture in the Computer Age*. London, UK: Duckworth.

Borges, J. L. (2001). The total library. In E. Allen & S. Levine (Trans.), *The Total Library: Non-Fiction 1922–1986* (New edition, pp. 214–216). London, UK: Penguin Classics.

Boring, E. G. (1929). *History of Experimental Psychology*. New York: Genesis Publishing Pvt Ltd.

Bostrom, N. (2016). *Superintelligence: Paths, Dangers, Strategies* (Reprint edition). Oxford, UK and New York: Oxford University Press.

Bourdeau, M. (2014). Auguste Comte. In E. N. Zalta (Ed.), *The Stanford Encyclopedia of Philosophy* (Winter 2014). Retrieved from http://plato.stanford.edu/archives/win2014/entries/comte/.

Bower, J. M., & Bolouri, H. (2001). *Computational Modeling of Genetic and Biochemical Networks*. Cambridge, MA: MIT Press.

Breuer, Y., & Shavit, E. (2014). *Hilarious Hebrew: The Fun and Fast Way to Learn the Language*. Brighton, UK: Pitango Publishing.

Bringsjord, S. (2008). The Logicist Manifesto. Retrieved from http://kryten.mm.rpi.edu/SB_LAI_Manifesto_091808.pdf.

Broekens, J., Heerink, M., & Rosendal, H. (2009). Assistive social robots in elderly care: a review. *Gerontechnology, 8*(2). doi:10.4017/gt.2009.08.02.002.00.

Brooks, R. A. (1991). Intelligence without representation. *Artificial Intelligence, 47*(1–3), 139–159. doi:10.1016/0004-3702(91)90053-M.

Brooks, R. A. (2017, October 6). Robotics Pioneer Rodney Brooks Debunks AI Hype Seven Ways. Retrieved December 8, 2017, from www.technologyreview.com/s/609048/the-seven-deadly-sins-of-ai-predictions/.

Brooks, R. A., Breazeal, C., Marjanović, M., Scassellati, B., & Williamson, M. M. (1999). The cog project: Building a humanoid robot. In C. L. Nehaniv (Ed.), *Computation for Metaphors, Analogy, and Agents* (pp. 52–87). Berlin and Heidelberg: Springer. doi:10.1007/3-540-48834-0_5.

Brown, A. (2010). *The Rise and Fall of Communism*. London, UK: Vintage.

Byers, E. S., Purdon, C., & Clark, D. A. (1998). Sexual intrusive thoughts of college students. Journal of Sex Research, 35(4), 359–369. doi:10.1080/00224499809551954.

Byrne, A. (2005). Introspection. *Philosophical Topics, 33*(1), 79–104.

Carr, J. E. (1985). Ethno-behaviorism and the culture-bound syndromes: The case of amok. In R. C. Simons & C. C. Hughes (Eds.), *The Culture-Bound Syndromes* (pp. 199–223). Netherlands: Springer. Retrieved from http://link.springer.com/chapter/10.1007/978-94-009-5251-5_20.

Chapman, A. (2013). *Slaying the Dragons: Destroying Myths in the History of Science and Faith*. Oxford, UK: Lion Books.

Chomsky, N. (1959). A review of BF Skinner's verbal behavior. *Language, 35*(1), 26–58.

Chomsky, N. (2017, August 15). Can We Save Our Democracy and History. Retrieved from www.youtube.com/watch?v=-aEFjtfFpLs&t=761s.

Chrisley, R. (2003). Embodied artificial intelligence. *Artificial Intelligence, 149*(1), 131–150. doi:10.1016/S0004-3702(03)00055-9.

Clark, A. (1998). *Being There: Putting Brain, Body, and World Together Again*. Cambridge: MIT Press.

Clark, A. (2013). Whatever next? Predictive brains, situated agents, and the future of cognitive science. *Behavioral and Brain Sciences, 36*(03), 181–204. doi:10.1017/S0140525X12000477.

Clark, A., & Chalmers, D. (1998). The extended mind. *Analysis, 58*(1), 7–19.

Collins, S. H., & Ruina, A. (2005). A bipedal walking robot with efficient and human-like gait. In *Proceedings of the 2005 IEEE International Conference on Robotics and Automation, 2005. ICRA 2005* (pp. 1983–1988). doi:10.1109/ROBOT.2005.1570404.

Costall, A. (2004). From Darwin to Watson (and cognitivism) and back again: The principle of animal-environment mutuality. *Behavior and Philosophy, 32*(1), 179–195.

Costall, A. (2006). 'Introspectionism' and the mythical origins of scientific psychology. *Consciousness and Cognition, 15*(4), 634–654. doi:10.1016/j.concog.2006.09.008.

Cowie, F. (2010). Innateness and language. In E. N. Zalta (Ed.), *The Stanford Encyclopedia of Philosophy* (Summer 2010). Retrieved from http://plato.stanford.edu/archives/sum2010/entries/innateness-language/.

Creath, R. (2014). Logical empiricism. In E. N. Zalta (Ed.), *The Stanford Encyclopedia of Philosophy* (Spring 2014). Retrieved from http://plato.stanford.edu/archives/spr2014/entries/logical-empiricism/.

Crosson, F. J. (1985). Psyche and the computer: Integrating the shadow. In S. Koch & D. E. Leary (Eds.), *A Century of Psychology as Science* (pp. 437–451). Washington, DC: American Psychological Association.

Daniel Dennet Discussion with Marvin Minsky: The New Humanists 2/2. (2012). Retrieved from www.youtube.com/watch?v=mbkvpJmHtDE&feature=youtube_gdata_player.

Dawkins, R. (2016). *The Selfish Gene: 40th Anniversary Edition* (4 edition). New York: Oxford University Press.

Dennett, D. (2003). Who's on first? Heterophenomenology explained. *Journal of Consciousness Studies, 10*(9–10), 19–30.

Dennett, D. C. (1989). *The Intentional Stance.* Cambridge: MIT Press.

Deryugina, O. V. (2010). Chatterbots. *Scientific and Technical Information Processing, 37*(2), 143–147. doi:10.3103/S0147688210020097.

Descartes. (1952). In J. Veitch (Trans.), *The Meditations and Selections from the Principles.* La Salle, IL: Open Court.

Diamond, J. (1998). *Guns, Germs and Steel: A Short History of Everybody for the Last 13,000 Years* (New edition). London, UK: Vintage.

Dowe, D. L. (2013). Introduction to Ray Solomonoff 85th memorial conference. In D. L. Dowe (Ed.), *Algorithmic Probability and Friends. Bayesian Prediction and Artificial Intelligence* (pp. 1–36). Berlin and Heidelberg: Springer. Retrieved from http://link.springer.com/chapter/10.1007/978-3-642-44958-1_1.

Dreyfus, H. L. (1965). *Alchemy and Artificial Intelligence.* Santa Monica, CA: Rand Corporation.

Dreyfus, H. L. (1979). *What Computers Can't Do / The Limits of Artificial Intelligence* (Revised). New York: Harper & Row.

Dreyfus, H. L. (1996). Response to my critics. *Artificial Intelligence, 80*(1), 171–191. doi:10.1016/0004-3702(95)00088-7.

Dreyfus, H. L. (2007). Why Heideggerian AI failed and how fixing it would require making it more Heideggerian. *Artificial Intelligence, 171*(18), 1137–1160. doi:10.1016/j.artint.2007.10.012.

Dreyfus, H. L. (2012). A history of first step fallacies. *Minds and Machines, 22*(2), 87–99.

Dreyfus, H. L., & Dreyfus, S. E. (1986). *Mind Over Machine: The Power of Human Intuition and Expertise in the Era of the Computer*. New York: Free Press.

Edwards, P. N. (1997). *The Closed World: Computers and the Politics of Discourse in Cold War America*. Cambridge: MIT Press.

Eksteins, M. (2000). *Rites of Spring: The Great War and the Birth of the Modern Age* (1st edition). Boston, MA: Mariner Books.

Ericsson, K. A., & Simon, H. A. (1981). Sources of evidence on cognition: An historical overview. In T. V. Merluzzi, C. R. Glass, & M. Genest (Eds.), *Cognitive Assessment*. Carnegie-Mellon University, Department of Psychology. Retrieved from http://octopus.library.cmu.edu/cgi-bin/tiff2pdf/simon/box00067/fld05162/bdl0001/doc0001/simon.pdf.

Ericsson, K. A., & Simon, H. A. (1993). *Protocol Analysis: Verbal Reports as Data* (2nd edition). Cambridge: MIT Press. Retrieved from http://capitadiscovery.co.uk/sussex-ac/items/543010.

Evangeliou, C. C. (2008). The place of Hellenic philosophy. *Proceedings of the Xxii World Congress of Philosophy*, *2*, 61–99.

Fantl, J. (2014). Knowledge how. In E. N. Zalta (Ed.), *The Stanford Encyclopedia of Philosophy* (Fall 2014). Retrieved from http://plato.stanford.edu/archives/fall2014/entries/knowledge-how/.

Feigenbaum, E. A. (1989). What hath Simon wrought. In D. Klahr & K. Kotovsky (Eds.), *Complex Information Processing: The Impact of Herbert A. Simon* (pp. 165–182). Hillsdale, NJ: Lawrence Erlbaum Associates.

Feynman, R. (1988). Richard Feynman's Blackboard at Time of His Death | Caltech. Retrieved October 21, 2015, from http://caltech.discoverygarden.ca/islandora/object/ct1%3A483.

Franssen, M., Lokhorst, G.-J., & van de Poel, I. (2013). Philosophy of technology. In E. N. Zalta (Ed.), *The Stanford Encyclopedia of Philosophy* (Winter 2013). Retrieved from http://plato.stanford.edu/archives/win2013/entriesechnology/.

Freed, S. (2013). Practical introspection as inspiration for AI. In V. C. Müller (Ed.), *Philosophy and Theory of Artificial Intelligence* (pp. 167–177). Berlin and Heidelberg: Springer. Retrieved from http://link.springer.com/chapter/10.1007/978-3-642-31674-6_12.

Freed, S. (2017). *A Role for Introspection in AI research*. University of Sussex. Retrieved from http://sro.sussex.ac.uk/66141/.

Freed, S. (2018). Is programming done by projection and introspection? In V. C. Müller (Ed.), *Philosophy and Theory of Artificial Intelligence 2017* (pp. 187–189). Cham, Switzerland: Springer Nature.

Freedman, H., & Maurice, S. (1961). *Midrash Raba (Genesis)*. London, UK: Sonico Press. Retrieved from http://archive.org/details/RabbaGenesis.

Froese, T. (2011). Validating and calibrating first- and second-person methods in the science of consciousness. *Journal of Consciousness Studies*, *18*(2), 38–64.

Fromm, E. (2011). *Escape from Freedom*. New York and Tokyo, Japan: Ishi Press.

Gadamer, H.-G. (1979). *Truth and Method* (2nd edition). London, UK: Sheed and Ward. Retrieved from http://capitadiscovery.co.uk/sussex-ac/items/40876.

Gadamer, H.-G. (2004). *Truth and Method* (2nd, revised edition). London, UK and New York: Continuum.

Gallagher, S., & Zahavi, D. (2012). *The Phenomenological Mind*. London, UK and New York: Routledge.

Gamez, D. (2008). Progress in machine consciousness. *Consciousness and Cognition, 17*(3), 887–910. doi:10.1016/j.concog.2007.04.005.

Gasset, J. O. Y. (1963). *Man and People* (Revised edition). New York: W. W. Norton & Company.

Goffman, E. (1971). *The Presentation of Self in Everyday Life*. Harmondsworth, UK: Penguin.

Goldie, P. (2012). *The Mess Inside: Narrative, Emotion, and the Mind*. Oxford, UK: Oxford University Press.

Gonzalez, H. B., & Kuenzi, J. J. (2012, August 1). Science, Technology, Engineering, and Mathematics (STEM) Education: A primer. Congressional Research Service. Retrieved from https://fas.org/sgp/crs/misc/R42642.pdf.

Gower, B. (1996). *Scientific Method: A Historical and Philosophical Introduction* (1st edition). London, UK and New York: Routledge.

Harari, Y. N. (2012). *From Animals into Gods: A Brief History of Humankind*. Charleston, NC: CreateSpace Independent Publishing Platform.

Harding, M. E. (2001). *Woman's Mysteries: Ancient & Modern* (Book Club). Boulder, CO: Shambhala.

Hasel, G. F. (1974). The polemic nature of the genesis cosmology. *The Evangelical Quarterly, 46*, 78–80.

Hassan, S. (1988). *Combatting Cult Mind Control*. Glasgow, Scotland: Aquarian press.

Hastings, M. (2014). *Catastrophe: Europe Goes to War 1914*. London, UK: William Collins.

Heidegger, M. (1962). *Being and Time*. (J. Macquarrie & E. Robinson, Trans.). Malden, MA and Oxford, UK: Blackwell.

Heidegger, M. (2009). The question concerning technology. In C. Hanks (Ed.), *Technology and Values: Essential Readings* (pp. 99–113). Oxford, UK: John Wiley & Sons.

Hernández-Orallo, J. (2017). *The Measure of All Minds: Evaluating Natural and Artificial Intelligence*. New York: Cambridge University Press.

Hesslow, G. (2012). The current status of the simulation theory of cognition. *Brain Research, 1428*, 71–79. doi:10.1016/j.brainres.2011.06.026.

Hockings, N., Iravani, P., & Bowen, C. R. (2014). Artificial ligamentous joints: Methods, materials and characteristics. In *Humanoids* (pp. 20–26). Retrieved from http://people.bath.ac.uk/nch28/pdfs/Artificial%20Ligamentous%20Joints%20-%20Methods%20Materials%20and%20Characteristics.pdf.

Hoefer, C. (2003). Causal Determinism. Retrieved from https://plato.stanford.edu/archives/win2017/entries/determinism-causal/.

Hurlburt, R. T. (2011). *Investigating Pristine Inner Experience: Moments of Truth*. New York: Cambridge University Press.

Hurlburt, R. T., Heavey, C. L., & Kelsey, J. M. (2013). Toward a phenomenology of inner speaking. *Consciousness and Cognition, 22*(4), 1477–1494. doi:10.1016/j.concog.2013.10.003.

Hyslop, A. (2014). Other minds. In E. N. Zalta (Ed.), *The Stanford Encyclopedia of Philosophy* (Spring 2014). Retrieved from http://plato.stanford.edu/archives/spr2014/entries/other-minds/.

IBM. (2014, March 20). IBM Collaboration Solutions Software - Lotus Software - United Kingdom [CT503]. Retrieved October 10, 2014, from www-01.ibm.com/software/uk/lotus/.

Irwin, R. (2010). *The Arabian Nights: Tales of 1,001 Nights: Volume 1*. (M. Lyons & U. Lyons, Trans.) (1st edition). London, UK, New York, USA, Toronto, Ontario, Canada, Dublin, Ireland, Victoria, Australia, New Delhi, India, North Shore, New Zealand, Johannesburg, South Africa: Penguin Classics.

Isensee, P. (2001). Genuine random number generation. *Game Programming Gems, 2*, 127.

Ismael, J. (2015). Quantum mechanics. In E. N. Zalta (Ed.), *The Stanford Encyclopedia of Philosophy* (Spring 2015). Retrieved from http://plato.stanford.edu/archives/spr2015/entries/qm/.

Jack, A., & Roepstorff, A. (Eds.). (2003). *Trusting the Subject: v. 1*. Exeter, UK: Imprint Academic.

Jack, A., & Roepstorff, A. (Eds.). (2004). *Trusting the Subject: v. 2*. Exeter, UK: Imprint Academic.

Johansson, P., Hall, L., Sikström, S., Tärning, B., & Lind, A. (2006). How something can be said about telling more than we can know: On choice blindness and introspection. *Consciousness and Cognition, 15*(4), 673–692.

Jung, C. G. (1984). *Dream Analysis: Notes of the Seminar Given in 1928–1930*. Princeton, NJ: Princeton University Press.

Klotzko, A. J. (2001). *The Cloning Sourcebook*. New York: Oxford University Press.

Knapp, S. (2008). Artificial Intelligence: Past, Present, and Future. Retrieved December 9, 2015, from www.dartmouth.edu/~vox/0607/0724/ai50.html.

Kremer-Marietti, A. (1993). Positivism. In *Encyclopedia of Religion* (Vol. 11). New York: Macmillan.

Kuhn, T. (2012). *The Structure of Scientific Revolutions* (50th anniversary edition). Chicago and London: University of Chicago Press.

Laird, J. E., & Rosenbloom, P. (1996). The evolution of the Soar cognitive architecture. In D. Steier & T. M. Mitchell (Eds.). *Mind Matters: A Tribute to Allen Newell* (pp. 1–50). Mahwah, NJ: Lawrence Erlbaum Associates.

Langley, P. (2006). *Intelligent Behavior in Humans and Machines*. Technical Report. Computational Learning Laboratory, CSLI, Stanford University. Retrieved from http://lyonesse.stanford.edu/~langley/papers/ai50.dart.pdf.

Lao-Tzu. (n.d.). Tao Te Ching (170+ translations of Chapter 1). Retrieved January 9, 2015, from www.bopsecrets.org/gateway/passages/tao-te-ching.htm.

Lenat, D. B., Prakash, M., & Shepherd, M. (1985). CYC: Using common sense knowledge to overcome brittleness and knowledge acquisition bottlenecks. *AI Magazine, 6*(4), 65.

LeVine, S., & Hinton, G. (2017, September 15). Artificial intelligence pioneer says we need to start over. Retrieved September 17, 2017, from www.axios.com/ai-pioneer-advocates-starting-over-2485537027.html.

Lucas, R. (2009, August 6). In defence of the dismal science. *The Economist*. Retrieved from www.economist.com/node/14165405.

Makari, G. (2016). *Soul Machine: The Invention of the Modern Mind*. New York: W. W. Norton & Company.

Malpas, J. (2013). Hans-Georg Gadamer. In E. N. Zalta (Ed.), *The Stanford Encyclopedia of Philosophy* (Summer 2013). Retrieved from http://plato.stanford.edu/archives/sum2013/entries/gadamer/.

Mandik, P. (2001). Mental representation and the subjectivity of consciousness. *Philosophical Psychology, 14*(2), 179–202. doi:10.1080/09515080120051553.

Markram, H. (2006). The blue brain project. *Nature Reviews Neuroscience, 7*(2), 153–160. doi:10.1038/nrn1848.

Markram, H. (2012). The human brain project. *Scientific American, 306*(6), 50–55. doi:10.1038/scientificamerican0612-50.

Matthews, M. R. (1994). *Science Teaching: The Role of History and Philosophy of Science.* New York and London,UK: Routledge.

McCorduck, P. (2004). *Machines who think: a personal inquiry into the history and prospects of artificial intelligence* (25th anniversary update). Natick, MA: A.K. Peters.

McCulloch, W. S., & Pitts, W. (1943). A logical calculus of the ideas immanent in nervous activity. *The Bulletin of Mathematical Biophysics, 5*(4), 115–133. doi:10.1007/BF02478259.

McHugh, J., & Minsky, M. (2003, August 1). Why A.I. is Brain-Dead. Retrieved January 8, 2016, from www.wired.com/2003/08/why-a-i-is-brain-dead/.

McKeon, R. (Ed.). (1941). *The Basic Works of Aristotle.* New York: Random House.

McLeod, P., Reed, N., & Dienes, Z. (2003). Psychophysics: How fielders arrive in time to catch the ball. *Nature, 426*(6964), 244–245.

McNeill, D., & Freiberger, P. (1994). *Fuzzy Logic: The Revolutionary Computer Technology that is Changing Our World* (1st edition). New York: Touchstone / Simon & Schuster.

Mhaskar, H., Liao, Q., & Poggio, T. (2016). Learning Functions: When is Deep Better Than Shallow. ArXiv:1603.00988 [Cs]. Retrieved from http://arxiv.org/abs/1603.00988.

Mill, J. S. (2013). *Auguste Comte and Positivism.* CreateSpace Independent Publishing Platform.

Miller, G. A. (1956). The magical number seven, plus or minus two: Some limits on our capacity for processing information. *Psychological Review, 63*(2), 81–97. doi:10.1037/h0043158.

Minsky, M. (1987). *The Society of Mind* (First Edition First Printing edition). New York: Simon & Schuster.

Minsky, M. (1991). Logical versus analogical or symbolic versus connectionist or neat versus scruffy. *AI Magazine, 12*(2), 34–51.

Mladenić, D., & Bradeško, L. (2012). A Survey of Chatbot Systems through a Loebner Prize Competition [Conference or Workshop Item]. Retrieved July 17, 2014, from http://eprints.pascal-network.org/archive/00009729/.

Mould, R. F. (1998). The discovery of radium in 1898 by Maria Sklodowska-Curie (1867–1934) and Pierre Curie (1859–1906) with commentary on their life and times. *The British Journal of Radiology, 71*(852), 1229–1254. doi:10.1259/bjr.71.852.10318996.

Müller, V. C. (2009). Pancomputationalism: Theory or metaphor? In R. Hagengruber (Ed.), *The Relevance of Philosophy for Information Science.* Berlin: Springer, Forthcoming. Retrieved from www.typos.de/pdf/2008_Paderborn_Pancomputationalism.pdf.

Murakami, M. (1995). The history of verb movement in English. *Studies in Modern English, 1995*(11), 17–45.

Nagel, T. (1974). What is it like to be a bat? *The Philosophical Review, 83*(4), 435–450. doi:10.2307/2183914.

Neisser, U. (1967). *Cognitive Psychology.* New York: Appleton-Century-Crofts. Retrieved from http://capitadiscovery.co.uk/sussex-ac/items/27273.

Newell, A., & Simon, H. A. (1956). The logic theory machine–A complex information processing system. *IRE Transactions on Information Theory, 2*(3), 61–79. doi:10.1109/TIT.1956.1056797.

Newell, A., & Simon, H. A. (1961a). Computer simulation of human thinking. *Science.* Retrieved from http://psycnet.apa.org/?fa=main.doiLanding&uid=1962-05907-001.

Newell, A., & Simon, H. A. (1961b). *GPS, a program that simulates human thought.* Defense Technical Information Center. Retrieved from http://octopus.library.cmu.edu/cgi-bin/tiff2pdf/simon/box00064/fld04907/bdl0001/doc0001/simon.pdf.

Newell, A., & Simon, H. A. (1976). Computer Science as Empirical Inquiry: Symbols and Search. *Communications of the ACM, 19*(3), 113–126. doi:10.1145/360018.360022.

Nietzsche. (1889). Full Text of "The Will to Power." Retrieved October 30, 2014, from https://archive.org/stream/TheWillToPower-Nietzsche/will_to_power-nietzsche_djvu.txt.

Nilsson, N. J. (2010). The Quest for Artificial Intelligence. Retrieved March 20, 2015, from www.cambridge.org/gb/academic/subjects/computer-science/artificial-intelligence-and-natural-language-processing/quest-artificial-intelligence.

Nisbett, R. E., & Wilson, T. D. (1977). Telling more than we can know: Verbal reports on mental processes. *Psychological Review, 84*(3), 231–259. doi:10.1037/0033-295X.84.3.231.

Nobelprize.org. (1978). The Prize in Economics 1978-Press Release. Retrieved from www.nobelprize.org/nobel_prizes/economic-sciences/laureates/1978/press.html.

O'Regan, J. K. (2011). *Why Red Doesn't Sound Like a Bell: Understanding the feel of consciousness.* New York: Oxford University Press.

Overgaard, M. (2006). Introspection in Science. *Consciousness and Cognition, 15*(4), 629–633. doi:10.1016/j.concog.2006.10.004.

Overgaard, M. (2008). Introspection. *Scholarpedia, 3*(5), 4953. doi:10.4249/scholarpedia.4953.

Partenie, C. (2014). Plato's myths. In E. N. Zalta (Ed.), *The Stanford Encyclopedia of Philosophy* (Summer 2014). Metaphysics Research Lab, Stanford University. Retrieved from https://plato.stanford.edu/archives/sum2014/entries/plato-myths/.

Payne, S. J., & Squibb, H. R. (1990). Algebra mal-rules and cognitive accounts of error. *Cognitive Science, 14*(3), 445–481. doi:10.1016/0364-0213(90)90019-S.

Pear, J. J. (2007). *A Historical and Contemporary Look at Psychological Systems* (1st edition). Mahwah, NJ: Psychology Press.

Piccinini, G. (2004). The first computational theory of mind and brain: A close look at Mcculloch and Pitts's "logical calculus of ideas immanent in nervous activity." *Synthese, 141*(2), 175–215. doi:10.1023/B:SYNT.0000043018.52445.3e.

Proops, I. (2017). Wittgenstein's logical atomism. In E. N. Zalta (Ed.), *The Stanford Encyclopedia of Philosophy* (Winter 2017). Metaphysics Research Lab, Stanford University. Retrieved from https://plato.stanford.edu/archives/win2017/entries/wittgenstein-atomism/.

Quine, W. v. O. (1976). Two dogmas of empiricism. In S. G. Harding (Ed.), *Can Theories be Refuted?* (pp. 41–64). Netherlands: Springer. Retrieved from http://link.springer.com/chapter/10.1007/978-94-010-1863-0_2.

Raatikainen, P. (2015). Gödel's incompleteness theorems. In E. N. Zalta (Ed.), *The Stanford Encyclopedia of Philosophy* (Spring 2015). Metaphysics Research Lab, Stanford University. Retrieved from https://plato.stanford.edu/archives/spr2015/entries/goedel-incompleteness/.

Rahula, W., & Demieville, P. (1997). *What the Buddha Taught* (New edition). Oxford: Oneworld Publications.

Raibert, M., Blankespoor, K., Nelson, G., Playter, R., & others. (2008). Bigdog, the rough-terrain quadruped robot. In *Proceedings of the 17th World Congress* (pp. 10823–10825). Retrieved from http://web.unair.ac.id/admin/file/f_7773_bigdog.pdf.

Ramberg, B., & Gjesdal, K. (2014). Hermeneutics. In E. N. Zalta (Ed.), *The Stanford Encyclopedia of Philosophy* (Winter 2014). Retrieved from http://plato.stanford.edu/archives/win2014/entries/hermeneutics/.

Ravenscroft, I. (2010). Folk psychology as a theory. In E. N. Zalta (Ed.), *The Stanford Encyclopedia of Philosophy* (Fall 2010). Retrieved from http://plato.stanford.edu/archives/fall2010/entries/folkpsych-theory/.

Rayner, K., White, S. J., Johnson, R. L., & Liversedge, S. P. (2006). Raeding wrods with jubmled Lettres there is a cost. *Psychological Science, 17*(3), 192–193. doi:10.1111/j.1467-9280.2006.01684.x.

Resnick, M. (1993). Behavior construction Kits. *Communications of the ACM, 36*(7), 64–71. doi:10.1145/159544.159593.

Reutlinger, A., Schurz, G., & Hüttemann, A. (2014). Ceteris paribus laws. In E. N. Zalta (Ed.), *The Stanford Encyclopedia of Philosophy* (Spring 2014). Retrieved from http://plato.stanford.edu/archives/spr2014/entries/ceteris-paribus/.

Richtel, M., & Dougherty, C. (2015, September 1). Google's driverless cars run into problem: Cars with drivers. *The New York Times*. Retrieved from www.nytimes.com/2015/09/02/technology/personaltech/google-says-its-not-the-driverless-cars-fault-its-other-drivers.html.

Robertson, J. (2007). Robo sapiens japanicus: Humanoid robots and the posthuman family. *Critical Asian Studies, 39*(3), 369–398. doi:10.1080/14672710701527378.

Romano, C. (2009, October 18). Heil Heidegger! *The Chronicle of Higher Education*. Retrieved from http://chronicle.com/article/Heil-Heidegger-/48806/.

Rothenberg, A. (1995). Creative cognitive processes in Kekulé's discovery of the structure of the benzene molecule. *The American Journal of Psychology, 108*(3), 419–438. doi:10.2307/1422898.

Russell, B. (1952). Is there a God? *Why I Am Not a Christian*.

Russell, S., & Norvig, P. (2013). *Artificial Intelligence: A Modern Approach* (3rd edition). Harlow, UK: Pearson.

Russell, S., & Norvig, P. (2016). 1293 Schools Worldwide That Have Adopted AIMA. Retrieved January 10, 2016, from http://aima.cs.berkeley.edu/adoptions.html.

Ryan, S. (2014). Wisdom. In E. N. Zalta (Ed.), *The Stanford Encyclopedia of Philosophy* (Winter 2014). Metaphysics Research Lab, Stanford University. Retrieved from https://plato.stanford.edu/archives/win2014/entries/wisdom/.

Safonov, Y. G., & Prokof'ev, V. Y. (2006). Gold-bearing reefs of the Witwatersrand Basin: A model of synsedimentation hydrothermal formation. *Geology of Ore Deposits, 48*(6), 415–447. doi:10.1134/S1075701506060018.

Schank, R. C., & Abelson, R. P. (1977). *Scripts, Plans, Goals, and Understanding: An Enquiry into Human Knowledge Structures*. Erlbaum. Retrieved from http://capitadiscovery.co.uk/sussex-ac/items/38886.

Schank, R. C. (1982). *Dynamic Memory: A Theory of Learning in Computers and People*. New York: Cambridge University Press.

Schickore, J. (2014). Scientific discovery. In E. N. Zalta (Ed.), *The Stanford Encyclopedia of Philosophy* (Spring 2014). Retrieved from http://plato.stanford.edu/archives/spr2014/entries/scientific-discovery/.

Schwitzgebel, E. (2004). Introspective training apprehensively defended: Reflections on Titchener's lab manual. *Journal of Consciousness Studies, 11*(7–8), 58–76.

Schwitzgebel, E. (2012). Introspection. In E. N. Zalta (Ed.), *The Stanford Encyclopedia of Philosophy* (Winter 2012). Retrieved from http://plato.stanford.edu/archives/win2012/entries/introspection/.

Schwitzgebel, E. (2014). Introspection. In E. N. Zalta (Ed.), *The Stanford Encyclopedia of Philosophy* (Summer 2014). Retrieved from http://plato.stanford.edu/archives/sum2014/entries/introspection/.

Searle, J. R. (1980). Minds, brains, and programs. *Behavioral and Brain Sciences, 3*(03), 417–424. doi:10.1017/S0140525X00005756.

Searle, J. R. (1992). *The Rediscovery of the Mind* (Massachusetts Institute of Technology edition). Cambridge, MA: A Bradford Book.

Seth, A. K. (2010). The grand challenge of consciousness. *Frontiers in Psychology, 1.* doi:10.3389/fpsyg.2010.00005.

Shakespeare, W. (n.d.). Macbeth. Retrieved July 26, 2018, from www.gutenberg.org/cache/epub/2264/pg2264-images.html.

Shamdasani, S. (1998). *Cult Fictions: C.G. Jung and the Founding of Analytical Psychology.* Psychology Press, London, UK.

Shanahan, M. (2016). The frame problem. In E. N. Zalta (Ed.), *The Stanford Encyclopedia of Philosophy* (Spring 2016). Metaphysics Research Lab, Stanford University. Retrieved from https://plato.stanford.edu/archives/spr2016/entries/frame-problem/.

Shanon, B. (2008). *Representational and the Presentational: An Essay on Cognition and the Study of Mind* (2nd edition). Exeter, UK and Charlottesville, VA: Imprint Academic.

Sharkey, A., & Sharkey, N. (2011). Children, the elderly, and interactive robots. *IEEE Robotics Automation Magazine, 18*(1), 32–38. doi:10.1109/MRA.2010.940151.

Shortliffe, E. H., Scott, A. C., Bischoff, M. B., Campbell, A. B., Van Melle, W., & Jacobs, C. D. (1984). An expert system for oncology protocol management. Rule-Based Expert Systems, BG Buchanan and EH Shortliffe, Editors, 653–665.

Simon, H. A. (1955). A behavioral model of rational choice. *The Quarterly Journal of Economics, 69*(1), 99–118. doi:10.2307/1884852.

Simon, H. A. (1976). *Administrative Behavior: A Study of Decision-Making Processes in Administrative Organization* (3rd edition). London, UK: Collier Macmillan. Retrieved from http://capitadiscovery.co.uk/sussex-ac/items/38710.

Simon, H. A. (1981). *The Sciences of the Artificial* (2nd edition). Cambridge, MA: MIT Press.

Simon, H. A. (1989). The scientist as problem solver. In D. Klahr & K. Kotovsky (Eds.). *Complex Information Processing: The Impact of Herbert A. Simon* (pp. 375–398). Hillsdale, NJ: Lawrence Erlbaum Associates.

Simon, H. A. (1996a). *Models of My Life.* Cambridge, MA: MIT Press. Retrieved from http://capitadiscovery.co.uk/sussex-ac/items/547214.

Simon, H. A. (1996b). *The Sciences of the Artificial* (3rd edition). Cambridge, MA: MIT Press. Retrieved from http://capitadiscovery.co.uk/sussex-ac/items/546838.

Simon, H. A., & Newell, A. (1958). Heuristic problem solving: The next advance in operations research. *Operations Research, 6*(1), 1–10.

Skinner, B. F. (1987). Whatever happened to psychology as the science of behavior? *American Psychologist, 42*(8), 780–786. doi:10.1037/0003-066X.42.8.780.

Smith, B. C. (2005, January 31). Digital Future: Meaning of Digital. Retrieved December 4, 2013, from http://c-spanvideo.org/program/FutureM.

Smith, D. W. (2013). Phenomenology. In E. N. Zalta (Ed.), *The Stanford Encyclopedia of Philosophy* (Winter 2013). Retrieved from http://plato.stanford.edu/archives/win2013/entries/phenomenology/.

Smullyan, R. M. (1993). *The Tao is Silent* (Reissue edition). San Francisco, CA: Harper.

Snow, C. P. (1964). *The Two Cultures: And a Second Look* (2nd edition). Cambridge, UK: Cambridge University Press.

Solomonoff, G. (2016). Ray Solomonoff and the Dartmouth Summer Research Project in Artificial Intelligence, 1956. Retrieved June 15, 2017, from http://raysolomonoff.com/dartmouth/dartray.pdf.

Solomonoff, R. J. (1968). The search for artificial intelligence. *Electronics and Power, 14*(1), 8. doi:10.1049/ep.1968.0004.

Sophocles. (2009). Antigone. Retrieved from http://classics.mit.edu/Sophocles/antigone.html.

Sponsel, A. (2002). Constructing a 'revolution in science': The campaign to promote a favourable reception for the 1919 solar eclipse experiments. The British Journal for the History of Science, 35(04), 439–467. doi:10.1017/S0007087402004818.

Sun, R. (2008). *The Cambridge Handbook of Computational Psychology* (1st edition). Cambridge and New York: Cambridge University Press.

Supertramp. (2009). Logical Song - Written and Composed by Roger Hodgson - Voice of Supertramp. Retrieved from www.youtube.com/watch?v=OQfjIw3mivc.

TheEconomist. (2013, May 14). Difference Engine: The caring robot. *The Economist.* Retrieved from www.economist.com/blogs/babbage/2013/05/automation-elderly.

Togelius, J., Lucas, S. M., & Nardi, R. D. (2007). Computational intelligence in racing games. In N. Baba, P. L. C. Jain, & H. Handa (Eds.), *Advanced Intelligent Paradigms in Computer Games* (pp. 39–69). Berlin and Heidelberg: Springer. doi:10.1007/978-3-540-72705-7_3.

Trump, D. J. (2015). TRUMP WORDS | User Clip | C-SPAN.org. Retrieved December 14, 2017, from www.c-span.org/video/?c4659877/trump-words.

Trump, D. J. (2017). FULL SPEECH: Donald Trump CIA Headquarters Statement FNN - YouTube. Retrieved December 14, 2017, from www.youtube.com/watch?v=GMBqDN7-QLg.

Tuchman, B. W. (1990). *The March of Folly: From Troy to Vietnam* (New edition). London, UK: Abacus.

Turing, A. M. (1953). Digital computers applied to games. In B. V. Bowden (Ed.), *Faster than Thought : A Symposium on Digital Computing Machines* (pp. 286–310). London: Pitman.

Turkle, S. (1984). *The Second Self: Computers and the Human Spirit.* London: Granada. Retrieved from http://capitadiscovery.co.uk/sussex-ac/items/1155840.

Turkle, S. (1991, March 17). Dangerous thoughts … and machines with big ideas. *The New York Times.* Retrieved from www.nytimes.com/1991/03/17/books/dangerous-thoughts-and-machines-with-big-ideas.html.

van der Zant, T., Kouw, M., & Schomaker, L. (2013). Generative artificial intelligence. In V. C. Müller (Ed.), *Philosophy and Theory of Artificial Intelligence* (pp. 107–120). Berlin and Heidelberg: Springer. Retrieved from http://link.springer.com/chapter/10.1007/978-3-642-31674-6_8.

Watson, I. (1999). Case-based reasoning is a methodology not a technology. *Knowledge-Based Systems, 12*(5–6), 303–308. doi:10.1016/S0950-7051(99)00020-9.

Watson, J. B. (1913). Psychology as the behaviorist views it. Psychological Review, 20(2), 158–177. doi:10.1037/h00744zzXxz28.

Watson, J. B. (1914). *Behavior: An Introduction to Comparative Psychology.* New York: H. Holt. Retrieved from http://archive.org/details/behaviorintroduc00watsuoft.

Watson, J. B. (1920). Is thinking merely action of language mechanisms1? (v.). *British Journal of Psychology. General Section, 11*(1), 87–104. doi:10.1111/j.2044-8295.1920. tb00010.x.

Watson, J. B. (1931). *Behaviorism* (Rev. edition). London: Kegan Paul. Retrieved from http://capitadiscovery.co.uk/sussex-ac/items/24582.

Watson, P. (2001). *Terrible Beauty: A Cultural History of the Twentieth Century: The People and Ideas that Shaped the Modern Mind: A History.* London, UK: Phoenix.

Watson, P. (2006). *Ideas: A History of Thought and Invention, from Fire to Freud.* New York: Harper Perennial.

Watts, A. (2009). *The Book: On the Taboo Against Knowing Who You Are.* London: Souvenir Press Ltd.

Weizenbaum, J. (1966). ELIZA - A computer program for the study of natural language communication between man and machine. *Commun. ACM, 9*(1), 36–45. doi:10.1145/365153.365168.

Wheeler, M. (2005). *Reconstructing the Cognitive World: The Next Step.* London: MIT. Retrieved from http://prism.talis.com/sussex-ac/items/911756.

Whitby, B. (2011). Do you want a robot lover? The ethics of caring technologies. In P. Lin, K. Abney, & G. Bekey (Eds.), *Robot Ethics: The Ethical and Social Implications of Robotics* (p. 233). Cambridge, MA: MIT Press.

Winograd, T. (1971). Procedures as a Representation for Data in a Computer Program for Understanding Natural Language.

Winograd, T. (1991). Thinking machines: Can there be? Are we? In J. J. Sheehan & M. Sosna (Eds.), *The Boundaries of Humanity: Humans, Animals, Machines.* Berkeley, CA: University of California Press.

Winograd, T., & Flores, F. (1986). *Understanding Computers and Cognition: A New Foundation for Design.* Norwood, NJ: Ablex. Retrieved from http://prism.talis.com/sussex-ac/items/272586.

Wittgenstein, L. (2001a). *Philosophical Investigations: The German Text with a Revised English Translation* (3rd edition). Malden, MA: Wiley-Blackwell.

Wittgenstein, L. (2001b). *Tractatus Logico-Philosophicus* (2nd edition). London and New York: Routledge.

Zadeh, L. A. (1965). Fuzzy sets. *Information and Control, 8*(3), 338–353. doi:10.1016/ S0019-9958(65)90241-X.

Zimmer, H. R. (1951). *Philosophies of India.* (J. Campbell, Ed.). Princeton, NJ: Princeton University Press.

Index

A

Action-oriented representations, 227–228
Action/output requirements, decision process, 211
Actions, 192
Actions set, AIF2, 222
Adhyasa/superimposition, 228
Agendas, truth, 92–93
Agre, P. E., 38–39, 144
AIF0, 191, 199, 212, 213, 217
    example run, statistics, 197–200
    human-like/anthropic, 201–202
    implementation, 196–197
    introspection
        distinct sources, 200–201
        parameters, 201
    similarity, 202
AIF1, 191, 202–203, 206
AIF2, 191, 207, 208, 221–223, 225–228
    anthropic AI, 216
    data types, 208–209
    example runs, 214
        learn 1, 214–215
        learn 2, 215
        learn 3, 215
    as Gadamerian, 218
    history database, 217
    implementation of, 211–212
    reinforcement learning, 216
    sequence data type, 217
AIF *vs.* CBR, 216–217
algebraic_form, 213
Ambitious introspection, 205
Analogue phenomena, 186
Analytical philosophy, 28, 76
Anatomy, subjectivity, 120
Antecedent conditions, 181
Anthropic AI, 85, 131, 157, 158, 164, 169, 184,
        185, 187–189, 200, 216, 219, 220, 229

data structures, 112–114
definition of, 105, 106
development of, 95–96
ethics of, 115–116
human-like AI
    advantage of, 104
    vs. Anthropic, 104–105
    characteristics of, 103–104
    human intelligence, versatility of,
        101–102
    human-like behaviour, 102–103
    rational/idealised AI, 100–101
human modelling
    cognitive level, 109
    discussion, multiple levels of,
        106–109
    human mind/brain, layers, 105–106
    multiple level computers, 110
human *vs.* ideal/rational, 99–100
introspection for, 94–97
meaningful theorems, 100
metaphysical non-problems, 114–115
plausible source for, 95
profitable avenues in, 93
technology-oriented efforts, 110–112
Anti-intellectualism, 113
Anxiety, 49, 54, 60–62
APIs, 106
Applied science, 88
Approximation, introspection usage
    analogue cannot arise out of digital, 186
    being analogue does not mean it is not
        digital, 186–187
    holes in introspection, 185–186
    opportunistic approximation, 186
Arbitrary
    parameters, 201
    precision, 186
Articulation, 180, 193, 196, 206